AF564641

Small Businesses in Tourism

Small Businesses in Tourism

Ravindra Ahuja

RANDOM PUBLICATIONS
NEW DELHI (INDIA)

Small Businesses in Tourism

ISBN 978-93-5111-962-3

Published in 2016 in India by

RANDOM PUBLICATIONS

4376-A/4B, Gali Murari Lal, Ansari Road
New Delhi-110 002
Phone : +9111-43580356, 011-23289044, 011-43142548
e-mail: sales@randompublications.com,
info@randompublications.com, randomexports@gmail.com

Type Setting by : Friends Media, Delhi-110089
Digitally Printed at : Replika Press Pvt. Ltd.

Preface

The tourism industry is a multi-billion dollar industry and it is continuously growing each year accounting for bulk of most countries GDP. If you want to enter the tourism industry, now may probably be the best time to do so as the industry is booming by the day.

Successful business performance is affected by a number of firm-specific factors including human and social capital. Although, small and medium firms comprise the vast majority of the tourism production system, research on small business performance in tourism is rather limited. Drawing on recent advances and empirical evidence from enterpreneurship and small business literature we control first, for the role of human and social capital and second, for the role of owners'/managers' perceptions of place attractiveness over small business performance.

Small and Medium Enterprises (SMEs) are the backbone of local economies and form the majority of businesses in the tourism industry. The potential risks affecting SMEs are the same as those faced by larger corporations, but the impacts of unmanaged risks can differ. Unless risks are adequately addressed, they could impair any of the key components of your business, such as product or services, inputs, processes and outputs.

Travel and tourism is a fun and rewarding industry. Starting with a good business plan will help you succeed in this exciting field. To get started, check out a sample business plan for an upscale travel agency, international travel agency, sightseeing tours business, and other travel related business.

The goal of the project is to contribute to increase the competitiveness of the micro and small enterprises (MSEs) and community-based organizations (CBOs) that are linked with the cruise ship tourism sector in Belize. Its purpose is to strengthen the capability of MSEs and CBOs to offer sustainable tourism products and improve their participation in integrated tourism business chains.

The book is designed to provide students, researchers, practitioners, individuals and organisations, a broad overview of planning and development issues in hospitality and tourism industry.

– Author

Contents

1

The Economics Development of Tourism

In a tourism context, the economics of tourism has been defined by one writer as being. The concerned with the use of scare resource, labour, capital, land, and environmental resources, to produce the product, tourism, and with the distribution of this product between different.

It should be noted that in this definition, environmental resources are differentiated as a separate resource (rather than included as part of the 'land' resource.) In so doing, the underlying critical importance to the tourism product of the environment in terms of air and water quality and the aesthetic beauty of nature and the landscape is recognised.

Indeed, Bull (1995) argues that the basis for tourism lies in building upon these 'free' resources (or 'renewable resources' as they are sometimes termed), with a mixture of public sector and private sector resources. These free resources, together with the other scarce resources, are combined to form what most tourists perceive as the tourist 'product' they consume and which suppliers produce. As Bull (1995) points out, in today's world there are few truly free resources since any human activity makes demands on the world's resources and, as a consequence, ultimately someone will have to pay a price. All the resources have competing demands made upon them so that, if they are used for one form of development, they cannot be used in others ways. For example, a large flat land coastal area might be suitable for the development of a resort area for tourism or as a site for heavy industry.

If tourism is chosen ahead of heavy industry, an opportunity to develop heavy industry on this site has been lost and the cost of this choice is known as the 'opportunity cost', which represents the potential economic returns that are being given up in favour of developing tourism.

Economics, then, can be viewed at two levels. The *micro* level considers individual business and consumers and the *macro* level considers the economy as a whole in a particular area or in relation to the national or international economy. *Microeconomics* in tourism is therefore, concerned with how economic decisions are reached at the level of the individual tourism business or the individual tourism consumer. Key questions to consider include:

- What makes consumers decide which tourism products they are going to buy, and in what quantities?
- How do specific tourism businesses, decide with tourism products are going to be sold and distributed to consumers and in what quantities?
- How are the market prices for buying and selling tourism products arrived at?

Microeconomics in tourism is concerned with the study of the total (usually termed aggregate) effects of economic phenomena affecting the local, national or international economy. Key questions include:

- What factors determine the level of aggregate tourist spending?
- What is aggregate economic effect of tourism on the economy through the so-called 'multiplier' effect?
- In this chapter we will consider some of these questions first at the micro level and thereafter at the macro level.

ECONOMIC CHOICES

The cornerstone of economic analysis at the micro level is the consideration of supply and demand and the interaction between them. Every individual demands goods and services (products) and, when all these demands are put together, the resulting aggregate demand is what the industry must supply if all consumers are to achieve satisfaction.

The interaction of the forces of supply and demand determine the price of a product. Products have a price because they are useful (or have *utility* to use the economists' jargon), and because they are scarce. Their usefulness is shown by the fact that consumers demand them and scarcity is revealed by the unwillingness of firms of provide unlimited amounts of a product. Neither demand nor supply are static but vary with changing condition. Furthermore, the nature of demand and supply will vary according to the nature of the product in question. Before going on to consider the nature of demand and supply in tourism, it is necessary to consider briefly where the interaction of these forces takes places in a market. Markets are situations where buyers and sellers of products come together in order to exchange. To an economist, the term 'market' does not represent the geographical place where buyers and sellers meet buy instead, refers to all those buyers and sellers who exert an influence on the price of a product. Some markets are worldwide, such as the markets for oil, gold or foreign exchange, whereas others are more localised, such as the markets for holidays or transportation.

In analysing markets, economists distinguish between *perfect* and *imperfect* competition in markets. All markets have some imperfections, but economics often study perfect markets as they provide useful insight to the theoretical behaviour of markets and demonstrate what would happen if all the imperfections were to be removed.

A perfect market exists where there are a large number of buyers and sellers and no individual buyer or seller has enough market power to influence the market price. In a perfect market:

- Individual firms must sell at the prevailing market price.
- All buyers and sellers have the same information about prices.
- The consumer will act rationally by purchasing at the lowest available price.
- The product is uniform across the market (*i.e.* it is homogeneous).
- There is freedom of entry into the market for new sellers.
- It is easy and cheap of transfer purchases from one seller to another.

These conditions, outlined above, ensure that price difference in the market are rapidly eliminated and that one market price is established for each product. In the world, of course, perfect markets do not exist, although some markets such as the market for foreign exchange, come close. All markets exhibit some degree of imperfection. Reasons for this include:

- Suppliers creating the impression that their products are different or better than those of their competitors.
- The loyalty of consumers to particular products preventing rational buying decisions being made.
- Buyers and sellers not having complete access to information on prices.
- An individual buyer or seller (or a group of buyers and sellers) being powerful enough to influence the price of the products on offer.

At the opposite end of the spectrum of market types from perfect markets are monopolistic markets where there is only one seller in the market, and the seller thereby has a very large influence on the price (unless the market is regulated by outside bodies). For example, the aviation market is heavily regulated by government agencies.

Having briefly considered the nature of markets, we can now move on to consider demand and supply and how they interact in markets through the *price mechanism.*

THE CONCEPT OF DEMAND

Demand represents the quantity of a product buyers are willing and able to buy at a particular price over a specified period of time.

Demand to an economist is not quite the same as wants. Everyone might want to go on a round-the-world cruise, but not everyone has the ability to pay for it. Thus, wants are unlimited, but demand is limited by the ability to pay. Several factors influence the total market demand for a product such as:

- The price of the product.
- The price of competing products.
- The size and distribution of household incomes.

- Fashion and tastes.
- Opportunities for consumption (*e.g.* leisure time).

Central to a consideration of demand is the theory of demand which states that: Other things being equal, the quantity of a good or service demanded is inversely related to its price. In other words, as the price goes down the quantity demanded goes up and, conversely, as the price goes up the quantity demanded goes down.

The Demand Curve

This relationship between demand and price is usually shown graphically as a demand curve. A demand curve can be drawn:

- For an individual consume.
- A *market* demand curve which represents the aggregate quantity of a product demanded by all consumers together, at a given price.

A demand curve is constructed from a *demand schedule,* which shows the quantities of a product that are demanded at different prices. The market demand curve generally slopes downwards to the right because:

- As prices fall the product becomes cheaper relative to other products and, therefore, expenditure will shift to the product whose price has fallen. That is, a fall in the relative price of a product increases the demand for it—*the substitution effect.* (An increase in the relative price of a product decreases the demand for it).
- A fall in the product's price means that people with lower incomes will be able to afford it and the overall demand therefore increase. That is, a fall in the absolute price of a product increases in the demand for it—*the price effect.* (The converse is also true if the product's price rises).

Analysis of a given demand curve gives a great deal of information about the nature of demand for a particular product. In particular two factors are of interest:

1. The shape or slope of the demand curve.
2. The position of the demand curve.

The shape or slope of the curve is a reflection of its steepness, and tells us how sensitive demand is to changes in price; that is, the *elasticity of demand.* The position of the curve refers to its position in relation to each axis. As already established, changes in price result in movements along the curve.

TOURISM AND ECONOMIC DEVELOPMENT

This chapter seeks to introduce some of the important concepts and concerns associated with expanding the economic benefits of tourism through investment in infrastructure. It is adapted from previous work by the author and colleagues, and was presented in part in a World Tourism Organization publication. There is growing recognition that innovative approaches must be adopted in order to maintain the economic health of many countries, communities and regions. While conditions vary from region to region, tourism has been seen as an important form of economic development. It has also been promoted as a somewhat benign agent of economic and social change, a promulgator of peace through interaction and dialogue, and a service-based industry capable of creating employment and income.

The perception that tourism has only positive economic benefits has lessened in recent years, due to the growing awareness and knowledge of the more intangible and indirect economic costs of tourism. While it can be argued that tourism does offer an important alternative form of economic activity, it must be seen as only one component of a larger series of development initiatives within any economic system. That is not to say that tourism in selected circumstances cannot be the major source of income and jobs in a community or region, but rather that the impact and role of tourism will vary from region to region.

Experience has shown that tourism may take many forms and meet a number of tourist motivations. Experience has also shown that destinations can rise and fall in popularity, driven by various factors in the destination's internal and external environment.

A destination that is entirely dependent on tourism is much more vulnerable to these shifts than an economy that is well diversified and has tourism as just one of its industries.

ECONOMIC EFFECTS OF TOURISM

The ability of a tourism destination to attract tourism revenues and investment in infrastructure is influenced by a complex number of characteristics, such as:

- Political constraints and incentives;
- The resources and conveniences offered;
- Market characteristics;
- Political stability;
- The ability of the destination to market and promote itself effectively.

The primary and secondary effects of tourism expenditures are discussed later in this chapter. In its simplest form, the economic impact of tourism can be measured as the difference in economic well-being between the income levels that would have existed without tourism activity and the income levels after tourism activity. There are a number of potential tangible and less tangible economic benefits and costs; these are summarized below.

The potential economic benefits of tourism development include:

- Increased resources for the protection and conservation of natural and cultural heritage resources;

- Increased income and improved standard of living from tourist expenditures;
- Increased induced income from tourism expenditures;
- New employment opportunities;
- Increased community visibility leading to other economic development opportunities;
- New induced employment opportunities;
- Increased tax base;
- Improved infrastructure and facilities;
- Development of local handicrafts.

The potential costs include:

- Seasonal employment;
- Low status/paying jobs;
- Inflation;
- Increased costs;
- Pollution;
- Increased traffic/congestion;
- Negative impacts on cultural and natural heritage resources;
- Increased crime;
- Increased taxes;
- Leakage of revenues and external domination;
- Over-dependence on tourism as a prime economic activity.

There are other costs that may have an indirect or long-term impact on the economic contributions of tourism. For example, land values may change as high-priced projects replace traditional and less profitable land uses. If agricultural landowners choose to sell or develop their land for tourism purposes, the tourism economy may have to rely on some food imports to feed the tourists and locals. The loss of traditional land values can also have an impact on the local heritage and sense of place. Moreover, conflict may arise between those landowners who do not wish to see the loss of the historic character of their community and area, and pro-tourism proponents.

Residents and speculators who suffer or benefit from rising land prices might join in the fray. Such conflict could escalate as tourism pressures increase, and the resulting scars on the community might take a long time to heal. This short example helps to illustrate that understanding and measuring economic impacts is more complex than simply measuring direct impacts. It is also important to view economic impacts from a long-term perspective. Environmental degradation and pollution will result in short-term environmental costs and associated economic costs incurred in repairing the damage caused by the pollution. There could also be considerable long-term economic costs to the local, regional, and national economies if the destination is no longer desirable due to the effects of degradation and pollution.

MEASURING ECONOMIC IMPACTS OF TOURISM

A major objective of any tourism planning and development process should be to minimize negative impacts and ensure that the benefits are realised in an equitable manner. While there are significant problems on the road to achieving this objective, there is growing recognition that sustainable tourism approaches will help in reaching this goal. There are a number of methods for measuring the economic impacts of tourism activity, some of which are discussed below. Measuring the economic impact and employment creation activities of tourism should be carried out in an integrated fashion, taking into account direct and indirect job creation as well as the economic well being of the community.

While employment creation is seen as an important objective, concern for the overall local economy must also be a major consideration. As has been discussed, this implies that jobs and economic benefits may be realised from a number of sources other than tourism. It may also imply that jobs are created as the result of private sector entrepreneurial activity as well as community initiative.

SUPPLY-DEMAND AND PRICE ELASTICITIES

The economic contribution of tourism activity to a community or region is influenced by a diverse number of factors within and outside the destination. Given that diversity, it is difficult to calculate impacts due to the wide range of effects associated with tourism economic activities, the diverse number of participants involved in those activities, and the complex interrelationships between various sectors. Tourism economic activity is often explained using the concept of supply and demand. A number of variables influence the demand and supply of a tourism product or service. For example, if the price of a hotel room increases, demand may decrease, as visitors seek other locations or accommodation sources, and the supply of available hotel rooms therefore increases.

The supply-demand relationship of tourism goods and services can be influenced by factors such as the price elasticity of demand for tourism. When demand is price elastic, a lower price could generate a higher demand and hence higher revenues.

Similarly, if demand is price inelastic, a lower price could result in lower overall revenues. Knowing the price elasticity of demand can aid tourism service providers in designing their product mix. However, a number of factors affect price elasticity, making it difficult to calculate.

DIRECT AND INDIRECT EFFECTS OF TOURISM EARNINGS

The economic benefits of travel and tourism can be derived directly or indirectly. The primary effect is direct benefits that result from direct tourist expenditures for goods and services in the destination. These are realised through business receipts, income, employment and government receipts from the sectors that directly receive the tourism expenditure. Indirect benefits are generated by the circulation of tourism expenditures in the destination country through domestic inter-business transactions. For example, indirect benefits can be generated from the investment and spending by the businesses that benefit directly from tourism expenditures. The direct business receipts, when re-funnelled as investments or used to purchase other goods and services from domestic suppliers, stimulate income and employment in other sectors. In addition, tourism spending within the destination area can create induced benefits.

As income levels rise due to the direct and indirect effects of change in the level of tourism expenditure, some of the additional personal income is spent within the destination. This results in induced benefits, such as local income and jobs in the local goods and service sector. Hence, the spending by tourists at the destination can create direct benefits in tourism-related services and sectors such as accommodation, hospitality, attractions, events and transportation. This spending can also create a significant amount of indirect and induced benefits in other sectors such as agriculture, construction and manufacturing. Indirect and induced benefits are also referred to as the secondary effect.

MULTIPLIER MODEL OF TOURISM REVENUE TURNOVER

Multipliers measure the effect of expenditures introduced into an economy. Tourism multipliers are used to determine changes in output, income, employment, business and government receipts, and balance of payments due to a change in the level of tourism expenditures in an area. For example, if tourism expenditures increase by 15 per cent due to attendance at a special event in the destination, some of this added revenue may be used by the event to purchase food and other goods from the local economy, as well as on payment of wages, salaries, government taxes etc.

The suppliers to the event may then spend the money received from the event on other goods, services, taxes etc., thus generating yet another round of expenditures. Employees from the events and local suppliers to the events may use the additional personal income, derived from the direct and indirect effects of the increase in tourism expenditures, to consume local goods and services.

Some of the added revenues from the increase in tourism expenditures may, however, undergo leakage. For example, revenues may leak out of the local economy in the form of payment for imports or monies saved. Import payments can take several forms, such as repatriation of profits to foreign corporations and salaries to non-local managers, as well as payment for imported goods and promotion and advertising by companies based outside the destination.

Tourism-related commodities and services could be purchased from within the destination, thereby reducing leakages through the creation of economic interrelationships among the goods and service providers in the destination. The net effect of the successive rounds of spending of added tourism expenditure is the multiplier effect. In essence, tourism multipliers attempt to describe the relationship between direct tourism expenditure in the economy and the secondary effect of that expenditure upon the economy. Some of the factors that affect the multiplier are the size of the local economy, the propensity of tourists and residents to buy imported goods or services, as well as the propensity of residents to save rather than spend. In mathematical terms.

Some common multipliers are:

- The income multiplier, which measures the extra domestic income generated by an extra unit of tourism expenditure;
- The employment multiplier, which measures the increased number of primary and secondary jobs created by an extra unit of tourism expenditure;
- The government multiplier, which measures the extra government revenue created by an extra unit of tourism expenditure.

Multipliers can be calculated for a country, region or community. However, the information provided by tourism multipliers has to be very carefully evaluated. Factors such as the size of the destination can significantly affect the multiplier. A smaller economy may have a much smaller multiplier than a larger one since more goods and services might be imported to meet the tourists' needs, resulting in a greater leakage of revenues out of the destination.

Hence, multipliers may vary greatly among communities within a country or region. Furthermore, since tourism multipliers can be calculated in a number of different ways, care must be taken when comparing the multipliers of different countries. Multipliers should be examined together with other measurements and indicators in order to determine the positive and negative economic impacts of tourism on the community.

INPUT-OUTPUT ANALYSIS

Studies of the economic impacts of tourism generally include inputoutput analysis. This kind of analysis helps to demonstrate how economic sectors are related, the number of linkages and the effect of these linkages. This form of analysis is, therefore, a means of analysing inter-industry relationships in the flow of goods and services in an area's economy, through the chain of producers, suppliers and intermediaries to the final buyer.

Input-output analysis commences with the development of a table that illustrates, in matrix form, how transactions flow through the economy over a given time period. The rows of the matrix show the sales of the total output by each sector to every other sector.

The columns demonstrate the inputs required by every sector from the other sectors.

When assessing tourism accommodation, the rows in the table would demonstrate the output, *i.e.*, the revenues generated by each industry from the sale of products or services, including accommodation, meals, tour guides and related services such as laundry, medical services etc. The columns would allow us to see the inputs that go into the output of the accommodation sector, including food, utilities, paper products, advertising and promotion services, wage and salary levels etc.

Using a combination of matrix manipulations, multipliers can be calculated to provide an assessment of the effects of different sectors on each other. While input-output tables are helpful in understanding the linkages of the sectors in the economy, it must be remembered that the information obtained provides a snapshot of inter-industry economic actions at only one point in time.

TOURISM SATELLITE ACCOUNTS

Satellite accounts provide comprehensive information on a field of economic activity, and are generally tied to the economic accounts of a nation or region. The Tourism Satellite Account is a relatively new phenomenon.

For example, the British Columbia Ministry of Development, Trade and Tourism has developed a Tourism Satellite Account as a separate input-output model designed to display tourism's contributions to the province related to the overall input-output model of the province.

A Tourism Satellite Account has also been developed by Statistics Canada in order to assess the significance of tourism to Canada. The account uses concise definitions of tourism and attempts to provide a clear and real measure of tourism-related economic activity. Both direct and indirect tourism activities are accounted for in areas such as, but not limited to, demand, supply, employment, taxes etc. Such a tool is crucial in determining the complex spending patterns of visitors as well as the goods and services that cater to their needs.

Some of the advantages of the Tourism Satellite Accounts can be summarized as follows:

- They help governments and businesses determine the value of tourism to the economy, and thereby develop strategies for ensuring competitive advantage;
- They identify the amount of benefit enjoyed by various sectors, and the employment, income, taxes and other benefits that flow from those sectors;
- They provide a comprehensive picture of the size and scale of tourism in a country, and can help to gather support for ensuring adherence to the principles of sustainable tourism development.

COST-BENEFIT EVALUATION

By applying a number of economic tools and methods, destinations are able to obtain a large array of economic information on tourism; this information can then be used to make decisions. In assessing this information, analysts, planners, and managers have to determine not just whether jobs and wealth are created, but also how the benefits are distributed, what costs result from the development process, and whether the benefits of tourism outweigh the economic, social and cultural costs.

It is clear that economic analysis needs to be integrated with other data in order to provide a reasonable indication of whether tourism is a good strategy for the destination. Cost-benefit analysis is an important activity to perform, but is also difficult to carry out, since a number of the costs are very difficult to quantify. How does one measure the "sense of place" or "spiritual happiness" of a population? How does one quantify the loss value of habitat fragmentation to ecological integrity? While strides are being taken to develop full-cost, environmentally-based accounting, some measures may need to remain qualitative rather than quantitative. Full-scale cost-benefit analysis, while recommended, can therefore be time consuming, expensive and difficult to conduct. Another challenge of cost-benefit analysis lies in identifying who benefits from, and who pays the costs of, tourism. Smaller cost-benefit analyses can be conducted on specific issues to provide information related to tourism.

OBSTACLES TO CREATING ECONOMIC DEVELOPMENT FROM TOURISM

There are a number of obstacles to creating economic development through tourism. These obstacles are discussed below.

Market Obstacles

The potential for a region or municipality to attract tourists on a long-term basis is a key factor. Tourism activities, to a very large degree, are dictated by what is considered "popular" at a given point in time.

In addition, the ability and interest of tourists to travel and how far they are willing to travel is dependent on a variety of factors, such as income levels, cost of fuel, job security, physical condition and mobility, and travel motivations. The ability of a destination to conduct a reliable market survey, identify a positioning strategy and promote itself is essential. However, this requires skill and knowledge that is often lacking in many areas. In addition, cooperation in the marketing effort is important but difficult to achieve in many urban and rural settings.

Community Obstacles

Negative perceptions of tourism are often found at the local level. Tourism activities are not generally viewed as “viable” or “appropriate” business ventures. Generally, tourism is viewed as a short-term activity until more appealing and profitable employment can be found, since many tourism positions pay low wages and are seen as low-status occupations. These perceptions act as a deterrent to local people participating in tourism-related employment.

Lack of Infrastructure

As is discussed later in this study there are a number of infrastructure elements that are crucial to the success of tourism at all levels of a country or region.

As tourism tastes change and become more sophisticated, and as the competitive environment further develops, countries and destinations will require adequate infrastructure to meet market demands as well as environmental regulations.

Environmental Obstacles

The emphasis in most tourism activities tends to be on attracting larger numbers of tourists to a region or site, posing problems for environmentally sensitive areas. It is clear that some environments may have to generate high-yielding tourist activities to generate sufficient income while protecting social and natural environments. This is difficult to accomplish in the highly competitive tourism market.

Lack of Integration

There is limited integration and cooperation between many tourism businesses given that, for the most part, the local tourism industry tends to be fragmented or lacking in tourism expertise.

Institutional Obstacles

There is very little coordinated governmental support and promotion for tourism development and initiatives. In addition, governmental activities are often poorly structured to help plan and manage tourism. In other instances, political and other ideologies make tourism planning and management difficult to implement.

Employment and Training Obstacles

There is a serious lack of training and education opportunities in tourism planning and management. The training that is available is often very narrow in focus, and does not address the broader context of tourism and the range of potential opportunities.

The scarcity of employment equity and opportunities for women is a serious obstacle in ensuring an equitable distribution of the benefits of tourism activity. In addition, access to education and training is limited for a number of disadvantaged groups. It is clear from this discussion that there are a number of factors and obstacles that need to be considered in the expansion of tourism. It is essential that an integrated approach be taken. The role of infrastructure in that particular process will be explored in the remaining portion of this study.

ECONOMIC IMPORTANCE OF TOURISM IN ASIA PACIFIC

Tourism is one of the most important sectors in the economies of Asia Pacific countries.

Currently, tourism is the most important sector and major source of foreign exchange earnings in Thailand, Australia, and New Zealand. It is ranked second in Hong Kong, Malaysia and the Philippines, and ranked third in Singapore and Indonesia. For example, in New Zealand, the tourism industry employs more than 200,000 people, with projections of a 14% annual growth till the year 2000. In Hong Kong, tourism employs 12% of the workforce and contributes about 7% to the economy. The tourism sector in Thailand supports over 1.5 million jobs and contributes 5% to the economy. Tourism is also gaining importance in China.

By the year 2000, China expects to receive 55 million visitors with foreign exchange earnings of US$14 billion, which will contribute 5% to China's economy, making tourism one of the most significant components of the national economy. In Singapore, the healthy overall balance of payments is attributed to the huge surplus achieved by the tourism sector which contributes about 10% to the economy. Despite Singapore's open economy, and its vulnerability to external shocks and import leakages, tourism has made a significant contribution to output, employment, and income.

Based on 1988 input-output tables, Khan *et al.* (1995) estimated that tourism contributed 11.9% to Singapore's GDP (Gross Domestic Product) in 1992, while employment accounted for 13.4% of the labour force. The employment effect of a million dollars in tourist expenditures would create 25 new jobs. The results its showed that every dollar of tourist expenditure would generate S$1.97 of output and S$1.05 in income.

The income multiplier for tourism was larger when compared to Hong Kong, Indonesia and Malaysia, while the tourism output multiplier was greater relative to other sectors of the Singapore economy. Comparisons with previous studies showed an increase in the contribution of tourism over time, a strong indication of the significance of tourism in the Singapore economy.

The estimated economic impact of tourism is also significant in South Korea. According to Lee and Kwon (1995), the total impact of tourism receipts of US$4.7 billion in 1993, generated US$11.7 of output, US$2.4 billion in income, and created 350,000 full time jobs. The secondary impacts were also found to have a considerable effect on the economy. The findings suggested that tourism should be promoted as a strategic export industry.

It is no surprise that the key to the success of tourism in the Asia Pacific region is a clear recognition by the host governments of the important role of tourism in the economic development of the country. Tourism serves as an important means to increase economic growth, raise the quality of life, create employment, and improve the overall balance of payments by helping to offset deficits in other sectors. Many Asia Pacific countries show a net surplus in their tourism balance of payment account.

Japan, Taiwan, and South Korea are major tourist generating countries in the region and this is reflected by the deficits in their respective travel balance of payments accounts. Mak and White (1992) attributed the travel account deficits for these high income countries to a higher allocation of disposable income to leisure travel. The relaxation of travel restrictions in Taiwan also had a significant impact on its travel account, due to the large increase in outbound travel. On the other hand, China, Thailand, and Singapore are major receivers of tourists, enjoying a huge surplus. As a percentage of exports, tourism contributes more than 13/n to the economies of Australia, New Zealand, and Thailand, again reflecting its ranking as the top export. Its contribution to the GDP is significantly greater in Singapore (10%) and Hong Kong (7%).

Almost all Asian nations are committing substantial manpower and resources to attract more arrivals whose expenditures represent significant contributions to national income and foreign exchange earnings. For example, Singapore has unveiled a new tourism blueprint titled "Tourism 21" that is expected to turn the nation into a world class tourism business centre and the tourism capital of the East. Plans call for increasing arrivals and receipts by 6.4% and 6.6% annually to 10 million and US$11.4 billion, respectively, by the year 2000.

Even Indonesia and Malaysia have raised their commitments towards developing the tourism sector. Indonesia plans to make tourism the nation's number one foreign exchange earner by the year 2004, when arrivals will hit 11 million and receipts reach US$15 billion from current levels of 4.3 million and US$5.4 billion, respectively. In the current Seventh Malaysia Plan, which ends in the year 2000, a number of strategies were formulated to turn tourism into a top revenue earner for the country. Millions of dollars will be allocated for tourism infrastructure in an effort to increase arrivals and receipts to 12.5 million and US$6.3 billion, respectively, by the end of this decade. With increasing competition for the tourist dollar, the national tourism organizations of New Zealand, Thailand, Australia and Hong Kong, among others, have also allocated an increase in tourism funding to tap the emerging tourism markets that promise new income and employment opportunities.

GROWTH FACTORS

A number of factors are responsible for the rapid growth and development of the tourism industry in the Asia Pacific region. These include the strong economic growth, increase in income, breakdown of political barriers, easing of travel restrictions, liberalization of air transport, and focused marketing campaigns. These factors are expected to accelerate the growth of tourism over the next decade.

Economic Growth

The rapid growth of the tourism industry is a reflection of the region's booming and diversified economies. Economic growth has ranged between an average of 6% to 9% in the last decade, in contrast to 3% to 4% growth achieved by the rest of the world. Only the industrialized countries of Australia, Japan, and New Zealand show a lower rate of growth than the rest of the region. China, which has achieved double-digit growth over the last 5 years, is poised to become one of the world's largest economies and surpass Japan in the next decade. The region is expected to maintain its growth at a rate between 6% to 8% over the next decade.

Strong economic growth in Asia is attributed to a focus on market reforms, export oriented industries, stable currencies, diversification of the economy, and massive injection of foreign capital. Billions of dollars are being poured into the tourism infrastructure to accommodate a burgeoning Asian tourism industry. This has intensified trade, investment, and travel within the region and with the rest of the world. Asian governments have also sought to avoid extremes of inflation and unemployment, and are keeping budget deficits small or running surpluses. It is no wonder that the region has attracted much attention from the rest of the world regarding its success. The opening up of Indochina, Myanmar, and China to tourism, and given the increasing number of companies setting up bases and new businesses in the region the volume of business travel will rise. This will provide ample marketing opportunities for travel-related businesses.

Income and Leisure Time

As a result of strong economic growth, disposable incomes have soared in Asian countries and along with it, the propensity to travel. Leisure consciousness has been enhanced with travel no longer seen as a luxury. In fact, it is now seen as an affordable commodity to be enjoyed by all who choose to engage in a variety of leisurely pursuits. Some Asians may see travel as a status symbol, while others see it as relief from the pressures of work. The introduction of a 5-day workweek in China will provide Chinese residents with more leisure time that will likely be devoted to travel.

A number of Asian countries have recorded significant growth in real per capita income over the last Syears with Singapore (7.3%), Thailand (6.8%), China (10.3%), 5. Korea (6.7%), and Indonesia (7.1%) showing the highest growth. Rising incomes have created a middle class of sophisticated and affluent Asians who are better educated, have more disposable income, and who appreciate the value of leisure. Research by Mak and White (1992) has shown travel propensity and tourism spending to be positively correlated a ed with per capita income among the major Asia Pacific countries. This means that increases in income levels will enable a greater proportion of Asians to travel overseas. Unlike previous generations, this generation of primarily young travelers are intent on enjoying the fruits of their labour. Although price conscious, they still demand high qualify products. Since Asians are more likely to travel in groups and families, more travel products and services, such as tour packages that incorporate activities, must be designed to cater to their needs. This may include travel to exotic places, soft-adventure travel, cruises, and sports related tours, among others. Disposable incomes will continue to rise, and thus fuel the demand for leisure travel. The trend among Asia Pacific countries is towards more frequent regional holidays to various destinations and resorts within the region.

Political Stability and Breakdown of Political Barriers

In recent years, the Asia Pacific region has become politically more stable than it has ever been, especially in the Philippines, where tourism was adversely affected by terrorism, civil strife, and natural disasters in the last decade. However, the political, social and economic reforms of the current government have reversed the fortunes of the tourism industry. Tourism investments in the Philippines over the last 3 years were estimated at U5$6.27 billion, with a large portion of the funds allocated towards resort development. To encourage more investment, the Philippines Department of Tourism is urging financial institutions to provide funding to investors involved in tourism-related projects.

Investors are showing confidence not only in the Philippines but also in Vietnam, Indonesia, and China. These nations, which were off-limits to foreigners at one time, are witnessing rapid hotel and resort developments. Even areas which were closed or long considered inaccessible in parts of China and Indonesia are now open to tourism. The opening of borders to both inbound and outbound travel, and the breakdown of political barriers, will provide tourists with opportunities to pursue their leisure interests. For example, South Korea's normalization of relations with China also is expected to boost arrivals from Seoul to major cities in China when non-stop air traffic routes are inaugurated.

TOURISM IN THE UNDERDEVELOPED WORLD

LDCs suffer from a history of colonial domination and what has been referred to as dependent development. A review of tourism literature reinforces the notion that there is a set evolutionary pattern of multinational interests in the tourism sector of the underdeveloped. Dependency, therefore, can be conceptualised as a process of historical conditioning which alters the internal functioning of economic and social subsystems within a less developed country. This dependency occurs not from processes within the LDC's economy, but rather from demand from overseas tourists and new foreign company investment in the LDC. For example, after a potential tourist destination has been identified (on the basis of unique biophysical or cultural conditions), the involvement of the multinationals increases. Foreign companies greatly influence the image of a destination country through development and promotion. Such efforts lead tourists to perceive the host country in terms of this image and the nature of hotel accommodation, attractions, and other tourist services as publicised.

Domination of the tourism sector in an LDC is most outwardly represented by the foreign ownership of airlines and hotels. However, the grip on the destination region often goes much deeper.

Because of the inability of agricultural and manufacturing producers in most underdeveloped economies to guarantee a good-quality supply of goods and services for international luxury-standard tourist facilities, there is a strong reliance on imported supplies for both the construction and the operation of tourist facilities.

Also, as Winpenny (1982) writes, middle and senior management levels of tourism developments in underdeveloped countries are often occupied by expatriates. The following scenario of metropolitan dominance serves as an example:

On arrival in a Caribbean island between plane and hotel, the tourists could well have passed through a terminal building presented by the people of Canada and have been driven along a road either built or improved 'thanks' to Canadian aid, on behalf of the expected Canadian tourists of course. At the hotel you will likely be greeted with rum punches the first of the few local products to be encompassed by the package.

At your first meal, a menu, perhaps designed in Toronto, Chicago or Miami will provide you with a selection of food imported for the greater part from North America—good familiar, homogenized, taste-free food, dressed up with a touch of local colour.

The question therefore is as follows: who owns and controls the various components of a holiday package? It has been found (Economic and Social Commission for Asia and the Pacific 1978:40) that where tour packages consist of a foreign air carrier, but include local hotel and other group services, destination countries receive on average only 40-45 per cent of the inclusive tour retail prices paid by the tourists in their home country. If both the airline and hotels are owned by foreign companies, a mere 22-25 per cent of the retail tour price stays in the destination country.

While Rajotte (1980) feels that tourism is less environmentally destructive than other forms of development that exist in tropical islands, there are still many significant effects that may be attributed to tourism. Many of these impacts are universal, but their intensity and severity are more noticeable in island environments (much of the past research on dependency and development has been linked to island environments).

Important is the notion that often with size comes ecological diversity. Nation states of the Caribbean, because of their small size, have tenuous floral and faunal vitality. Tourism can stress these systems through yearly visitation levels that exceed the local population of an island; for example, Hayward *et al.* write that in 1979, more than 600,000 tourists visited Bermuda, some ten times the population of the island.

A key area of research for the future is the need to document whether or not developing countries such as Brazil, Costa Rica, Dominica, the countries of Eastern Africa, and Ecuador undergo the same social, ecological, and economic dysfunctions from ecotourism as outlined above from the perspective of mass tourism.

For example, Kusler (1991) writes that ecotourism in the LDCs is marked by limited dollars, government-directed financing, foreign visitation, foreign ownership of hotels and other facilities, and non-existent land use planning. In this sense, ecotourism as an intervention may or may not improve the socio-economic conditions of a country from the example of mass tourism outlined above. It is important to realise, as outlined by Kusler, that the LDCs and their developed-country counterparts are separated by a number of key structural differences. These include finances, the political climate of a country, accessibility to opportunities, discretionary income, and resources for the acquisition and planning of land.

CORE-PERIPHERY CONCEPT

One of the main theoretical approaches used to explain development is the concept of core and periphery, which Freidmann and Alonso (1974) describe as characterised by a dynamic, growing central region, and a slower-growing or stagnating periphery. The core is marked by high-growth potential whereas peripheral areas are often marked by declining rural economies with low agricultural production (loss of primary resource).

Shields refers to peripheralised regions as marginal places, regions that 'are not necessarily on geographical peripheries but, first and foremost, they have been placed on the periphery of cultural systems of space in which places are ranked relative to each other'.

Important in his discussion is the fact that margins, from social, political, economic, and perceptual perspectives, are systems of centres and peripheries and are, therefore, locationally oriented.

These spatial systems are established in a series of binary relationships (economic, society, and so on) of centre and periphery, so that margins signify everything that the centre denies or represses.

Our socio-economic paradigm is constantly exercising this binary relationship, and it reaches to the furthest outposts of physical space and humanity. In a touristic sense, a classic example of the core-periphery idea can be found in Christaller's (1963) analysis of tourism location in Europe. Christaller wrote that tourism avoids central places and is drawn to the periphery, reaching the natural resource base not found in cities.

This idea has been further developed by a number of authors. In particular, Battisti (1982) reflected on the principles established by Christaller on tourist space organisation, noting that tourism is part of the continual process carried out by humankind in order to specialise and to diversify the exploitation of the soil. Battisti made reference to the distinction between peripheral regions and peripheral places. The first represents a wide range of possibilities in choosing a recreational place.

The second indicates real destinations of tourist flows, where the 'fruition of space for recreational purposes is accomplished'. The core-periphery concept has also been applied more recently to the analysis of adventure travel regions from a spatial context. Zurick (1992) suggested that the movement of adventure travellers in Nepal takes place through a complicated hierarchy of gateways.

Tourists from the core move through an international gateway (semi-periphery), to a national gateway (periphery), and further to a regional gateway (periphery frontier), said to be the adventure region. In this latter region there is often a clash between traditional interests and national development goals. As frontier regions succumb to further intrusions, the uniqueness of these areas diminishes, as does the potential for travel to untouched areas in the future as these areas become fewer in number.

One of the key defining elements of travellers to outward peripheries is the need to experience something different in a remote setting. Along with this, perhaps, is the need to escape the mainstream of tourism, which can only be achieved by taking the road less travelled.

Although there are few data at hand to support this idea, the traveller's mind-set may alter upon reaching successive outward peripheries of a destination.

Fennell (1996) thought that the following factors contributed to this feeling:

- *Familiarity with the destination*: A lack of knowledge or familiarity with a region's environment/culture may add to the uniqueness of such an area and therefore represent a perceived periphery.
- *Unscheduled change*: Movement that occurs spontaneously or that is not pre-planned (e.g. from a core region to a peripheral region).
- *Psychological and/or physiological change*: Personal adaptations that have to be made in order to feel comfortable or maximise feelings of satisfaction/pleasure, including culture, language, personal hygiene, food, and shelter.

- *Distance from amenities*: This factor reinforces the notion that a particular peripheral region does not, cannot, or will not offer goods and services that can be found at regions closer to the core.
- *Adaptation*: As tourists move out to a new periphery, the accompanying shortage of goods and services such as shops and facilities—found at regions closer to the core—becomes more accepted. The state of the infrastructure, therefore, plays less of a role in satisfying the tourist. Poor weather may also not pose a problem because a more 'frontier-like' attitude is adopted.
- *Population density*: Regions with a lower tourist and local population density may provide an indication that the periphery has been, or is being, reached.
- *Authenticity*. As population density decreases, the authenticity and/or incidence of natural and cultural attractions may increase in relation to the characteristics of the region. The character of the region is important, as Costa Rica may have a higher species diversity in urban areas than Shetland has at the periphery.
- *Symbolism*: The periphery may be represented by experiential, environmental, or cultural phenomena (symbols). Such phenomena may include lochs, mountains, wind, solitude, barrenness, a rainforest, or lack of banking machines. Consequently, the more these symbols are experienced, the greater might be the feeling of reaching the perimeter. Fear may also act as a symbol, as may the realisation that there is a lack of knowledge of a region and its charact-eristics.

Fear or anxiety of the unknown is an important feature of adventure tourism (characteristics that Csikszentmihalyi (1990) has reported on regarding risk-taking in rock climbers).

- *Scale of attraction*: It is the region itself that may take on characteristics of 'attraction' in the outer periphery. For example, while cities have many attractions and goods and services to offer tourists and locals alike, small, peripheral islands may have comparatively few or no structural attractions, and because of this the nature of the island's limited infrastructure, small size, and distance from the mainland may be the attraction itself.
- *Distance from home*: This factor occurs in combination with other factors. For example, travel to Sydney, Australia, from rural Canada represents a large distance, but may not necessarily represent a mental change from core to periphery.

Thus the relationship between core and periphery has not only a psychological component but, as discussed earlier, a spatial one. This spatial component occurs at a variety of scales. Examples include small islands of the South controlled by the North, and huge territories of the North controlled politically, economically, and socially by decision-makers of the core. The Northwest Territories of Canada has been identified by Keller (1987) as an example of a peripheral region caught in transition regarding the development of its tourism industry.

To Keller, differing authorities in control of development in this region become important actors in both decision-making and implementation of a viable tourist industry. These hierarchies of control occur at local, regional, national, and international levels. As the sphere of tourism development becomes international, Keller suggests, the more the periphery has become 'a playground for exogenous investors, and the peripheral government an observer of its own fate'. It is stated by Keller that to avoid a transgression of the above scenario, the periphery (Northwest Territories) must act to control the decision-making in the development of a tourist industry, and limit the development to a scale of growth in tune with the resources, capital, manpower, and culture within the periphery. The implications of the core-periphery concept to ecotourism are that, often, remote travel regions are dependent on national and international markets, inbound and outbound tour operators, as well as externally based transport modes and schedules. With the inability and lack of resources fully to plan and implement ecotourism on their own, the cycle of tourism dependency continues for peripheral regions.

This lack of an ability to link directly with the market in the developed world is one of the main reasons why the benefits of ecotourism do not percolate down to the community level; and it is precisely why those who are able to coordinate ecotourism activities—whether they be expatriates or local—between the LDCs and the developed world stand greatly to gain economically.

In such a case the power to make ecotourism happen in a developing country lies in the hands of a few, and perpetuates the phenomenon of a typical LDC economic situation, with much of the money and resources lying in the hands of a few, and the majority of the population, in the absence of a prominent middle class, living in impoverished conditions.

While the preceding discussion has emphasised the significance and impact of externally based control in the development of tourism and ecotourism enterprises at a macro level, the discussion of community development to follow offers an alternative to many of the tourism development concerns outlined above. Community development, then, may be considered as a viable means by which to offset the conventional tourism development models of the past and redistribute control and decision-making among the individuals within the community, not to those from outside.

COMMUNITY DEVELOPMENT

Community development, as described by Smith (1990a), originated in the self-help programmes that were developed during the depression years in

Canada, the United States, and the United Kingdom. A defining characteristic of community development is that it is based on local initiatives, in that it advocates a site-specific approach to finding solutions to community problems using community members and community resources. Bujold (1995:5) defines it as 'the process by which the efforts of the people themselves are united with those of governmental authorities to improve economic, social, and cultural conditions of communities'.

Typical community development encompasses all aspects of the community and focuses on the best quality of life possible for its members, and may involve creating new business and employment, increasing cultural awareness, or providing a range of opportunities for all members of the community. However, Joppe (1996) alludes to the fact that it is important to understand that there exists a fundamental division between conventional community development and community economic development (CED) models.

While conventional economic development focuses on the attraction of new businesses to the community (seen as an outward-directed approach to development), conversely a CED focus is on being small, green, and social, and is more inward in its orientation by striving to 'help consumers become producers, users become providers, and employees become owners of enterprise', through the principles of economic self-reliance, ecological sustainability, community control, meeting individual needs, and building a community culture.

Tourism is increasingly seen as a key community development tool in the 1990s, with the recognition of its economic contribution in bolstering stagnating economies and diversifying existing sectors, and its ability to unify community members. Such is the case in the Shetland Islands, Scotland, where tourism is being relied upon to sustain an economy that was once dominated by North Sea oil development, or the Finnish island of Åland, where all tourism initiatives are owned or controlled by local people.

With this realisation, researchers have begun to explore community development as it relates to tourism and ecotourism from many different perspectives. As an example, Christensen (1995) examines the role that tourism can play in securing quality of life within the community. At the foundation of any tourism development strategy is the realisation that

If tourism development is to be viable as a long-term economic strategy, these concerns [social and ecological] must be addressed, and the resource base must be protected in the process. The host community is the economic, social, cultural, and infrastructural resource base for most tourism activity, and resident quality of life is a measure of the condition of the resource.

Christensen proposes a community quality of life framework that addresses both objective and subjective indicators, at the individual and community scale. A tourism development project is said to affect change in the quality of life of members of the community, which in turn cause impacts at different social scales. Such impacts need to be evaluated both by individuals and by the community, depending on the scale of reference to the individual. There is a deliberate hierarchy established with respect to agents of change, suggesting that appropriate solutions need to be implemented at the individual social scale first, followed by neighbourhood groups, coalitions, responsible industry, policy, and governmental regulation.

The tactical approaches used by regions (local or national governing bodies) will make or break how ecotourism is perceived by local people, according to MacKinnon (1995). She sites a number of examples of communities in Mexico which have adopted or been identified to develop ecotourism in the country. One such community is Tres Garantías in the Yucatán peninsula. This region was initially set out as a hunting reserve by an international development team, but the area's residents found that non-consumptive recreation was more attractive to tourists than consumptive forms.

The project, however, was conceived using a top-end approach, and even though there have been isolated benefits derived from ecotourism, MacKinnon suggests that social integration within the community is not complete, and will not be complete until benefits are more widespread and the perception of ownership is given to the community. MacKinnon further uses the example of Los Tuxtlas, Veracruz, to illustrate that ecotourism has been successfully integrated into a community through more of a grassroots approach (initiated through the efforts of a local woman who set out to build empowerment slowly and deliberately). In this latter case, the community has been more quickly able to realise benefits which have been spreading on a more regional scale.

According to MacKinnon, the traditional mass tourism development model perpetuates the widening gap between rich and poor in countries like Mexico. Conversely, community-based tourism 'lends itself to being environmentally sustainable. Locals are the first to recognize the benefits of conserving their natural-resource base—much more so than large developers who don't live in the area'. While the interests of the community from a social standpoint are certainly paramount in the development of small-scale ecotourism, Williams (1992) feels that all factions within the community need to cooperate effectively in ensuring that a high-quality product is delivered without diminishing the ecology of the resource base. He advocates the development of an institutional structures strategy with the capacity to respond to tourism development before such development runs out of control.

This strategy includes the following:

- Development of a grassroots planning process, driven by local interests and including aboriginal involvement;
- Understanding and appreciation of ecotourism market requirements;
- An inventory of the region's resources to determine areas that are suitable for ecotourism and ones that are not;

- The establishment of goals and objectives in line with concerns related to the cultural and natural impacts of ecotourism, with the creation of a vision statement to act as a control mechanism for the future; and
- The establishment of a formal Tourism Management Board, to work with both the operators and the public, with the responsibility of monitoring change, communication, local benefits, etc.

Despite the fact that there will be direct and indirect beneficiaries and participants in the ecotourism industry, it is important to recognise that the entire community should be involved to some level. Participation therefore plays a key role in the initiative, as it empowers people to play a role in the decision-making process, where in many cases it is only those who are politically connected or affluent who are involved in the control and management of the enterprise. Such involvement can take the form of community representatives who speak for various elements of the population. This 'management committee' is very much like the proposed Tourism Management Board outlined by Williams (1992). The community ecotourism initiative needs to be founded on the notion of trust and transparency.

Actions and decisions need to be communicated to the community through bulletin boards or other means. Money and finances are identified by Sproule as critical elements in dividing a community. To be open about expenditures and to share information in an attempt to dispel feelings of mismanagement or corruption is to be transparent in one's approach to management. Specifically, Sproule's community-based ecotourism (CBE) refers to ecotourism enterprises that are owned and managed by the community. Furthermore, community-based ecotourism implies that a community is taking care of their natural resources in order to gain income through operating a tourism enterprise and using that income to better their lives. It involves conservation, business enterprise and community development.

A final example of how management may be used to control the development of ecotourism initiatives within a community is outlined by Drake (1991).

She defines local participation as 'the ability of local communities to influence the outcome of development projects such as ecotourism that have an impact on them'. Important in this process is the demonstrated benefit to the community both through community members' participation and through their realisation that some aspect of their community has been treated or protected (e.g. natural resources).

The following is proposed as a model of local participation in the development of ecotourism projects:

- *Phase 1: Determine the role of local participation in project*: This includes an assessment of how local people can help achieve set goals through efficiency, increasing project effectiveness, building beneficiary capacity, and sharing project costs.

- *Phase 2: Choose research team*: The team should include a broad multidisciplinary approach and include people in the social sciences and those within the media.
- *Phase 3: Conduct preliminary studies*: Political, economic, and social conditions of the community should be studied in the context of the environment, from existing documents, and by other survey-related work. Identification and assessment of the following is important: needs, key local leaders, media, the community's commitment to the project, intersectoral involvement, traditional uses of the land, the type of people interested in the project and why, the role of women, who will manage and finance the project, land ownership, and cultural values.
- *Phase 4: Determine the level of local involvement*: Local involvement occurs along a continuum from low-intensity to high-intensity involvement. This must be determined in addition to when the involvement is to occur. In cases where government is not supportive of local government, intermediaries (e.g. NGOs) can be used to facilitate local participation.
- *Phase 5: Determine an appropriate participation mechanism*: This is affected by the level of intensity of the participation, the nature of existing institutions (e.g. government, NGOs, citizens' groups), and the characteristics of the local people (how vociferous they may or may not be). This phase may include information sharing and consultation, which usually takes the form of a citizen advisory committee with representatives from many groups within the community. The committee is charged with the task of commenting on goals and objectives or other project-related aspects.
- *Phase 6: Initiating dialogue and educational efforts*: The use of the press is important in this phase as a means by which to build consensus through public awareness. Key community representatives can be used in this process. The ecotourism team should explain the goals and objectives of the project, how the project will affect the community, the values of the area, any history of threats, and the benefits of the project. Various audiovisual techniques should be used to emphasise these points. Workshops or public meetings could be organised to identify strengths and weaknesses of the project.
- *Phase 7: Collective decision-making*: This is a critical stage that synthesises all research and information from the local population. The ecotourism project team present the findings of their research to the community, together with an action plan. Community members

are asked to react to the plan, with the possible end result being a forum through which the team and local people negotiate to reach a final consensus based on the impacts of the project.

- *Phase 8: Development of an action plan and implementation scheme*: In this phase, the team and community develop an action plan for implementing solutions to identified problems. For example, if members of the community express the need to increase the community's standard of living, the team may respond by purchasing agricultural produce from local people at market rates or on a contractual basis. They may also develop a variety of positions to be occupied by local people including gift shops, research positions, park management positions, and private outfitting companies for the local people. This local action plan must then be integrated into the broader master plan of the project.
- *Phase 9: Monitoring and evaluation*: Monitoring and evaluation, although often neglected, should occur frequently and over the long term. The key to evaluation is to discover whether goals and objectives set out early in the project's life cycle have been accomplished or not.

Community development initiatives have a better chance of being accepted by local people if developers begin to acknowledge the fact that different groups within the community want different things, depending on their role in, affinity within, and utilisation of the community. This perspective is discussed by Jurowski (1996), who feels that because the impacts of tourism are not the same for all residents, residents' individual values need to be recognised by tourism developers in order for their projects to be successful.

The first unique group identified by Jurowski is the 'attached resident'. Such a person is likely to be a long-term resident or an older individual who loves living in the community because of its social and physical benefits. To these people, control over the form and function of their community is important. In general, tourism developers can gain support for their projects from this group by involving citizens in the planning process, establishing a focal point and common theme, developing projects that emphasise heritage themes, and showing that the project has social and ecological benefits for the community.

The second type established by Jurowski, the 'resource user', typically includes people like anglers and other recreationists who, although ambivalent about the economic impacts of tourism, can be won over by developers. The developers can gain their support by providing skill opportunities for youth, involving this group in events related to their interests (e.g. bike races), protecting 'their' sites for participation, and allocating tourism funds for the development of facilities and services they desire. The final group outlined by Jurowski is the 'environm-entalist'. Although this group is the most likely to focus on the negative aspects of the development, it is in the best interests of development teams to do the following:

- Provide information on how the project will protect the environment;
- Incorporate ecological education programmes;
- Encourage the participation of environmentalists in development; and
- Prompt citizens to develop their own educational programmes for tourists. Projects that reflect the interests and concerns of the community, therefore, are said generally to stimulate volunteer activity and minimise conflict.

This research is attractive because it acknowledges that people residing in the local community are indeed different from one another. This is in contrast to much tourism research which considers the local community as one homogeneous group. A key principle underlying the process of community development is the element of leadership.

Mabey (1994) suggests that unlike the older model of leadership, seen as an individual influencing a group towards an end, newer leadership paradigms involve collaboration and partnerships between community individuals, groups, and organisations.

This means devolving power to the followers, according to Mabey, and being fluid in the connection of people and resources. Belasco and Stayer (1993:18) likened this new style of leadership to what happens in a flight of geese:

I could see the geese flying in their 'V' formation, the leadership changing frequently, with different geese taking the lead. I saw every goose being responsible for getting itself wherever the gaggle was going, changing roles whenever necessary, alternating as a leader, a follower or a scout.... I could see each goose being a leader.

This example illustrates the importance of a common purpose in removing obstacles and establishing responsibility within the community ecotourism initiative. In essence the process of empowerment—holding the will, resources, and opportunity to make decisions within the community—allows people, either internal or external to the community, to step in and provide assistance in a respectful manner, while allowing local people to shape and control the pace of tourism development within their communities.

Where this is especially relevant is in marginal places where there exists a tremendous void between those who can and those who cannot access information and resources. As such, education must play a key role in this empowerment process of revitalisation through ecotourism (e.g. providing the needed means to enable people to be informed of certain choices).

An excellent example of education's role in empowerment lies in the Community Baboon Sanctuary project of Belize. Through education and partnerships, local farmers have stopped their conventional practice of clearing and denuding the land for agriculture purposes in favour of a land management strategy that is more environmentally sound. In so doing they have been able to attract international tourists fascinated by the ecological and cultural diversity of this part of the world.

Education, therefore, helps to rekindle people's love and appreciation of the land, which is indeed important for both community-building and nation-building. A similar case study involves the Havasupai reservation adjacent to the Grand Canyon National Park in northern Arizona, where education and tourism have played a significant role in diversifying the local economy.

PARTNERSHIPS

A partnership, as defined by Uhlik (1995:14) is 'an on-going arrangement between two or more parties, based upon satisfying specifically identified, mutual needs. Such partnerships are characterized by durability over time, inclusiveness, cooperation, and flexibility.' More specifically, Uhlik (1995) developed a six-stage model of partnership development that concentrates on the conditions that will lead to a successful partnership agreement.

These include:

- Education of self and others;
- Needs assessment and resource inventory;
- Identifying prospective partners and investigating their needs and inventories;
- Comparing and contrasting needs and resources;
- Developing a partnership proposal; and
- Proposing a partnership.

Clements *et al.* (1993) suggest that because tourism is starting to be recognised as a community development tool, development must be sensitive to the requirements of many stakeholder groups, including tourism providers (e.g. hotels), public providers (e.g. recreation and park providers), and residents. Their view is that partnerships must be struck to ensure that a high-quality product is delivered, and is based on the notion that tourism experiences rely on all aspects of the community.

The overall effectiveness of the delivery system is only as strong as its weakest link, and communities intent on the development of a tourism industry will increasingly rely on the positive benefits of partnerships in being accountable to the local and non-local public. The partnerships developed for ecotourism, according to Sproule (1996), must also fit into systems that have been developed at regional and national levels. There are potentially many partnerships that can be struck to facilitate an atmosphere of cooperation and trust.

Potential partners include:

- Organisations within the established tourism industry, particularly tour operators;

- The government tourism bureau and natural resource agencies, especially the park service;
- Non-governmental organisations (NGOs), especially those involved with environmental issues, small business management, and traditional community development;
- Universities and other research organisations;
- Other communities, including those with a history of tourism and also those that are just beginning; and
- Other international organisations, public and private funding institutions, national cultural committees, and many others; the tourism industry literature is replete with examples of stakeholder groups that have conventionally been at odds.

In Canada, the United States, Australia, and many other countries around the world, there exists a significant degree of incompatibility between parks and aboriginal peoples.

McNeely (1993) feels that despite what has occurred in the past, partnerships must be forged between these two groups in order that both may prosper in the late twentieth century and beyond.

He feels that the following ten principles must be followed in order to help the cooperative efforts of these stakeholder groups:

- Build on the foundations of local culture.
- Give responsibility to local people.
- Consider returning ownership of at least some protected areas to indigenous people.
- Hire local people.
- Link government development programmes with protected areas.
- Give priority to small-scale local development.
- Involve local people in preparing management plans.
- Have the courage to enforce restrictions.
- Build conservation into the evolving new national cultures.
- Support diversity as a value.

Rather than emphasise what has not worked in the past, the partnership ideal must embrace the present and future needs of the groups involved in any transaction. For those in the realm of parks it may be biodiversity and the establishment of more protected areas. From the perspective of aboriginal people, decision-making and culture may be issues that top the list.

ABORIGINAL INTERESTS

As outlined above, the relationship between parks and aboriginal people has often been one based on conflict, and stems from the physical displacement and socio-economic fragmentation of aboriginal people. In Canada, the relationship has been one of mistrust, where peripheral lands (occupied by aboriginals) have been run outside the control and sphere of influence of local native authority. This in itself is a perpetuation of the rift that has existed between Ottawa in the south and those living in the 'north'. Part of the problem exists because the concept of 'park' never existed in aboriginal languages, at least in North America, and the fundamentals of our Western view of park management (i.e. balancing recreational use with preservation) are completely alien to aboriginal culture, as oulined by Notzke:

The distinction between work and leisure is largely an artifact of industrial society. The fragmentation and compartmentalization of life and environment which is part and parcel of western culture, is totally alien to aboriginal cosmologies, which view the world in an essentially holistic and unified manner.

This view is supported by Sadler (1989), who suggests that aboriginals think of space primarily from a holistic perspective, which is contrary to the dichotomous Western perspective associated with conservation. Park management therefore proceeded to exclude Aboriginals entirely from the park planning process. This has led to an indifferent, even hostile, attitude towards the existence of parks close to or adjacent to aboriginal lands. The Clearwater River Provincial Park in northwestern Saskatchewan is an example of this indifference.

Even though there is an abundant population of indigenous people in the vicinity of the park, there is little use of park resources (e.g. fish, game) by such people, in large part because of the park's political status (B. Wilson, personal communication, December 4, 1996). In order for parks to become accepted by the aboriginal population, therefore, some feel that a revision must be made to the preservation mandate that currently exists in some types of parks, changing it to one that is conservation oriented, which will be more consistent with the social, economic, and ecological requirements of the First Nations people in Canada.

TOURISM AND INDIAN ECONOMY

Tourism contribution to the Indian economy is major. Tourism is among India's important export industries. Even with comparatively low levels of international tourist traffic, tourism has already emerged as an important segment of the Indian economy. Tourism also contributed to the economy indirectly through its linkages with other sectors like horticulture, agriculture, poultry, handicrafts and construction.

Foreign exchange earnings from tourism during 2003-04 were US $ 3,533 million (₹16,429 crore). Besides being an important foreign exchange earner, tourism industry also provides employment to millions of people in India both directly and indirectly (through its linkage with other sectors of the economy.) It is estimated that total direct employment in the tourism sector is around 20 million.

POTENTIAL OF INDIAN TOURISM

India has significant potential for becoming a major global tourist destination. The country witnessed foreign tourist arrivals of 2.75 million in 2001. The industry is waking up to the potential of domestic tourism as well, with an estimated 4.7 billion domestic trips in 2001. Tourism spending within India in 2001 was US$ 22 billion. There is considerable government presence in the travel and tourism industry.

Each state has a tourism corporation, which typically runs a chain of hotels/ motels and operates package tours, while the central government runs the India Tourism Development Corporation. Divestment of these state-run tourism corporations have either already taken place or are in process. Incoming foreign tourist arrivals have shown a 6 per cent compounded annual growth rate over the last 10 years. The government has realised the potential and has advanced several incentives to promote infrastructure growth in the tourism sector.

During 2004, India for the first time breached the three million mark and the number of tourists who came to this country stood at 3.37 million reflecting an increase of 23.5 per cent over 2003. Foreign exchange earnings did better with ₹21,828 crore, up by 32.9 per cent and this momentum has continued during the first half of 2005. Till May end, arrivals have increased to 1.52 million, a growth of 23.5 per cent over the corresponding period in 2004 and foreign exchange earnings touched ₹10,571 crore, an increase of 26.7 per cent. The domestic tourism has continued to be upbeat.

During 2004, domestic visits, according to provisional figures crossed the 360 million mark compared to the 2003 record of 309 million. More Indians are travelling abroad also, much more than inbound travellers. During 2003, the number of Indians going abroad was 5.3 million but this grew to 6.2 million in 2004 according to provisional estimates showing a growth of 15.2 per cent. For instance, the number of Indian visitors to Malaysia in April 2004 was 10,480; this went up by 47.5 per cent in the corresponding period in 2005 to 15,464.

People increasingly have been looking at the Net to plan their leisure travel for both international and domestic sectors. This trend is on the rise with growing Internet penetration (about 5 million) in the country. In India, most of the booking is still done through travel agents though the airlines are now ready with e-ticketing platforms. The travel trade in India has understood the importance of the Net and now has comprehensive information on fares, packages and other travel related matter on their Web sites.

In the field of tourism another trend is that more families are travelling together. This is because family get-togethers are getting rarer as family members find it difficult to take time off to visit parents and siblings. Family groups consisting of 30 and more, along with grandparents, from places such as Hyderabad, Bangalore and even interior Tamil Nadu have opted to travel overseas. Short stays are another new travel trend. Executives employed in high pressure jobs, which do not allow them to take long vacations, are more likely to take short holidays, closer to their place of work. Sri Lanka, Singapore, Maldives are some such getaways.

Sri Lanka Tourist Board holds the opinion that India topped the list of arrivals into Sri Lanka in April 2005 at 9,024 compared to the 5,784 in April 2004. The dynamics of the Indian travel scene has changed with the coming of the low-cost airlines. The low fares have changed the way people look at air travel. Air travel is no longer considered a luxury but a necessity. The advent of low-cost carriers has created a new boom in the Indian travel scene offering more options for the Indian traveller, who now has access to better and cheaper air connectivity plus attractive package deals for new destinations. Leisure traffic to India is yet to pick up in a big way.

A Federation of Hotel and Restaurant Association survey shows that more than 50 per cent of the occupancy in hotels comes from corporate travellers. The average room rate (ARR) from corporate occupancy is higher than that of the leisure travellers.

India ranks 50th in the global growth ranking by the World Travel and Tourism Council, below Malaysia which is ranked third and China which is ranked 11th. To fall in line with internationally benchmarked tourism models, India needs at least 90,000 more rooms (in the five star segment) and therefore an investment of ₹80,000 crore. India also needs to increase inbound traffic from 3.3 million to at least 10 million in the next six to seven years.

Tourism Policy Initiatives

The Tourism Policy, released in May 2002 has outlined the following policy initiatives for the tourism sector:

- This policy was built around the 7-S Mantra of Swaagat (welcome), Soochanaa (information), Suvidhaa (facilitation), Surakshaa (security), Sahyog (cooperation), Sanrachnaa (infrastructure) and Safaai (cleanliness).
- The focus of this policy was on making tourism a catalyst in employment generation, wealth creation, development of remote and rural areas, environment preservation and social integration. Its aim was to spruce up economic growth and promote India's strengths as a tourism destination that is both safe and at the same time exciting.
- The policy proposed the inclusion of tourism in the concurrent list of the Constitution so as to enable both the central and state governments to participate in the development of the sector.
- No approval was required for foreign equity of up to 51 per cent in tourism projects. Enhanced equity is considered on a case-to-case basis. NRI investment was allowed up to 100 per cent.
- Approvals for Technology agreements in the hotel industry are

available on an automatic basis, subject to the fulfilment of certain specified parameters.

- Concession rates on customs duty of 25 per cent for goods that are required for initial setting up, or for substantial expansion of hotels.
- 50 per cent of profits derived by hotels, travel agents and tour operators in foreign exchange were exempt from income tax. The remaining profits were also exempt if reinvested in a tourism related project.
- Approved hotels were entitled to import essential goods relating to the hotel and tourism industry up to the value of 25 per cent of the foreign exchange earned by them in the preceding licensing year. This limit for approved travel agents/tour operators was 10 per cent. Hotels located in locations other than the four major metro cities were entitled to 30 per cent deduction from profit, for a ten-year period. The expenditure tax had been waived in respect of hotels located in the hills, rural areas, places of pilgrimage or specified place of tourist importance.

INVESTMENT IN INDIAN TOURISM

India requires considerable investment into infrastructure which could only be met with foreign direct investment. The shortage of rooms in Delhi is adversely affecting the flow of tourists to the capital as well as to other destinations. The accommodation constraints in Delhi will have serious implications on the arrangements for the 2010 Commonwealth Games. It is estimated there will be a requirement of about 40,000-50,000 rooms in the budget category for the tourists visiting Delhi and surrounding areas during the Games.

The issue of giving tax benefit, under section 80 IA of Income Tax Act by declaring them as infrastructure projects for three and four star hotels, which are constructed prior to 2010, has been taken up with ministry of finance. Tourism industry is approximately a $200-billion industry and India doesn't even touch eight per cent of this. We are looking to get a larger chunk of it. The government of India was considering offering tax incentives for attracting attract investment into building convention centres and halls. Pointing out the country was facing severe shortage of hotel accommodation in the wake of its preparation for 2010 Commonwealth games.

The government has outlined plans to facilitate land procurement by hoteliers in order increase number of budget hotels, bed and breakfasts (BandBs) and self-service apartments.

Steps to Promote Tourism

Recently, Indian government adopted a multi-pronged approach for promotion of tourism, which includes new mechanism for speedy implementation of tourism projects, development of integrated tourism circuits and rural destinations, special capacity building in the unorganized hospitality sector and new marketing strategy. A nation wide campaign, for creating awareness about the effects of tourism and preservation of our rich heritage and culture, cleanliness and warm hospitality through a process of training and orientation was launched during 2004-05.

The aim was to rebuild that sense of responsibility towards tourists among Indians and re-enforces the confidence of foreign tourist towards India as a preferred holiday destination. More than 6500 taxi drivers, restaurant owners and guides trained under the Programmes.

Government also took several other initiatives to promote Indian tourism industry and increased the plan allocation for tourism *i.e.* from ₹325 crore in 2003-04 to ₹500 crore in 2004-05. Road shows in key source markets of Europe, Incredible India campaign on prominent TV channels and in magazines across the world were among the few steps taken to advertise Indian tourism. In addition a task force was set up to promote India as prominent health tourism destination. However, in order to attract more visitors, India still needs to upgrade its airports, roads and other infrastructure to global standards.

Even with the recent surge, tourist arrivals are just a mere per centage of those in such popular Asian destinations like Bangkok and Thailand. It is boom time for India's Tourism and Hospitality sector. Driven by a surge in business traveller arrivals and a soaring interest in India as a tourist destination, the year 2005 has been the best year till date, with foreign visitor arrivals reaching a record 3.92 million, resulting in international tourism receipts of US$ 5.7 billion.

Boom time India

According to global hotel and hospitality consulting firm, HVS International, the strong performance in tourist arrivals in 2005 can be attributed to a strong sense of business and investment confidence in India inspired by:

- India's strong GDP performance
- Strengthening of ties with the developed world, and
- Opening of sectors of the economy to private sector/foreign investment.
- The efforts made by the Ministry of Tourism and Culture in the last few years have had a salutary effect on India's tourism industry.
- Foreign tourist arrivals are expected to witness a growth of 78 per cent in 2006 over 2001 (last 5 years)
- Growth in foreign exchange earnings is expected to be of the order of 122 per cent during this period.
- As per estimates (Ministry of Tourism), on an average, about 3.1 million additional jobs per year have been created directly and indirectly in the tourism sector in the last four years.

India is fast emerging as one of the most enticing destinations for the global leisure traveller. The Readers Travel Awards 2006, conducted by Condé Nast Traveller has recently placed India at number four among the world's must-see countries, up from number nine in 2003. The Incredible India campaign has also been a huge success.

An Economic Growth Engine

As an engine for economic growth, the tourism and hospitality sector cuts across the rural-urban divide, and bridges economic boundaries. According to The World Travel and Tourism Council's 2006 Travel and Tourism Economic Research, the travel and tourism sector in India is expected to generate a total demand of US$ 53,544.5 million of economic activity in 2006, accounting for nearly 5.3 per cent of GDP and 5.4 per cent of total employment.

According to the report, the sector is expected to grow at a rate of 8.4 per cent in 2006 and by 8 per cent per annum, in real terms, between 2007 and 2016.

- GDP
- Employment
- Visitor Exports
- Personal TandT
- Capital Investment
- Government Expenditure
- Outlook for 2006 (Real Growth)
  - 7.8 per cent
  - 1.4 per cent
  - 10.9 per cent
  - 6.9 per cent
  - 8.3 per cent
  - 7.7 per cent
- (Outlook for the next 10 years 2007-2016)
  - 6.6 per cent
  - 1.0 per cent
  - 7.8 per cent
  - 6.7 per cent
  - 7.8 per cent
  - 6.1 per cent

A Room-full of Opportunity

As travellers surge into India, the demand for rooms, across segments, has skyrocketed. Hotels in the luxury and business traveller segment are recording nearly 100 per cent occupancy, spiralling tariffs, and a strain on capacity and manpower. Anticipating this demand, around 10,856 hotel rooms in Delhi, 9,318 rooms in Mumbai, 7,794 rooms in Bangalore and 7,408 rooms in Hyderabad are expected to be added by 2011, according to estimates by HVS International.

A Policy Thrust

The objective of the existing Tourism Policy of the Government of India is to position tourism as a major engine of economic growth and to harness its direct and multiplier effects for employment and poverty eradication in an environmentally sustainable manner.

The present government's major policy initiatives include:

- Liberalization in aviation sector
- Pricing policy for aviation turbine fuel which influences internal air fares
- Rationalization in tax rates in the hospitality sector
- Tourist friendly visa regime
- Immigration services
- Procedural changes in making available land for construction of hotels
- Allowing setting up of Guest Houses

The Indian Ministry of Tourism has identified 31 villages across the country to be developed as tourism hubs. The states in which these villages have been identified include Himachal Pradesh, Gujarat, Maharashtra, Bihar, Karnataka, Madhya Pradesh, Andhra Pradesh, Kerala, Tamil Nadu, Orissa, Assam, Sikkim, Rajasthan and West Bengal.

Open Skies, Open Arms

The government's Open Skies policy, permission for domestic airlines to commence international flights, start-up of various low-cost carriers, and fleet expansion by domestic players has created a huge incentive for domestic travellers to explore far-off destinations within and outside India. The booming aviation business is bringing an ever-increasing number of passengers to India, and pulling Indians out of their homes and into hotels.

The numbers, according to the Ministry of Tourism, speak for themselves:

- The number of domestic and international passengers has increased fifteen-fold to 73.34 million in 2005/06 since 1970.
- Domestic air passenger traffic grew by 16.8 per cent in 2005/06 compared to 2004/05.
- International passenger traffic observed a growth of 16.9 per cent in the same period.
- Private airlines accounted for 77.0 per cent of the total domestic traffic.

Health Tourism

India is gradually gathering popularity as a health tourist destination. A study by McKinsey and Confederation of Indian Industry (CII) says that at its current pace of growth, healthcare tourism alone can rake over US$ 1.7 billion additional revenues by 2012. Medical tourism is now a US$ 299 million industry, as about 100,000 patients come each year. The country needs to exploit the cost advantage it can offer to a health tourist, the study said. The biggest driver for healthcare tourism is the disparity in costs.

- A heart surgery in the US costs US$ 30,000 as compared to US$ 6,000 in India.
- A bone marrow transplant in the US costs US$ 250,000 and US$ 26,000 in India.

"With yoga, meditation, ayurveda, allopathy, and other systems of medicine, India offers a unique basket of services to an individual that is difficult to match by other countries," the CII study said. Clinical outcomes in India are at par with the world's best centres since India has internationally qualified and experienced specialists.

2

Development and Growth of Tourism in 21st Century

TOURISM AND DEVELOPMENT

Development can be viewed from various dimensions, however, for the purpose of this current session, we use the following definition of economic development: Economic development is a process of economic transition that involves the structural transformation of an economy and a growth of the real output of an economy over a period of time. It is a long run concept. Structural transformation is achieved through modernization and industrialization and is measured in terms of the relative contribution to gross domestic product of agriculture, industry and service sectors. The potential of tourism to contribute to development is widely recognized in the industrialized countries, with tourism playing an increasingly important role and receiving government support. Tourism along with some other activities like financial services and tele-communications is a major component of economic strategies. Tourism has become a favoured means of addressing the socio- economic problems facing rural areas on one end, while enhancing development of urban areas on the other.

TOURISM AND NATIONAL DEVELOPMENT

Tourism emerged as a global phenomenon in the 1960s and the potential for tourism to generate economic development was widely promoted by national governments. They appreciated that tourism generated foreign exchange earnings, created employment and brought economic benefits to regions with limited options for alternative economic development. National tourism authorities were created to promote tourism and to maximize international arrivals. However, an awareness of the negative environmental, social and some other impacts also increased. The importance of economic benefits at the local level, environmental and social sustainability was also widely accepted. It was observed that tourism presents excellent opportunities for developing entrepreneurship, for staff training and progression and for the development of transferable skills. Tourism development focuses on national and regional master planning. It also focuses on international promotion, attracting inward investment. The primary concern has been with maximizing foreign exchange earnings. These earnings enable the government to finance debt and also to finance some investment in technology and other imports for economic development.

NO TRADE BARRIERS TO TOURISM

Unlike many other forms of international trade, tourism does not suffer from the imposition of trade barriers, such as quotas or tariffs. Mostly, destination countries have free and equal access to the international tourism market. This position has become strengthened by the inclusion of tourism in the General Agreement on Trade in Services, which became operational in January 1995.

REDISTRIBUTION OF WEALTH

Both internationally and domestically, tourism is seen as an effective means of transferring income, wealth and investment from richer, developed countries or regions to less developed, poorer areas. This redistribution occurs as a result of both tourist expenditures in destination areas and also of investment by the richer, tourist generating countries in tourist facilities. Thus it appears as if, the developed countries support the economic growth and development of less developed countries.

TOURISM AND POVERTY REDUCTION

Tourism can contribute to development and the reduction of poverty in a number of ways. Economic benefits are generally the most important element, but there can be social, environmental and cultural benefits and costs as well. Tourism contributes to poverty reduction by providing employment and various livelihood opportunities. This additional income helps the poor by increasing the range of economic opportunities available to them. Tourism also contributes to poverty alleviation through direct taxation of tourism generated income. Taxes can be used to alleviate poverty through education, health and infrastructure development. Some tourism facilities also improve the recreational and leisure opportunities available for the poor themselves at the local level. Tourism is not very different from other productive sectors but it has four potential advantages for pro-poor economic growth:

- It has higher linkage with other local businesses because customers come to the destination;
- It is relatively labour intensive and employs a large proportion of women workers;

- It has high potential in poor countries and areas with few other competitive exports;
- Tourism products can be built on natural resources and culture, which might sometimes be the only assets that people have.

The contribution of tourism to the local economy is also important to note. It has five kinds of positive economic impacts on livelihood, any or all of which can form part of a poverty reduction strategy:

- Collective income which may include profits from a community run enterprise, land rent, dividends from joint ventures. These incomes can provide significant development capital and provide finance for corngrinding mills, a clinic, teachers housing and school books
- Dividends and profits arising from locally owned firms and business units
- Earnings from selling goods and service or casual labour
- Infrastructure gains, for example, roads, water pipes, electricity and communications.
- Wages from formal employment

At this point it must also be mentioned that there are some disadvantages of tourism as well. For example, leakages and volatility of revenue. These are also common to other economic sectors. However, tourism may involve greater trade-offs with local livelihoods through more competition for natural resources, particularly in coastal areas.

STRATEGY FOR DEVELOPING COUNTRIES

Tourism plays a very important role in the economies of many countries. Earnings from tourism-related activities contribute a considerable portion to their GDPs. Tourism is now being viewed as a significant tool and an important strategy in achieving economic growth in these countries. The WTO is convinced that tourism has considerable potential for growth in many developing countries and Less Developed Countries where it is a significant economic sector and promising high growth rate; and that it has advantages when compared with other economic sectors. This case can be summarized as follows: Comparative Advantages of Tourism as a Development Strategy for Developing Countries.

- Access to international markets is a serious problem for developing countries particularly in traditional sectors like food, agriculture and textiles where they confront tariff and non-tariff barriers. This is not the case for the tourism sector, where barriers would involve visa restrictions and related taxes only. The example of Cuba is instructive in this regard. Whilst Cuba has struggled to find export markets for its sugar and tobacco, it has been much more successful in maintaining a dynamic tourism industry.

- In many developing countries, for example South Africa, China, Philippines and India, domestic tourism is growing rapidly and like international tourism brings relatively wealthy consumers to areas where they constitute an important local market. Domestic tourism can be accessed by people with lower budgets and is often equally valuable to the economy.
- Most export industries depend on financial, productive and human capital. The tourism industry not only depends on these, but also on natural capital and culture, which are sometimes the only assets owned by the poor.
- Tourism has particular potential in many countries with few other competitive exports.
- Tourism is a much more diverse industry than many others and can build upon a wide resource base. This diversity results in wider participation of the informal sector, for example a farming household produces and sells local handicrafts.
- Tourism is consumed at the point of production. This results in great opportunities for individuals and micro-enterprises, in urban or marginal rural areas, to sell additional products or services to the potential consumers.
- Tourism is often reported to be more labour intensive than other productive sectors. Data from six countries with satellite tourism accounts does indicate that it is more labour intensive than nonagricultural activities, particularly manufacturing, although less labour intensive than agriculture.
- Tourism provides various employment opportunities especially to women as compared to some of the other sectors.

Perceived Disadvantages of Tourism as a Development Strategy:

- Foreign private interests drive tourism and it is difficult to maximize local economic benefits due to the high level of foreign ownership, which means that there are high levels of leakages and few local linkages. But that might not be the case many times.
- Many small enterprises and individual traders sustain themselves around hotels and other tourism facilities and these small companies are not foreign owned. There is often confusion about levels of foreign ownership as local ownership is often masked by franchise agreements and management contracts. WTO is studying this issue in collaboration with UNCTAD as part of its poverty elimination research.
- Tourism can impose substantial non-economic costs on the poor. For example, loss of access to resources, displacement from agricultural land, social and cultural disruption and exploitation.

- Many forms of development bring with them disadvantages that need to be managed. The economic and non-economic negative impact needs to be determined and the issues addressed. It is for this reason that the WTO supports a holistic livelihood approach to assessing the impact of tourism-positive and negative–on the poor. Issues like environmental management and planning at local level need to be addressed through the good governance agenda.
- Tourism is a vulnerable industry. It reacts immediately to factors like changes in economic conditions in the originating markets, levels of economic activity in tourism in the destination markets. Thereby affecting international visitor arrivals. It is also very vulnerable to civil unrest, crime, political instability and natural disasters in destination countries.
- It has been observed that the volatility of export markets for tourism is not significantly greater than other commodities. Many times tourism has the advantage noted that it is not subject to tariff or other non-tariff barriers and that the destination has some control over civil unrest, crime and political instability
- Tourism requires highly sophisticated marketing. International tourism marketing is expensive, although there are more efficient and less costly forms of marketing available today. Many government agencies at the national level, tie ups of domestic hotels and resorts with international participants, word of mouth publicity, target marketing are some of the methods used.

Tourism in many developing countries and many LDCs has been growing strongly in recent years and there are strong reasons to think that these trends will continue. Many developing countries have comparative advantages in tourism where tourism constitutes one of their better opportunities for development. The disadvantages, which are often identified in relation to international tourism in developing countries, are few when tourism is compared with other sectors of the economy. WTO believes that tourism is considered alongside other industries as a development option and that where tourism presents the best opportunity for local economic development and antipoverty strategies, development banks, bilateral and multilateral development agencies should back it with determination.

DEVELOPMENT IN TOURISM

The concept of sustainability originated in the context of renewable resources like forests and fisheries and was subsequently adopted by the environmental movement. In most cases it is understood to mean "the existence of the ecological conditions necessary to support human life at a specific level of well being through future generations." However, in addition to ecological conditions there are social conditions that influence ecological sustainability in a nature-people interaction.

The social connotations have been described by Barbier (1987) who has defined social sustainability as "the ability to maintain desired social values, traditions, institutions, cultures or other social characteristics." The term sustainability came into usage in 1980 when the IUCN presented the World Conservation Strategy where sustainable development was linked to conservation of living resources. However, the fundamental goals have often been lost sight of because of operational goals (e.g. food, water, shelter, health are fundamental goals to be realised through self reliance, cost effectiveness, appropriate technology, people centred-ness etc.)

Consequently, the WCED made its definition brief: Social Development is development that meets the needs of the present without compromising the ability of future generations to meet their own needs. They did not make any assumptions on the direction in which changes in demand would take place. (e.g. equity, social justice, self-determination, or cultural diversity).

India's tourism policy follows the mainstream SD (Sustainable Development) thinking by adopting all the critical objectives: revive growth change the quality of growth meet essential needs for jobs, food, energy, water and sanitation ensure sustainable levels of population conserve and enhance the resource base reorient technology and management risk merge environment and economics in decision making reorient international economic relations make development more participatory.

These objectives are responsible for building a very broad consensus on the issue of sustainable development, yet the debate at the operational level continues. Most participants in the debate now accept that many human activities are reducing the long-term ability of the natural environment to provide goods and services, which will eventually affect human health and well being.

Enviromental Degradation

Many also accept that poverty is devastating the lives of millions in the Third World since there is no consensus between what is environmentally necessary and what is economically and developmentally feasible. The level of inter-dependence between the two insights is yet to be incorporated in the concept of Social Development. Some problem areas are: Environmental degradation, already affecting millions in the Third World, is likely to reduce human well being across the globe.

Who is responsible for this rapid degeneration? Is it the poor or the rich? The poor have no option but to exploit resources for short-term survival. If we take the example of forests and their resources, which have been traditionally outside the market system and in the sphere of tribal or indigenous peoples rights, they are today seen as exploiters of the forests as against tourists, with all their demand for infrastructure and superstructure, who are seen to be conservationists. The inter-linked nature of the problem of sustainability is such that the impact of degradation will be quicker on the poor than on the rich.

Can Sustainable Development be the metafix it claims to be in reconciling increasing industrial, agricultural and resource use productivity with environmental needs. The weakness of the Social Development argument lies in the techno-economic approach to solutions with regard to common property resource management, through know how transfers, resource pricing, subsidy policies and building management capabilities. (World Bank, 1987) Deeper processes such as land reforms, industrial demands on raw materials, over consumption, changing legal and political structures are either ignored or looked at in a cursory manner.

For instance how can we claim a consensus between those who are concerned for the survival of future generations with those who are concerned with the survival of wild life, or human health and subsistence? Unless we can identify the trade-offs necessary for each specific objective of sustainability, we will not have clarity in the discussion. We will also fail to understand why, even when there is a broad consensus, projects on the ground result in conflicts. Suggested refinements could be:

1. A distinction between ecological and social sustainability and in the process an identification of the inter-linkages a distinction between renewable and non-renewable resources, between environmental processes crucial to human life and crucial to other forms of life dependent on the resources. a distinction between the techno-economic aspects of social sustainability (infrastructure, services, government) with political and cultural sustainability.
2. A distinction between equitable development and local participation, and decentralisation, what many have called NGOisation of sustainable development. This is because no rigorous testing of local participation leading to social equity or to sustainable resource use have been reported.

Environmental Impact

Case studies reflect personal, organisational or political preferences. Tourism is one of the activities which have caused concern because of the effects of increasing human traffic on fragile environments. Countries which are looking towards Tourism as a means of economic growth, like India, have limited resources and cultural restraints and they have the greatest need to pay heed to the possible negative impacts of tourism. The environmental impact of tourism is a basic issue, whether we are looking at a developed or an underdeveloped area, region or country.

The costs of tourism for a country like India include extensive investment in fixed assets with a low rate of return for infrastructure, transportation, accommodation, cultural institutions, exhibition centres, and park facilities. To this maybe added the social and cultural costs like additional demands on infrastructure like land, water, health services; the creation of new jobs for displaced people; the cost of positive community relationships; the disparity between the lifestyle of visitors and those who serve them; the possible friction between local residents and new users of valued local resources; the perception of local residents of the spending of scarce capital resources on what they consider low priority areas like tourism; cultural cost of alterations in local ceremonial or traditional values; loss of privacy for local communities as tourists come to gape at their living conditions and rituals.

Tourism also causes increasing congestion and pollution as thousands of visitors flock to parks and sanctuaries in motorised vehicles; there are changes in accessibility, landscape and the ecological balance between man and nature; there is the cost, both monetary and human, of creating conservation zones (core/buffer) with unforeseen or undesirable side effects; which have been observed in the Eco-tourism movement.

The benefit of revenue from tourism does not always redress these problems but goes towards the cost of administering the project. The tourism industry is generally self-centred and not given to educational, cultural or exchange Programmes on a philanthropic basis. The natural environment, with the best will in the world, cannot escape damage with the volume of visitors. As more and more tourists, both domestic and international seek the exotic and remote destinations around the world, the likelihood of the environment suffering as a result become greater.

Forests can suffer from trampling, fires, tree felling for facilities and waste. Wildlife, despite the protection in national parks, has suffered a loss of habitat, hunting and poaching, viewing and photographing, leading to an interruption of feeding and breeding patterns or hunting for food undisturbed. These are the prized moments for the viewer. The trade in wild life trophies or tourist souvenirs is the more deliberately destructive aspect of such tourism.

Sanctuaries

The building of tourist lodges in materials that are not integrated with the environment and the pressure they put on the land and water bodies is also wilfully destructive. Management techniques that include being less user friendly or control of numbers by closing access or by multiplying the number of attractions and areas or charging higher admission fees are generally not popular with the tourist or the tour operator and are also difficult to implement because of high administrative costs. Equations, through its involvement in the field have had a variety of experiences relating to the debate on Eco-tourism and sustainable development. The major issues that have emerged after the policy of notification of wild life sanctuaries and their management by the Forest Departments are quite disturbing. Wherever notification has led to displacement of people the experience of rehabilitation has not been successful and the conservation aims have not been met. Several sanctuaries have witnessed militant action by displaced communities against the developers of tourism. In many cases the tourism aims have also not been met in making the sanctuary accessible to viewers, naturalists, wild life photographers. Tourism has not been able to counteract poaching and the most extensive and the oldest conservation project, Project Tiger has not been able to save the tiger population.

The commercialisation of the experience, like the privileging of one species, for example the tiger, has led to congestion and noise pollution and this has put a pressure on the management of the sanctuary to organise tiger shows which are putting a pressure on the feeding and mating habits of the tiger. These are very invasive techniques of experiencing the wild. On the plus side, the concept of beneficiary led development has helped indigenous people to organise against their displacement and exploitation as well as to fight for the retention of their traditional rights and life styles.

Environmentalists have not only been involved in such organisations and movements but have done valuable documentation. This has influenced many urban visitors to be more sensitive to the wild and to follow the rules when participating in eco-tourism. This has also led to the development of a code of conduct for the tourist, the industry and the administrator. These attempts are in a very nascent stage. The kind of co-ordination that is required between the environmentalist and economist is just beginning to emerge and have still to counter the myths of neo-classical economists in the field of tourism. But a beginning has been made.

Coastal Issues

The Coastal Regulation Zone (CRZ) came into existence on February 19, 1991, with the gazetting of the notification by the Union Ministry of Environment and Forests (MoEF) under Sec. 3(1) and Sec. 3(2)(v) of the Environment Protection Act, 1986, and Rule 5(3)(d) of the Environment Protection Rules, 1986. Through the Notification the Central Government declared the coastal stretches of seas, bays, estuaries, creeks, rivers and backwaters, which are influenced by tidal action (in the land ward side), up to 500m. from the high tide line (HTL) and the land between the low tide line (LTL) and HTL as CRZ. In the case of rivers, creeks and backwaters, the Notification stated that the CRZ could be modified on a case by case basis, on the basis of reasons to be recorded during the preparation of the coastal zone management plan (CZMP). However, the width of the CRZ from each bank could not be less than 100 m., or the width of the water body, whichever was less.

Activities Prohibited in the CRZ:

1. Setting up of new industries and expansion of existing ones, except those directly related to waterfront or requiring foreshore facilities.
2. Manufacture, handling, storage or disposal of hazardous substances.
3. Setting up and expansion of fish processing units including warehousing (excluding hatchery and natural fish drying in permitted areas).
4. · Discharge of untreated wastes and effluents from industries, cities, towns or other human settlements. The existing practices would have to be phased out by the concerned authorities within three years.
5. Dumping of ash or any waste from thermal power plants.
6. Land reclamation, bunding or disturbing the natural course of sea water with similar obstructions. Exceptions are made for activities required for the control of coastal erosion, the maintenance of water ways to ports; clearing sand bars; and for the construction of regulators, storm water drains and structures for the prevention of salinity ingress.
7. Mining of sand, rocks and other substrata materials, except those raw minerals not available outside the CRZ areas.
8. Drawing or harvesting of groundwater and construction of mechanism within 200 m. of the HTL. Between 200 and 500 m. it will be permissible only if done manually through ordinary wells for drinking, horticulture, agriculture and fisheries.
9. Construction activity in ecologically sensitive areas.
10. Any construction activity between LTL and HTL except facilities for carrying treated effluents and waste water discharge into the sea, facilities for carrying sea water for cooling purposes, oil, gas and similar pipelines and facilities essential for facilities permitted under the notification.
11. Dressing or altering of sand dunes, hill, natural features including landscape changes for beautification, recreation and other such purposes, except as permitted under the notification.

Regulated activities (requiring environmental clearance from MoEF):

1. Construction activities related to Defence requirements for which foreshore facilities are essential. Residential office, hospital, workshops will not normally be permitted in the CRZ, except in very special cases.
2. Operational construction for ports and harbors and light house.
3. Foreshore facilities of thermal power plants for transport of raw materials, in-take of cooling water and out fall for discharge of treated wastewater or cooling water.
4. All other activities with investment exceeding. 5 crores.

Coastal Zone Management Plan (CZMP)

All the coastal states have to prepare, within one year, CZMPs identifying and classifying CRZ areas as per the Notification guidelines. These plans have to be approved by MoEF All further development activities should be within the framework of these plans. In the interim period, before the approval of the plans, development activities should not violate the provisions of the Notification. Violations are punishable under the provisions of the Environment Protection Act of 1986. For regulating developmental activities, the coastal stretches within 500m of the HTL are classified into CRZ-1, CRZ-11 and CRZ-III.

CRZ-I — Areas that are ecologically sensitive and important (national parks, coral reefs, mangroves, areas close to the breeding and spawning grounds of fishes, areas of high natural beauty, historical heritage, high genetic diversity, and those likely to be inundated by global warming, 'etc.); and areas within the LTL and HTL.

Regulations in CRZ-I

1. No new construction shall be permitted within 500 m of the HTL.
2. No construction activity except for facility for carrying treated effluents and waste water into the sea or carrying sea water for cooling, oil, gas or similar pipelines will be permitted between the LTL and the HTL.

CRZ-II

Areas that have already been developed up to or close to the shoreline. 'Developed areas' that come within municipal limits or other legally designated urban areas which have been substantially built up and which have been provided with infrastructural facilities like drainage, approach road, water supply and sewage mains.

Regulations in CRZ-III

1. Buildings will not be permitted in the seaward side of existing roads (or those proposed in the CZMP) nor on the seaward side of the existing authorised structures.
2. Reconstruction of authorised buildings to be permitted subject to the existing floor space and without change in existing use CRZ III Areas that are relatively undisturbed and do not belong to either CRZ-I or CRZ-II. This will include coastal zones in the rural areas and also areas within municipal limits or urban areas that are not substantially built up.
3. Areas up to 200 m. from the HTL earmarked as no development zone (NDZ). No construction will be permitted within this zone except for repairs of existing authorised structures not exceeding the existing plinth area and covered apace. Raising of horticultural crops, gardens, pastures, parks, play fields, forestry and salt manufacture from sea water permitted in this zone.

4. Development of vacant plots between 200 m. 500 m. from the HTL, in designated areas with prior approval of MoEF, permitted for hotels and beach resorts.
5. Construction or reconstruction of dwellind units between the 200m and 500m of the HTL permitted so long as it is within the ambit of traditional rights and customary uses such as existing fishing villages and gouthans.

   Building conditions would be based on the conditions that the total number of dwelling units does not increase more than double of the existing units; the total covered area is not more than 33 per cent of the plot area; the overall height is not more than two floors and 9 m. Guidelines for development of beach resorts in the designated areas of CRZ-III · No construction within 200 m. from the HTL and in the area between LTL and HTL.
6. The total plot size should not be less than 0.4 hectare and the covered area should not be more than 33 per cent. · The total height of the construction should not be more than 9 m. and the building should not be more than two floors.

   Groundwater cannot be tapped within 200m of the HTL. Between 200 and 500 m. it can be tapped with the concurrence of the State or Central Groundwater Board.
7. Extraction of sand, leveling or digging of sandy stretches, except for the structural foundation will not be permitted within 500 M. of the HTL.
8. The quality of treated effluents, solid wastes, emissions and noise levels etc. must be within the standards laid down by the central or state pollution control boards. Untreated effluents and solid wastes should not be discharged into the water or beach.
9. To allow public access there should be a gap of 20m. width between two hotels. Two consecutive gaps should not be more than 500 m. apart.

NEW STAGE IN HOTEL-TOURISM DEVELOPMENT

In the late 1980s, as part of the global restructuring in the hotel-tourism industry, new investors entered the L.A. real estate market from the developing nations in the Pacific Rim. This second stage involved a relatively limited amount of new construction; instead, existing properties have been purchased and then resold to new investors. In the 1980s, Japanese investment began to diversify, particularly into the entertainment field and in other real estate investments.

For example, the Sony corporation purchased Columbia Pictures and the Matsushita conglomerate purchased MCA, which included Universal Studios, a major L.A. tourist venue. Korean and Taiwanese capital interests also invested overseas and the U.S. was one of the major investment destinations. Since 1989, three hotels in L.A., including the Westin Bonaventure, were sold to Taiwanese corporations. Korean capital interests recently purchased two hotels. The L.A. Omni (formerly known as the L.A. Hilton) in downtown L.A. was purchased in 1989. In 1991, an L.A. Hyatt Hotel was sold to wealthy Korean investors.

What stands out about L.A. is the rapid diversification of different sources of growth in foreign investment. Of the 24 major L.A.-area luxury hotels (excluding Santa Monica and Los Angeles Airport that are part of another HERE local's jurisdiction), 75% are owned by non-U.S. investors. In addition to Korean, Taiwanese, and Hong Kong investment, the Sultan of Brunei, who is worth an estimated $30 billion, owns the opulent Beverly Hills Hotel.

Investment in hotels is highly speculative. Real estate values rise and fall rapidly due to a number of economic factors. In addition to long-term players in the tourism industry, there are investors who seek to make a quick return on their investment through the buying and selling of property. This creates rapid swings in property values with boom-and-bust cycles becoming a common occurrence. The dizzying pace of property transference is exemplified by the following two examples.

The Bonaventure Hotel was built in 1977 for $110 million. In 1989, it was offered for $290 million to potential Japanese investors during the last Japanese buying binge of U.S. real estate. In 1994, the original owner went into bankruptcy due to a collapse in the domestic commercial real estate market during the 1990-1992 recession. The hotel recently sold for $50 million to a Taiwan-based company (interview with HERE researcher). The Bel Air Hotel was sold in 1995 for a reported $50 million, less than one-half of what it was sold for in the late 1980s.

The boom-and-bust cycle of real estate speculation in L.A.'s hotel industry cannot be explained solely by the local context of the real estate market. Most investment decisions regarding a particular property take place at the global level by international speculators. Investment decisions may be influenced by a variety of factors. Aoyama (1990) examined the reasons for Japanese investment in the L.A. real estate market and found that the limited availability of real estate property in Japan creates steep land prices and is very rarely sold. Investment in real estate overseas is motivated by differences in return on investment; for example, in Japan the return on equity investment is between two per cent and four per cent. In the U.S. during the 1980s, however, return on equity was between five per cent and eight per cent on real estate properties (Ibid.). Japanese capital left the country due to the lack of investment opportunities and was pulled toward the higher yields of L.A. properties. An additional pull factor from L.A. is that there is a strong presence of Japanese manufacturing and banking sectors that are based in Southern California.

At the local level, commercial real estate interests play an important intermediary role. They assist global capital in the complicated process of buying and selling hotels as well as other properties. Their clients are primarily international investors. Ownership in the L.A. hotel industry is primarily based overseas. The hotel management companies, on the other hand, have historically been based in the U.S. This group includes well-known corporations such as Hilton, Westin, and Marriott. This pattern of ownership and management is changing rapidly.

There is a blurring of any clear pattern in the globalized hotel industry. It is common to find a U.S.-based management company operating a hotel for a partnership of foreign investors that is financed by a Japanese lending institution. Determining ownership and accountability has become increasingly difficult. Many companies use offshore dummy corporations located in corporate tax-free places like the Grand Cayman Islands to conceal investments and profits.

Management, financing, and ownership are integral components of the increasingly diffuse global hotel and tourism industries. Generally, foreign owners tend to stand aloof from the local area and their involvement with the daily operations of their U.S. investments is minimal. How has the growth of foreign ownership affected the lives of tourism workers?

Tourism Profits from Immigrant Labour

Coupled with the rapid investment of international capital in the L.A. hotel-tourism industry, there has been a corresponding growth in immigrant labour. In 1960, 35 years ago, the population of L.A. County was 85% white. By 1990, Latinos comprised 37.8%, African Americans 11.2%, and Asian 10.8% of the population. This dramatic demographic change was spurred on by the loosening of immigration restrictions in the 1965 Immigration Act, to accommodate the needs of capital for inexpensive low- and high-skilled labour from the developing world. L.A. became a magnet for immigrants from Asia and Latin America, including a massive influx of workers from Mexico seeking jobs and a more economically secure way of life, and from Central Americans fleeing from war and deteriorating economic conditions in their own countries. By the 1980s, Latino and Asian immigrant workers had become the dominant sector in the local work force in the service and light manufacturing industries.

As a result of the economic and political calamities in Latin America, coupled with the relaxation of immigration restrictions, millions of young Latino/a workers have moved north to work in L.A.'s restructured economy. Unlike some of the older highly industrialized cities where high rates of poverty are associated with joblessness, in Latino and low-income Asian communities in L.A., poverty is related to the quality of employment. Labour-force participation rates are relatively high, as demand has been consistently heavy for low-wage workers, but poverty rates are also extremely high in immigrant communities, with 75% of the poor in L.A. spending half their income on rent. The restructuring of L.A. with low-wage immigrant labour has meant increased profits for the corporate community, but limited economic mobility for the service workers who keep the system functioning day to day. The restructuring process helps create the conditions for the widening gap of poverty in L.A. The effect of labour migration is illustrated by an examination of the tourism industry. In the 1980s, Latino immigrants became the largest segment of the tourism industry in L.A. Foreign-born room cleaners rose from 34% to 62% of all cleaners in the hotel industry between 1980 and 1990.

The hotel industry is composed of large numbers of first-generation immigrants, with the ethnic composition being 70% Latino, 10% Asian and Pacific Islander, 10% African American, and 10% white. Besides the high percentage of immigrant workers, another characteristic of the L.A. tourism industry is that wage levels are extremely low. Wage levels among room cleaners and dishwashers are barely above the minimum wage in nonunion places. What these low wages translate into is large numbers of workers being forced to live in poor working-class communities, including Pico Union, East Hollywood, East L.A., and South L.A., which surround downtown. Many hotel workers, unable to afford high rents, are forced to share apartments with other families. Numerous hotel workers work two and three jobs at the same time, juggling work and family responsibilities.

The lack of medical benefits also forces nonunionized workers to utilize the county public health-care system. Currently, there are over two million uninsured Angelenos who use the public hospitals. This creates an even greater strain on the county hospitals that are overflowing with an unemployed, underemployed, and low-wage work force that can't afford private health care.

The increase in the prevalence of low wages, inadequate health care, and poor living conditions for low-wage Latino workers corresponds to the expansion of the tourism industry. International capital, seeking to maximize return on investment, has increased the inequalities in the tourism industry by hiring low-wage Latino labour and added to the social and economic inequalities in L.A.

THE WORLD SCENARIO OF TOURISM

In recent years tourism has emerged as a major economic activity that is employment oriented and earns foreign exchange. Its share in the worlds GDP in 1994-95 was 10 per cent which is more than the world military budgets put together. In global terms, the investment in tourism industry and travel trade accounts for 7 per cent of the total capital investment. Today 21.2 crore people around the globe are employed in travel trade and tourism. In future, this industry is likely to see unprecedented growth. According to the World Tourism Council at Brussels, the revenues from travel and tourism in Asia Pacific region will grow at the rate of 7.8 per cent annually over the next decade. Amongst the economic sectors, the tourism sector is highly labour intensive. A survey by the Government of India notes that the rate of employment generation (direct and indirect) in tourism is 52 persons employed per Rs.10 lakh investment (based on 1992-93 Consumer Price Index). This is much higher than the rates of employment generation in most other economic sectors.

Indian tourism industry has also recorded phenomenal growth. The rate of international arrivals in India in recent years has been to the tune of about 19 lakh arrivals per year. The unprecedented growth in tourism in India has made it the third largest foreign exchange earner after gem and jewellery and ready-made garments. This is not surprising since India possesses a whole range of attractive normally sought by tourists and which includes natural attractions like Iandscapes, scenic beauty, mountains, wildlife, beaches, major rivers and manmade attractions such as monuments, forts, palaces and havelis. However, in global terms, in spite of such attractions, tourist arrivals in India are a mere 0.30 per cent of the world arrivals. Receipts are similarly low, just a 0.50 per cent of the world receipts. We are still quite far from the target of 50 lakh tourist arrivals per year. Travel and Tourism is the world's largest industry and creator of jobs across national and regional economies. WTTC/WEFA research show that in 2000, Travel and Tourism will generate, directly and indirectly, 11.7 per cent of GDP and nearly 200 million jobs in the world-wide economy. Jobs generated by Travel and Tourism are spread across the economy - in retail, construction, manufacturing and telecommunications, as well as directly in Travel and Tourism companies. These jobs employ a large proportion of women, minorities and young people; are predominantly in small and medium sized companies; and offer good training and transferability. Tourism can also be one of the most effective drivers for the development of regional economies. These patterns apply to both developed and emerging economies.

Contributing to Sustainable Development

The 1992 United Nations Conference on Environment and Development (UNCED), the Rio Earth Summit, identified Travel and Tourism as one of the key sectors of the economy which could make a positive contribution to achieving sustainable development. The Earth Summit lead to the adoption of Agenda 21, a comprehensive Programmes of action adopted by 182 governments to provide a global blueprint for achieving sustainable development. Travel and Tourism is the first industry sector to have launched an industry-specific action plan based on Agenda 21.

Travel and Tourism is able to contribute to development which is economically, ecologically and socially sustainable, because it:

1. Has less impact on natural resources and the environment than most other industries;

2. Is based on enjoyment and appreciation of local culture, built heritage, and natural environment, as such that the industry has a direct and powerful motivation to protect these assets;
3. Can play a positive part in increasing consumer commitment to sustainable development principles through its unparalleled consumer distribution channels; and
4. Provides an economic incentive to conserve natural environments and habitats which might otherwise be allocated to more environmentally damaging land uses, thereby, helping to maintain bio-diversity.

There are numerous good examples of where Travel and Tourism is acting as a catalyst for conservation and improvement of the environment and maintenance of local diversity and culture. (Some of these are set out in Section B of this paper and a fuller illustration of the range of industry action can be found on the World Travel and Tourism Council's Of course, there are also examples where development has not been sustainable. (Some of the lessons learnt from these poor practices are illustrated in Section C of this paper.)

Providing Infrastructure

To a greater degree than most activities, Travel and Tourism depends on a wide range of infrastructure services - airports, air navigation, roads, railheads and ports, as well as basic infrastructure services required by hotels, restaurants, shops, and recreation facilities (e.g. telecommunications and utilities).

It is the combination of tourism and good infrastructure that underpins the economic, environmental and social benefits. It is important to balance any decision to develop an area for tourism against the need to preserve fragile or threatened environments and cultures. However, once a decision has been taken where an area is appropriate for new tourism development, or that an existing tourist site should be developed further, then good infrastructure will be essential to sustain the quality, economic viability and growth of Travel and Tourism. Good infrastructure will also be a key factor in the industry's ability to manage visitor flows in ways that do not affect the natural or built heritage, nor counteract against local interests.

Challenge for the Future

Travel and Tourism creates jobs and wealth and has tremendous potential to contribute to economically, environmentally and socially sustainable development in both developed countries and emerging nations. It has a comparative advantage in that its start up and running costs can be low compared to many other forms of industry development. It is also often one of the few realistic options for development in many areas. Therefore, there is a strong likelihood that the Travel and Tourism industry will continue to grow globally over the short to medium term.

Of course, if Travel and Tourism is managed badly, it can have a detrimental effect - it can damage fragile environments and destroy local cultures. The challenge is to manage the future growth of the industry so as to minimise its negative impacts on the environment and host communities whilst maximising the benefits it brings in terms of jobs, wealth and support for local culture and industry, and protection of the built and natural environment.

Objectives

The main objective of the States Tourism Policy will be to undertake intensive development of tourism in the State and thereby increase employment opportunities. The following related objectives are dovetailed with main objectives:

1. Identify and develop tourist destinations and related activities.
2. Diversifications of tourism products in order to attract more tourists through a varied consumer choice.
3. Comprehensive development of pilgrimage centres as tourist destinations.
4. Create adequate facilities for budget tourists.
5. Strengthen the existing infrastructure and develop new ones where necessary.
6. Creation of tourism infrastructure so as to preserve handicrafts, folk arts and culture of the state and thereby attract more tourists.

Approach and Strategy

In addition to the facilitation role assigned to itself by the Government in the development of tourism, the Government will adopt the following strategy towards the private sector with the objective of securing its active involvement in leading the development of tourism in the State.

1. The tourism will be given the status of industry in order that the facilities and benefits available to the industry are also made available to tourism projects.
2. A special incentives package will be made available for encouraging new tourism projects as well as expansion of existing tourism units.
3. Infrastructural facilities will be strengthened and developed within the State, particularly in Special Tourism Areas which will be notified latter and which will be developed by adopting an integrated-area.
4. Effective mechanisms will be set up to build meaningful co-ordination with the Central Government and the State Governments agencies, the local self-government bodies and the NGOs.
5. Government will encourage building effective linkages with the relevant economic agents and agencies such as the national and

international tour operators and travel agents of repute, hotel chains and global institutions connected with tourism such as WTO.

So far, the lending from the State Financial Institutions has been largely confined to hotels only. In reality, the range of activities for tourism projects is far larger than just hotels as can be seen from the following illustrative list

Ten Commandments

1. Respect the frailty of the earth. Realize that unless all are willing to help in its preservation, unique and beautiful destinations may not be here for future generations to enjoy.
2. Leave only footprints. Take only photographs. No graffiti! No litter! Do not take away souvenirs from historical sites and natural areas.
3. To make your travels more meaningful, educate yourself about the geography, customs, manners and cultures of the region you visit. Take time to listen to the people. Encourage local conservation efforts.
4. Respect the privacy and dignity of others. Inquire before photographing people.
5. Do not buy products made from endangered plants or animals, such as ivory, tortoise shell, animal skins, and feathers. Read Know Before You Go, the U. S. Customs list of products which cannot be imported.
6. Always follow designated trails. Do not disturb animals, plants or their natural habitats.
7. Learn about and support conservation-oriented Programmes and organizations working to preserve the environment.
8. Whenever possible, walk or use environmentally-sound methods of transportation. Encourage drivers of public vehicles to stop engines when parked.
9. Patronize those (hotels, airlines, resorts, cruise lines, tour operators and suppliers) who advance energy and environmental conservation; water and air quality; recycling; safe management of waste and toxic materials; noise abatement, community involvement; and which provide experienced, well-trained staff dedicated to strong principles of conservation.
10. Encourage organizations to subscribe to environmental guidelines. ASTA urges organizations to adopt their own environmental codes to cover special sties and ecosystems.

Travel is a natural right of all people and is a crucial ingredient of worl.

DEVELOPMENTS OF TOURISM IN 21ST CENTURY

There has been an upmarket trend in the tourism over the last few decades, especially in Europe, where international travel for short breaks is common. Tourists have high levels of disposable income, considerable leisure time, are well educated, and have sophisticated tastes. There is now a demand for a better quality products, which has resulted in a fragmenting of the mass market for beach vacations; people want more specialised versions, quieter resorts, family-oriented holidays or niche market-targeted destination hotels.

The developments in technology and transport infrastructure, such as jumbo jets, low-cost airlines and more accessible airports have made many types of tourism more affordable. WHO estimates that up to 500,000 people are on planes at any time. There have also been changes in lifestyle, such as retiree-age people who sustain year round tourism. This is facilitated by internet sales of tourism products. Some sites have now started to offer dynamic packaging, in which an inclusive price is quoted for a tailor-made package requested by the customer upon impulse. There have been a few setbacks in tourism, such as the September 11 attacks and terrorist threats to tourist destinations, such as in Bali and several European cities.

Also, on December 26, 2004, a tsunami, caused by the 2004 Indian Ocean earthquake, hit the Asian countries on the Indian Ocean, including the Maldives. Thousands of lives were lost and many tourists died. This, together with the vast clean-up operation in place, has stopped or severely hampered tourism to the area. The terms tourism and travel are sometimes used interchangeably. In this context, travel has a similar definition to tourism, but implies a more purposeful journey. The terms tourism and tourist are sometimes used pejoratively, to imply a shallow interest in the cultures or locations visited by tourists.

SUSTAINABLE TOURISM

"Sustainable tourism is envisaged as leading to management of all resources in such a way that economic, social and aesthetic needs can be fulfilled while maintaining cultural integrity, essential ecological processes, biological diversity and life support systems." (World Tourism Organization) Sustainable development implies "meeting the needs of the present without compromising the ability of future generations to meet their own needs" (World Commission on Environment and Development, 1987) Sustainable tourism can be seen as having regard to ecological and socio-cultural carrying capacities and includes involving the community of the destination in tourism development planning.

It also involves integrating tourism to match current economic and growth policies so as to mitigate some of the negative economic and social impacts of 'mass tourism'. Murphy (1985) advocates the use of an 'ecological approach', to consider both 'plants' and 'people' when implementing the sustainable tourism development process. This is in contrast to the 'boosterism' and 'economic' approaches to tourism planning, neither of which consider the detrimental ecological or sociological impacts of tourism development to a destination.

However, Butler (2006) questions the exposition of the term 'sustainable' in the context of tourism, citing its ambiguity and stating that "the emerging sustainable development philosophy of the 1990s can be viewed as an extension of the broader realization that a preoccupation with economic growth without regard to it social and environmental consequences is self-defeating in the long term." Thus 'sustainable tourism development' is seldom considered as an autonomous function of economic regeneration as separate from general economic growth.

ECOTOURISM

Ecotourism, also known as ecological tourism, is responsible travel to fragile, pristine, and usually protected areas that strives to be low impact and (often) small scale. It helps educate the traveller; provides funds for conservation; directly benefits the economic development and political empowerment of local communities; and fosters respect for different cultures and for human rights.

PRO-POOR TOURISM

The pro poor tourism has to help the very poorest in developing countries has been receiving increasing attention by those involved in development and the issue has been addressed either through small scale projects in local communities and by Ministries of Tourism attempting to attract huge numbers of tourists. Research by the Overseas Development Institute suggests that neither is the best way to encourage tourists' money to reach the poorest as only 25% or less (far less in some cases) ever reaches the poor; successful examples of money reaching the poor include mountain climbing in Tanzania or cultural tourism in Luang Prabang, Laos.

RECESSION TOURISM

Recession tourism is a travel trend, which evolved by way of the world economic crisis. Identified by American entrepreneur Matt Landau (2007), recession tourism is defined by low-cost, high-value experiences taking place of once-popular generic retreats. Various recession tourism hotspots have seen business boom during the recession thanks to comparatively low costs of living and a slow world job market suggesting travellers are elongating trips where their money travels further.

MEDICAL TOURISM

When there is a significant price difference between countries for a given medical procedure, particularly in Southeast Asia, India, Eastern Europe and where there are different regulatory regimes, in relation to particular medical procedures (*e.g.* dentistry), travelling to take advantage of the price or regulatory differences is often referred to as "medical tourism".

EDUCATIONAL TOURISM

Educational tourism developed, because of the growing popularity of teaching and learning of knowledge and the enhancing of technical competency outside of the classroom environment. In educational tourism, the main focus of the tour or leisure activity includes visiting another country to learn about the culture, such as in Student Exchange Programmes and Study Tours, or to work and apply skills learned inside the classroom in a different environment, such as in the International Practicum Training Programme.

CREATIVE TOURISM

Creative tourism has existed as a form of cultural tourism, since the early beginnings of tourism itself. Its European roots date back to the time of the Grand Tour, which saw the sons of aristocratic families travelling for the purpose of mostly interactive, educational experiences.

More recently, creative tourism has been given its own name by Crispin Raymond and Greg Richards, who as members of the Association for Tourism and Leisure Education (ATLAS), have directed a number of projects for the European Commission, including cultural and crafts tourism, known as sustainable tourism. They have defined "creative tourism" as tourism related to the active participation of travellers in the culture of the host community, through interactive workshops and informal learning experiences.

Meanwhile, the concept of creative tourism has been picked up by high-profile organizations such as UNESCO, who through the Creative Cities Network, have endorsed creative tourism as an engaged, authentic experience that promotes an active understanding of the specific cultural features of a place. More recently, creative tourism has gained popularity as a form of cultural tourism, drawing on active participation by travellers in the culture of the host communities they visit. Several countries offer examples of this type of tourism development, including the United Kingdom, the Bahamas, Jamaica, Spain, Italy and New Zealand.

DARK TOURISM

One emerging area of special interest has been identified by Lennon and Foley (2000) as "dark" tourism. This type of tourism involves visits to "dark" sites, such as battlegrounds, scenes of horrific crimes or acts of genocide, for example: concentration camps. Dark tourism remains a small niche market, driven by varied motivations, such as mourning, remembrance, education, macabre curiosity or even entertainment. Its early origins are rooted in fairgrounds and medieval fairs.

DOOM TOURISM

Also known as "Tourism of Doom," or "Last Chance Tourism" this emerging trend involves travelling to places that are environmentally or otherwise threatened (the ice caps of Mount Kilimanjaro, the melting glaciers of Patagonia, The coral of the Great Barrier Reef) before it is too late. Identified by travel trade magazine TravelAge West editor-in-chief Kenneth Shapiro in 2007 and later explored in The New York Times, this type of tourism is believed to be on the rise. Some see the trend as related to sustainable tourism or ecotourism due to the fact that a number of these tourist destinations are considered threatened by environmental factors such as global warming, over population or climate change. Others worry that travel to many of these threatened locations increases an individual's carbon footprint and only hastens problems threatened locations are already facing.

GROWTH IN TOURISM INDUSTRY

The World Tourism Organization (UNWTO) forecasts that international tourism will continue growing at the average annual rate of 4%. With the advent of e-commerce, tourism products have become one of the most traded items on the internet. Tourism products and services have been made available through intermediaries, although tourism providers (hotels, airlines, etc.) can sell their services directly.

This has put pressure on intermediaries from both on-line and traditional shops. It has been suggested there is a strong correlation between tourism expenditure per capita and the degree to which countries play in the global context. Not only as a result of the important economic contribution of the tourism industry, but also as an indicator of the degree of confidence with which global citizens leverage the resources of the globe for the benefit of their local economies.

This is why any projections of growth in tourism may serve as an indication of the relative influence that each country will exercise in the future. Space tourism is expected to "take off" in the first quarter of the 21st century, although compared with traditional destinations the number of tourists in orbit will remain low until technologies such as a space elevator make space travel cheap. Technological improvement is likely to make possible air-ship hotels, based either on solar-powered airplanes or large dirigibles. Underwater hotels, such as Hydropolis, expected to open in Dubai in 2009, will be built. On the ocean, tourists will be welcomed by ever larger cruise ships and perhaps floating cities.

SPORTS TOURISM

Since the late 1970s, sports tourism has become increasingly popular. Events such as rugby, Olympics, Commonwealth games, Asian Games and football World Cups have enabled specialist travel companies to gain official ticket allocation and then sell them in packages that include flights, hotels and excursions.

LATEST TRENDS

As a result of the late-2000s recession, international arrivals suffered a strong slowdown beginning in June 2008. Growth from 2007 to 2008 was only 3.7% during the first eight months of 2008. The Asian and Pacific markets were affected and Europe stagnated during the boreal summer months, while the Americas performed better, reducing their expansion rate but keeping a 6% growth from January to August 2008. Only the Middle East continued its rapid growth during the same period, reaching a 17% growth as compared to the same period in 2007.

This slowdown on international tourism demand was also reflected in the air transport industry, with a negative growth in September 2008 and a 3.3% growth in passenger traffic through September. The hotel industry also reports a slowdown, as room occupancy continues to decline.

As the global economic situation deteriorated dramatically during September and October as a result of the global financial crisis, growth of international tourism is expected to slow even further for the remaining of 2008, and this slowdown in demand growth is forecasted to continue into 2009 as recession has already hit most of the top spender countries, with long-haul travel expected to be the most affected by the economic crisis. This negative trend intensified as international tourist arrivals fell by 8% during the first four months of 2009, and the decline was exacerbated in some regions due to the outbreak of the influenza AH1N1 virus.

HOTEL INDUSTRY MANAGEMENT OF 21ST CENTURY

From last a decade or two, Hotel Industry in world has also touched a remarkable height. Many hotels have been also built during last few years in India. The new hotel era was first dominated in India by the Oberoi group, ITC, ITDC, Hotel Corporation of India and other large luxurious group of hotels quickly followed. Keeping with this trend the hotel business proliferated throughout India and State Tourism Corporations also many establishments for providing food and accommodation the growing tourists and business traffic. Today, while, the building costs in the hotel sector are certainly substantial, the industry has gradually become more attractive to private investors with assurance of financial incentives from government.

CATEGORIES OF HOTELS

Partnership

Partnership is the relation between persons who agreed to share the profits of a business carried on by all or any of them acting for all. In this type of hotel business the business is started with atleast two persons and capital is provided by them to own the hotel on agreement basis. This type of agreement is known as *partnership agreement, partnership deed* or *articles of partnership*. The agreement points out the aims, objects, rights and duties, authorities and responsibilities of each partner. It also includes a clause for setting differences between partners and the circumstances and the manner in which the contract can be terminated. This type of hotel is generally bigger than individual type of hotel and smaller than joint stock company basis. One of the feature of partnership hotel is that all the partners are liable for debts of the partnership. The firm's creditors have the right to sue all or any of the partners to the limit of their personal and business resources. It is notable that a relieved partner is also liable for debts incurred during the period in which he was a partner unless the other partners release him, but incoming partner will be free from liability for existing partnership debts. He will be liable for future debts in the normal way. Partnership based hotel can be closed after the expiry of the period of time set by the partners or when the business proves unlawful.

Co-owner Chain

In this type of hotel an agreement is made between the parent company and the local investor. In this category of partnership 50% of the stock of the hotel is owned by the local investor and 50% by the parent organization. The parent company is responsible of selection of site, designing, financing building and furnishing and the supervision of the hotel management.

Chain Type Hotels

A group of three or more hotels, or resorts operated under a common name are known as chain type of hotels. During last few years chain type of hotels have become very common and are very popular due to its efficiency. Statler, Hilton and Sheraton groups of hotels got a remarkable momentum and began to grow rapidly. Chain type of hotels have so many advantages for capitalising group as a means of increasing business and reducing duplication, inefficiency and waste. Chain hotels saves money in purchasing anything from food stuffs to furniture. It can be in a position to get the services of top specialists in every phase of hotel operation—engineers, food controllers, decorators, architectural planners, its large income sources. The chain hotels can easily advertise itself through magazines and newspapers than single hotels because the expen e is divided among numerous hotel and thus they receive full benefit of national coverage at the fraction of total cost. Reservation system is very easy for chain hotels as about the fourth of all room reservations are made through free teletype reservation services which permits a chain access to the various hotels in the group while it is out of reach of independent hotels. In India Welcome group, Taj, Oberoi, ITC groups and in foreign Holiday Inn, Hilton, Sheraton and Intercontinental are the dominant international groups which have changed the organizational structure and management of hotel enterprises throughout the world.

Multinational Hotels

Multinational hotels earn revenues from accommodation—the suites, flat lets and studio rooms and from catering services. Their restaurants provide entertainment also to the customers alongwith good food service. Multinational hotels have limited capability. There is a need for limited hotels in a particular region. These hotels are openable in the largest of communities where there are prosperous businessmen.

Sole Proprietorship

Sole-Proprietorship means *one man ownership of a business* etc., especially of a hotel. In special reference to hotel industry, sole-proprietorship hotels can be defined as such type of hotels, where all required capital is provided by one person and he takes all the risk, manages the hotel and is single authority to receive the total profit after providing for the expenses of operation and the cost of borrowings needed for the running of hotel business. 'One-man-business' is very common because of the nature of hotel business. In this type of business the owner enjoy all the profits in case of business prospers but in the case of failure he goes alone to the bankruptcy court. He has to pay for the debts and losses incurred by the operation. The main problem of individual type hotel is the lack of capital. The hotel owner has only his own resources so has to face the problem in the expansion and development of business

Heritage Hotels

Heritage Hotel is a new category of hotel introduced by the Indian Hotel Industry for its quick and efficient development. Heritage hotels can be defined as hotel running in *palaces, castles, forts, and residence of any size which were built prior to 1950.* As it was not possible for the Indian princes in independent India to maintain their large and stylish palaces so they have changed their palaces into luxury hotels to make ends meet. It is essential for a Heritage Hotel that the outward appearance, architectural features and general construction of the building will have the distinctive qualities, ambience and decor in keeping with the traditional way of the place. Parking space for cars is also an essential feature for this type of hotel. It is required that all public rooms and areas will be well maintained and well equipped with carpets, furniture, fittings etc. Reception cash and information counter are attended by trained personnel which provide money changing facilities and many other facilities. A well equipped, well furnished and well maintained dining room and a well equipped bar is essential for a Heritage Hotel. Apart from these facilities a well maintained ground and garden is a symbol of Heritage Hotel. In this type of hotel, food and beverage services are of high standard. Housekeeping is also of highest standard and there is good arrangement for medical assistance in case of need. Thus, a heritage hotel is a hotel of distinctive and traditional life-style of the area.

Time Sharing Resorts

With the changing need of tourists and travellers Time Sharing Resorts' or Resort hotels have acquired valuable place in the field of hotel industry. For the purpose of suitable climate the rich go out in summer as well as in winter. Apart from this group a number of families travel during vacations and so a place is needed to stay and relax during holidays. Although travelling is sometimes limited to a particular season of the year, most of the hill and beach resorts are getting vacation spots for summer as well as winter. So there are year-round resorts also existence alongwith time-sharing resorts. Resort hotels are generally located in tourist resort areas.

A resort hotel have rooms less than fifty and it is classed as luxury type hotel due to size of guest rooms and provision of facilities such as dining, restaurants, bar, recreation, etc. Resort hotels are mainly of three types:

(a) *Natural Recreational Resort Hotels:* Some hotels are located near natural recreational areas such as sea shore, large lakes, national shrines, parks, ski slopes, hill resorts, legalized gambling areas etc. These hotels are known as Natural Recreational Resort Hotels. These hotels are based on either European plan or modified American plan.

(b) *Self-Contained Resort Hotels:* These resorts are American plan based resorts and provide all the recreational facilities for its guests such as: Indoor and outdoor pools, Horse back riding, Tennis courts, entertainment, Golf courses, etc.

(c) *Summer Resorts:* Summer resorts in India are operated during May, June, July. As this season is very short so the operation depends upon the elements like rain etc. Shimla, Srinagar, Mussoorie, Nainital, Darjeeling hill stations are best example of summer resorts.

(d) *Ski Resort Hotels:* The third type of resort hotel is ski-resort hotels. These hotels are located far away from the cities where the areas for the various functions depend upon the anticipated number of hotel guests plus the amount of a patronage expected from the community.

(e) *Warm Winter Resorts:* Warm Winter Resorts means a resort where the traveller can enjoy the hot sun, the golden beaches etc.

(f) *The Year Round Resorts:* These resorts are located at those places where the climate at those places is pleasant during the whole year. So the travellers of can enjoy here a twelve month season.

(f) *Cold Winter Resorts:* These are places mainly having facilities for winter sports like skating. Gulmarg is the best example of such resorts.

Most resorts, hotels are seasonable establishments who may be closed in the off season. The hotel industry aims building up a regular holiday trade because it is more valuable to sell the house in advance year by year. These resorts are no being made to open during summer or winter by capitalising skiing and other seasonal sports. Off season prices are lower and are often sold in combination with special rate, combination of transportation entertainment etc. These hotels frequent encourage business by cooperation with airlines and of carriers to offer a single price covering travel, lodging, meals a often entertainment.

Franchise

Organization: Franchise is a technical word that means to name from a reputed firm or organization in return of a agreement. In regard with hotel business, Franchise agreement between a hotel company and an independent owner whereby for a fee the owner is allowed to use the trade marks and various services offered by the chain, continuing relationship in which a franchiser provides a privilege to do business plus assistance in organizing, merchandising and operation management, in return consideration from the franchisee. Franchise system provides a large scale of opportunity to go into business as the parent organization assist the newcomer at any and all times. They provide the advantage of brand name or trade mark in advertising, sales promotion and advance registration.

On the other hand the parent organization is also benefited by Franchise system. At first, franchising provides an opportunity for an organization to spread its name rapidly and widely throughout the country at a minimum amount of expenses. Secondly, franchise operations act booking agents for the hotels of the organization and thus the referral business proves a two-way street and excellent sources of rooms and food and beverage business for the metropolitan hotels. Apart from these two benefits the hotel companies receive a great deal of money through this system. As every franchisee pays a franchise fee and a daily charge to the organization, there is plenty of money to be made in franchising. Holiday Inn, Hyatt, House Sheraton Inn, Hilton, Congress Inn, Howard Jonshon's, Quality Courts, Albert Pick, Down Towner, Marriott, Ramada Inns are some of the well-known franchise chains.

Services: There are many services offered by a franchiser to a franchisee such as:

(a) *Methods:* At first, operating procedures established by the franchiser are used by the franchisee to run the business successfully. Training programme, deputation of regional manager are the forms of operating procedures provided by the franchiser to a franchisee.

(b) *Technical Assistance:* Technical assistance are provided by the franchiser in return of payment of additional services provided.

Assistance during the development of potential sites, assistance in obtaining finance, preparation of cost budgets and feasibility studies are various forms of technical assistance. Besides this architectural services, interior design services, purchasing services, project management and construction supervision can also be obtained from franchiser as technical assistance.

(c) *Marketing:* Marketing is one of the important service, provided by the franchiser. It is an important ingredient in a agreement. Advertising, sales and reservation are the three sources of providing marketing services.

3

The Economic Impact of Tourism

The adoption of tourism as an economic development strategy has not been without debate and questioning. The justification of large-scale public investment via EU Regional Development Funds, Development Agencies has led to numerous impact studies. The essential premise underlying the use of tourism in economic development is the economic advantage that is measured. Impact studies attempt to measure the number of jobs created, the kind of jobs created, the impact tourism has on the maintenance of amenities, and physical regeneration plus the more nebulous benefits of the impact of tourism on the image of the area and its general attractiveness to economic investment.

A key development in the "coming of age" of tourism in the eyes of policy makers was undoubtedly the development of tourist multiplier models as first developed by Archer (1973) in his study of Anglesey, "The Impact of Domestic Tourism". This model and developments of it have been applied by a wide range of authors in the 1970s and 1980s, including Archer (1976, 1977a, 1977b); Henderson (1975); Wheller and Richards (1974); Vaughan (1977); Archer, Shea, and Vane (1974). The attraction to policy-makers is that this is a technique that will produce. Thus claims for the number of jobs or income can be shown courtesy of a scientific study.

Such a study was undertaken for the Department of Environment Inner Cities Directorate, Tourism and the Inner City: An Evaluation of the Impact of Grant Assisted Tourism Projects, which concluded that, "Tourism projects have had a positive net impact on the areas in which they have been undertaken". The 20 projects they examined created 1200 permanent jobs and 348 seasonal or casual jobs, plus indirect employment. In the case of the Albert Dock and Merseyside Maritime Museum they estimated the secondary effects created an additional 70% over and above the direct jobs at the project, whereas in the case of Hull Marina and Post House, they estimated that secondary jobs accounted for an additional 44% of jobs. These secondary effects are referred to as the multiplier effect and measured by the multiplier.

It cannot be over-emphasised how important the development and use of tourist multipliers has been in the education of policy-makers in the importance of tourism at the national and sub-national level. Moreover, it has acted as a catalyst for the belief that tourism can and should be part of the regeneration of run-down urban areas in the UK. A typical example would be the plans for the Dearne Valley in South Yorkshire, a former coal mining and steel-producing region where the opportunities for tourism development are a key part of the plans for economic redevelopment. One of the more obvious examples of the importance and apparent success of tourism in economic regeneration has been in old industrial cities with a poor image and scarred landscapes, as illustrated by the urban tourism movement from the old industrial cities of "Baltimore, Cleveland, Detroit and Pittsburgh in the USA and Bradford, Birmingham, Liverpool and Manchester in the UK, to cities like Duisburg and Lyons in continental Europe".

In a matter of a couple of decades we seem to have come from a position where tourism was written off by policy-makers and researchers as an unimportant part of economic regeneration because the jobs were seasonal and part-time, almost to the other end of the spectrum where tourism is seen as an important export industry for cities and sub-national areas and most of the jobs are permanent. A useful overview of the economic importance of tourism can be found in World Tourism Organization (1998) Tourism Economic Report.

Although the multiplier has been refined over the years the most recent development being satellite accounting, the concept is much in evidence in the literature. The geographic range of studies shows that the multiplier is a global concept, there is also a range of techniques with even examples of export base models still being utilised, as well as the more ubiquitous key nesian adhoc and input-output models.

Within the literature there is also a growing concern over the misuse of multiplier analysis. In this paper we are going to develop a critique of the multiplier technique as applied to tourism studies which will suggest that the contribution of tourism to economic regeneration is over-stated and over-estimated. The more generous interpretation being that of Yu and Turco (2000): "Overemphasis on presentation of the total impact, rather than on interpretation of the resulting estimates and description of the application limitations, has often resulted in misunderstanding of the study results".

Whereas Hudson (2001) sees a more disturbing trend because: the accuracy of these studies is very dependent on the methodology followed by the individual author, who is required to make numerous, often discretionary decisions that will affect the final conclusion... Anyone with an even vaguely suspicious nature should be immediately on his or her guard when a study" so dependent on the authors discretion is published or funded by one of the interested parties in a debate.

There is also growing concern in a number of quarters of the accuracy of the number of jobs related to the tourist industry. Leiper (1999) quotes the example of dentistry in Australia where the number of jobs in dentistry directly related to the tourist industry comprises almost entirely of aggregated sum of minute fractions evenly skimmed off every job in a dental clinic around the country in which tourists were treated. It is suggested that in Australia, because of these inaccuracies a mythical image has spread of tourism as a "million-jobs" where 694 000 persons are directly employed while another 334,000 jobs are fully supported indirectly by multiplier effects. It is argued that although many are employed, the number of real jobs in tourism industries is below the widely quoted statistics.

The reality is that economic impact analysis is a best guess rather than being inviolably accurate. The problem, as Crompton, Lee, and Shuster (2001) note, is that the results of economic impact studies are often used mischievously or strategically to deliberately mislead and generate large numbers. The underlying pressure being that most research projects are less predicated on a search for the truth and more often they are undertaken to legitimise a position.

THE MULTIPLIER CONCEPT

The concept of the multiplier is based upon the recognition that sales from one firm require purchases from other firms within the local economy (*i.e.*, the sectors of an economy are interdependent). The key is that a change in the level of final demand for one sector output, such as tourism, will not only affect that particular industry but also all the other sectors that supply goods/ services to the tourism sector and in turn to the other sectors that supply goods/ services to those sectors.

Because firms in the local economy are dependent upon other firms for their supplies, any change in tourism expenditure will bring about a change in the local economy's level of economic activities (comprising production, household income, employment and government revenue). The concept of the tourism multiplier is the measure of the ratio of the changes (*i.e.*, the change in income, employment or output to the change in tourist expenditure). The impact can be divided between the direct, indirect and individual effects.

It is well known that the value of any tourism multiplier is meaningless unless one understands the methodology used to estimate it and the type of multiplier involved. Cooper, Fletcher, Gilbert, and Wahill (1998) describe five types of multipliers: transactions (or sales multiplier); output multiplier; income multiplier; employment multiplier; government revenue multiplier. In terms of methodology Cooper *et al.* (1998) describe the four major techniques which have been employed to measure the value of the tourist multiplier. These include base theory, Key nesian multiplier, ad hoc and input-output. It is generally recognised that input-output is the preferred methodology but that the data requirements are so large that in many cases they are impracticable to use. This led Archer (1973) to develop the ad hoc multiplier that lies between the Key nesian multiplier and input-output in terms of sophistication and data requirements.

It is well recognised that there are a range of weaknesses in and limitations to multiplier models, in particular data deficiencies, restrictive assumptions and operational limitations and supply constraints. In this paper we are criticising not so much the methodology of the multipliers but how methodological limitations of the multiplier and the interpretation of the results may overstate the importance of tourism in the process of economic regeneration.

Our starting point is the economic base multiplier, these days usually ignored on the grounds that the model is far too simplistic to be accurate in calculating tourism multiplier values. However, the theory underlying the economic base multiplier gives us a useful way of analysing the relationship between the so-called export sector and the local sectors of an economy. An early debate on the role and importance of the export sector in sub-national economies between North (1955, 1964) and Tiebout (1956, 1964) raises a number of key points fundamental to the role of exports in regional economic growth.

The economic base model starts from the premise that economic activity can be separated into three sectors/stages, often referred to as the Fisher Clark thesis. According to this theory of economic development there is a "natural" process of industrialisation starting with the primary industries (*e.g.*, agriculture, fishing, forestry and mining) which then evolves into manufacturing/secondary economic and then into the service/tertiary sector. The underlying assumption appears to be that services are in some sense "parasitic" and contribute little to the growth of local and regional economies.. At the extreme Fourastie, for example, argues that if a regional economy develops the tertiary sector beyond the level at which it can be supported by the primary and secondary sectors this will cause economic decline rather than growth.

The debate concerning deindus trialisation throughout the 1980s reflects this view of an export-base world. The fundamentals of an economic-base/export-base theory is the paradigm that an area needs to generate export sales in order to grow, and hence the rationale of dividing economic sectors into basic or non-basic within the economic base multiplier. The "basic" industries have to consist of the primary and secondary sectors, particularly the extractive industries and manufacturing industry, whereas the service sector is perceived as non-basic, (*i.e.*, industries that serve only the local market). An extreme view is that the service is wholly dependent on the wealth generated by the high-wage manufacturing sector.

However, the growing dominance of the service sector has led to a wide-scale criticism of the simplistic assumptions underlying economic base theory. The growing view appears to be that such a dichotomy of basic and non-basic is incorrect.

The service industries are now too diverse to be explained by the crude basic/non-basic dichotomy, Goe and Shanahan (1990) This is because the basic/non-basic dichotomy cannot adequately capture the heterogeneous nature of many service activities that in practice possess widely different economic characteristics. Some services, for example, are obviously export sectors in the sense that much of their production is sold outside the home region (*e.g.*, call centres) and, as has been argued for a long time, tourism. Williams (1996) argues that the basic sector should not be recognised as comprising any activity which earns export income for the region via the sale of tangible and intangible services such as tourism. Although recently postulated, this view underlies the concept of the tourist multiplier, and a very early tourist economic base multiplier by Nathan and Associates (1966) was used to calculate the short-run employment effects created by tourism expenditure in each of 375 counties and independent cities of Appalachia.

EARNER OF FOREIGN EXCHANGE

Tourism has major economic significance for a country. The receipts from international tourism are a valuable source of earning for all countries, particularly, the developing. Visitor-spending generates income for both public and private sectors, besides affecting wages and employment opportunities.

Although tourism is sensitive to the level of economic activity in the tourist-generating countries, it provides more fixed earnings than primary products. The income from tourism has increased at a higher rate than primary products. The income from tourism has tended to increase at a higher rate than merchandise export in a number of countries especially in countries having a low industrial base. Now there is practically an assured channel for financial flows from the developed countries to the developing countries raising the latter's export earnings and rate of economic growth. Tourism, therefore, provides a very important source of income for a number of countries, both developed and developing. The figures from World Tourism Organization indicate that, among the world's top 40 tourism earners about 18 were developing countries including India, in the year 1995. Regarding the number of visitor arrivals, in some countries there were more visitor arrivals than the population.

France with a population of 57 million received 74.5 million visitors in the year 2000. Similarly Spain with a population of 37 million received 48.5 million visitors during the same year. Several island countries, like the Caribbean Islands, depend greatly on tourist income resulting from visitor arrivals. These earnings form a major part of the gross domestic product. Even developed countries like Canada which derived over 13 per cent of its gross domestic product from international visitors in the year 1999, rely heavily on income from tourism.

Tourism forms a very important source of foreign exchange, for several countries. Although the quantum contributed in foreign currency per visitor varies from destination to destination, the importance of receipts from tourism in the balance of payment accounts and of tourist activities in the national revenue has become considerable for a number of countries. The major economic benefit in promoting the tourism industry is in the form of earning foreign exchange.

Income from these foreign-exchange earnings adds to the national income and, as an invisible export, may offset a loss of the visible trading account and be of critical importance in the overall financial reckoning. This is truer in the case of developing countries particularly the small countries, which depend heavily upon primary products such as a few basic cash crops where tourism often offers a more reliable form of income. In the case of some European countries, namely Spain, Portugal, Austria, France and Greece, the invisible earnings from tourism are of a major significance and have a very strong positive effect on the balance of payments. Tourism is therefore a very useful means of earning the much-needed foreign currency.

It is almost without a rival as an earning source for many developed as well as developing countries. These earnings assume a great significance in the balance of payment position of many countries. The balance of payments shows the relationship between a country's total payments to all other countries and its total receipts from them. In other words, it may be defined as a statement of income and expenditure on international account.

Payments and receipts on international account are of three kinds:

- The visible balance of trade relating to the import and export of goods
- Invisible items
- Capital transfers.

The receipts from foreign tourism form an 'invisible export', just like other invisibles which come from transportation and shipping, banking and insurance, income on investments, etc. Because most countries at times have serious problems with their international payments, much attention comes to be focused on tourism because of its potentially important contribution to, and also effect upon, the balance of payments. The receipts from international tourism, however, are not always net. Sometimes expenditures are involved which must be set against them.

Net foreign exchange receipts from tourism are reduced principally by the import cost of goods and services used by visitors, foreign exchange costs of capital investment in tourist amenities and promotion and publicity expenditure abroad. Peters, "Certain imports associated with tourist expenditures must be deduced... the importation of material and equipment for constructing hotels and other amenities, and necessary supplies to run them; foreign currency costs of imports for consumption by international tourists; remittances of interests and profits on overseas investment in tourism enterprises, mainly hotel construction; foreign currency costs of conducting a tourism development programme, including marketing expenditure overseas". Reliance on imports to meet the tourist's needs does not, in any way deny developing countries the opportunity of earning foreign exchange in supplying such goods and services. Imports are, to a large extent, essential to the operation of the tourist sector as to that of other sectors. The important question is whether the value added domestically on an item or service in is maximized? Maximization of import substitution without due regard to the effect on overall tourism receipts may be counter-productive.

Also, differences in the pattern and level of reliance on imported goods and services, capital equipment and manpower are very wide, depending upon the level of development of a country. In some cases, this reliance is simply due to a lack of resources that transform into items which are to be sold by the industry. In others, the industry has not yet drawn on such supply potential, for which it may be an important stimulus. There is a general need for careful programmes of positive import substitution.

MULTIPLIER EFFECT

The discussion in earlier paragraphs clearly indicates that earnings from tourism occupy an important place in the national income of any country. Without taking into account receipts from domestic tourism, international tourism receipts alone contribute to a great extent. The flow of money generated by tourist spending multiplies as it passes through various parts of the economy.

In addition to an important source of income, tourism provides a number of other economic benefits, which vary in importance from one country to another; depending upon the nature and scale of tourism. The benefits from infrastructure investments, justified primarily for tourism such as airports, roads, water supply and other public utilities, may be widely shared by the other sectors of the economy.

This enables us to understand how tourism impacts development in the economy. Tourist facilities such as hotels, restaurants, museums, clubs, sports complexes, public transport, and national parks are also used by domestic tourists and visitors, businessmen and residents, but still a significant portion of the costs are sometimes borne by international tourists. Tourists also contribute to tax revenue both directly through sales tax and indirectly through property, profits and income taxes.

Tourism provides employment, develops infrastructural facilities and may also help regional development. Each of these economic aspects can be dealt with separately, but they are all closely related and are many times considered together. Let us first look at the income aspect of tourism. Income from tourism cannot be easily measured with accuracy and precision. This is because of the multiplier effect. The flow of money generated by tourist spending multiplies as it passes through various parts of the economy through the operation of the multiplier effect. The multiplier is an income concept. The Concept: The 'multiplier' measures the impact of extra expenditure introduced into an economy by a person. It is, therefore, concerned with the marginal rather than average changes.

In the case of tourism, this extra expenditure in a particular area can take the following forms:

- Spending on goods and services by tourists visiting the areas
- Investment of external sources in tourism infrastructure or services;
- Government spending
- Exports of goods stimulated by tourism

The expenditure can be analysed as follows:

- *Direct Expenditure*: In the case of tourism, this expenditure is made by tourists on goods and services in hotels and other supplementary accommodation units, restaurants, other tourist facilities like buses, taxis coaches, railways, domestic airlines, and for tourism-generated exports, or by tourism related investment in the area.
- *Indirect Expenditure*: This covers a sum total of inter-business transactions which result from the direct expenditure, such as purchase of goods by hoteliers from local suppliers and purchases by local suppliers from wholesalers.
- *Included Expenditure*: This is the increased consumer spending resulting from the additional personal income generated by the direct expenditure, *e.g.*, hotel workers using their wages for the purchase of goods and services. Indirect and induced expenditure together are called secondary expenditure.

There are several different concepts of the multiplier. Most multipliers in common use incorporate the general principle of the Keynesian model.

The four types of multipliers are intrinsically linked as follows:

- *Sales Multiplier*: This measures the extra business turnover created by an extra unit of tourist expenditure. Output Multiplier: This is similar to the sales multiplier but it also takes into account inventory changes, such as the increase in stock levels by hotels, restaurants and shops because of increased trading activity.
- *Income Multiplier*: This measures the income generated by an extra unit of tourist expenditure. The problem arises over the definition of income. Many researchers define income as disposable income accruing to households within the area, which is available to them to spend. However, although salaries paid to overseas residents are often excluded, a proportion of these salaries may be spent in the local area and should therefore be included.

Income Multipliers can be expressed in two ways:

- The ratio method which expresses the direct and indirect incomes generated per unit of direct income;
- Normal method, which expresses total income generated in the study area per unit increase in final demand created within a particular sector.

Ratio multipliers indicate the internal linkages which exist between various sectors of the economy, but do not relate income generated to extra sales. Hence, on their own, ratio multipliers are valueless as a planning tool. Employment Multiplier:

The employment multiplier can be expressed in one of the two ways:

- As a ratio of the combination of direct and secondary employment generated per additional unit of tourist expenditure;
- Direct employment created by tourism per unit of tourist expenditure. Multipliers can be further categorized by the geographical area which is covered by the research, such as local community, a region within a country or the country as a whole.

The multiplier mechanism has also been applied to tourism and, in particular, to tourist expenditure. The nature of the tourism multiplier and its effect may be described in the example: "The money paid by a tourist in paying his hotel bill will be used by the management of the hotel to provide for the costs which the hotel had incurred in meeting the demands of the visitor, *e.g.*, such goods and services as food, drink, furnishing, laundering, electricity, and entertainment. The recipients, in turn, use the money they have thus received to meet their financial commitments and so on.

Therefore, tourist expenditure not only supports the tourist industry directly but also helps indirectly to support many other industries which supply goods and services to the tourist industry. In this way money spent by tourists is actually used several times and spreads into various sectors of the economy. In sum, the money paid by the tourist, after a long series of transfers over a given period of time, passes through all sectors of the national economy, stimulating each in turn throughout the process".

On each occasion when the money changes hands, it provides 'new' income and these continuing series of exchanges of the money spent by the tourists form what economists term the multiplier effect. The more often the conversion occurs, the greater its beneficial effect on the economy of the recipient country.

However, this transfer of money is not absolute as there are 'leakages' which occur. Such leakages may occur as a result of importing foreign goods, paying interest on foreign investments, etc.

The following are some examples of such leakages:

- Payment for goods and services produced outside, and imported into, the area;

- Remittance of incomes outside the area, for example, by foreign workers;
- Indirect and direct taxation where the tax proceeds are not re-spent in the area;
- Savings out of income received by workers in the area.

Any leakages of these kinds will reduce the stream of expenditure which, in consequence, will limit and reduce the multiplier effect. Income generated by foreign tourist expenditure in countries possessing more advanced economies, which generally are more self-sufficient and less in need of foreign imports which are less self-sufficient and need to support their tourist industries by substantial import. If the developing countries are desirous of gaining maximum economic benefits from tourism, they should strictly control the imported items for tourist consumption and keep foreign investment expenditure at a reasonable level. If the leakages are not controlled then the benefits arising from tourism will be greatly reduced or even cancelled.

The most important leakage would arise from expenditure on import of agricultural products like food and drink. In a primary macro-economic approach to the prospects opened up by tourism establishment in a developing country, it is regarded as advantageous that a good portion of tourist consumption should consist of food products. It is estimated that the major part of these products can be found in those countries, whose economic structure is largely agricultural in character. In this sense tourist consumption, derived from international flow, can offer an assured outlet to a production which is already active within the domestic economy, without raising problems connected with export of such products and could thus be substituted for imported foodstuffs and a significant saving effected thereafter. The host country derives maximum economic benefits from the tourism industry as these savings help in increasing the benefits from the tourism multiplier. This aspect of the question is all the more important as the multiplier effect maintains its efficacy and effectiveness as long as no importation takes place. It follows that if the national economy is to derive the maximum benefit from the impact of international and national tourism, there is an elementary obligation to find all those products needed for tourist consumption. The dynamics of agricultural production in recent years confirms the ability of developing countries to produce the major part of their agricultural products required for tourist consumption without resorting to massive imports. The tourist economy of any country, if it is to remain healthy, must rely upon local agricultural production and this condition seems today to be on its way to realization in most of the developing countries.

Multiplier of Tourism Income

To sum up, Multipliers are a means of estimating how much extra income is produced in an economy as a result of initial spending or after cash is injected.

Every time the money changes hands it provides new income and the continuing series of conversion of money spent by the tourists form the multiplier effect. The more often the conversion occurs, the greater its beneficial effect on the economy of the recipient country.

GROWTH OF INFRASTRUCTURE

A significant benefit of tourism is development and improvement of infrastructure. The benefits from infrastructure investments, justified primarily for tourism–airports, roads, water supply and other public utilities–may be widely shared by the other sectors of the economy. In addition to development of new infrastructure, the improvements in the existing infrastructure which are undertaken in order to attract tourists are also of great importance. These improvements may benefit the resident population by providing them with amenities which they desire. Furthermore, the provision of infrastructure may provide the basis or serve as an encouragement for greater economic diversification. A variety of secondary industries may be promoted which may not directly serve the needs of tourism.

Therefore, it is evident that tourist expenditure is responsible for stimulating other economic activities. One of the characteristics of under development is that of deficiencies in the basic infrastructures, which lie at the root of a series of problems related to the development of tourism. Development of infrastructure requires a certain size of investment. Tourism provides the size of demand which justifies the development of infrastructure. On the basis of this minimum demand for such facilities and for such social capital, the size of such infrastructural services evolves. Construction of primary infrastructures represents the foundation of any future economic growth, even though they are not directly productive. The tourism industry shows the elementary need for basic infrastructure.

It has today the important benefit of being able to profit from the existing infrastructures and thus to make a decisive contribution to the growth of the national economy. The international and national tourist traffic, moreover, represents a reward for the capital invested and can now contribute to the financial efforts required for maintenance. The satisfactory degree of development achieved in this specific sector now permits major tourist progress, while also giving further proof of the complementary character of tourism in relation to other economic sectors. Creation of basic infrastructures for tourist usage will also be of service to the other sectors of the economy such as industry and agriculture. This results in better equilibrium of general economic growth.

TOURISM AND TAXATION

Tourism also results in tax revenues both at national and local levels. Taxes can provide the financial resources for the development of infrastructure, enhancing and maintenance of some types of attractions and other public facilities and services, tourism marketing and training required for developing tourism, as well as to help finance poverty alleviation programmes by governments both at local and national levels.

In addition, tourism-related tax revenues help finance general community improvements and services used by all residents. WTO's 1998 report on tourism taxation emphasizes that taxation policies in a country must be carefully evaluated in an integrated manner to ensure that tourism-related taxes are giving the necessary substantial revenues. However, taxes should not be so high for the country's international competitive position to be counter productive and produce a loss of tourist traffic.

The aim should be to strike a balance between, a level of taxation that maintains a competitive position for the country and reasonable profits for the industry, and, receiving adequate revenues to support investment in and maintenance of the tourism sector, and to contribute towards general community welfare.

BALANCED REGIONAL DEVELOPMENT

Another important domestic effect relates to the regional aspects of tourist expenditure. Such expenditure is of special significance in marginal areas, which are relatively isolated, economically underdeveloped, and have unemployment problems. The United Nations Conference on International Travel and Tourism held in Rome in 1963 stated that tourism was important not only as a source of earning foreign exchange, but also as a factor determining the location of industry and in the development of underdeveloped regions. It further stated that in some cases the development of tourism may be the only means of promoting the economic advancement of less-developed areas lacking in other resources. In fact underdeveloped regions of the country usually greatly benefit from tourism development. Many of the economically backward regions contain areas of high scenic beauty and of cultural attractions. These areas, if developed for use by tourists, can bring in a lot of prosperity to the local people.

Tourism development in these regions accordingly becomes a significant factor in redressing regional imbalances in employment and income. Tourist expenditure at a particular tourist area helps the development of the many areas around it. Many countries both developed as well as developing have realised this aspect of tourism development and are contemplating developing tourist facilities in underdeveloped regions with a view to bringing prosperity there. Khajuraho in India, which is now an internationally famous tourist spot, is an example of one such region.

To show, Khajuraho, a remote and unknown small village about forty years ago, is now on the world tourist map which attracts thousands of tourists, both domestic as well as international. Today, Indian Airlines flies a jet plane between the capital city of New Delhi and Khajuraho and seats are not easy to come by. Thousands of tourists visit the place by air, rail and road transport every month to see the architectural beauty of temples and erotic sculptures whose creators were the Chandela kings, who ruled in North India from the 9th to the 13th centuries. Today 22 glorious temples remind us of the classic Indian architecture and culture of those times and represent the finest expression of the art of medieval India. The area around Khajuraho is well developed and full of life. The place has provided employment to hundreds of local people in hotels and shops.

There is a thriving clay-model industry devoted to making replicas of the famous temple sculptures and a number of shops dealing with items of presentation, handlooms and handicrafts, have created jobs for many. Tourists love to purchase various souvenirs to take home.

Thus local people are recipients of additional income which has increased the prosperity of the region. Subsequently areas around Khajuraho have also prospered and reaped the benefits from the tourist multiplier. There is no dearth of areas which could, after they are developed for tourism, become great assets to the region in particular and to the country as a whole. The French government has created a series of new resorts particularly to bring prosperity to the areas which traditionally have been underdeveloped. The Italian government is likewise attempting to develop tourism in Southern Italy in order to help redress the economic imbalances which have long existed between the northern and the southern parts of Italy. Tourism is to be regarded not as an area of peripheral investment whose benefits will help in creating employment opportunities and in the regeneration of backward regions. In India a similar approach needs to be adopted to develop areas with great tourism potential.

GENERATION OF EMPLOYMENT

Employment is an important economic effect of tourism. The problems of unemployment and under-employment are more active in the developing countries. Tourism can be looked upon in this light as a major industry which employs manpower on a large scale.

The problems which the industrialized countries face in recruiting manpower for the tourists industry confirm that, in any productive process consisting of services, human labour remains the basic need. If a comparison is to be drawn with the productive sector none of the technological progress achieved has succeeded in rendering the human factor less indispensable than in this sector, and this is true to an absolutely indisputable extent.

The high social impact of the tourist industry is well known, for it has repercussions in every other national economic sector through the multiplier effect, which is particularly marked in those services that are complementary to the tourist accommodation industry. The tourist industry is a highly labour-intensive service industry and hence is a valuable source of employment. It employs a large number of people and provides a wide range of jobs which extend from the unskilled to the highly specialized. In addition to those involved in management there are a large number of specialist personnel required to work as accountants, housekeepers, waiters, cooks and entertainers, who in turn need a large number of semi-skilled workers such as porters, chambermaids, kitchen staff, gardeners, etc. Tourism is also responsible for creating employment outside the industry in its more narrowly defined sense and in this respect those who supply goods and services to those directly involved in tourism are beneficiaries from tourism.

Such indirect employment includes, those involved in the furnishing and equipment industries, souvenir industries and farming and food supply. Construction industry is another very big source of employment. The basic infrastructures-roads, airports, water supply and other public utilities and also construction of hotels and other accommodation units create jobs for thousands of workers, both unskilled and skilled. In many of the developing countries, where chronic unemployment often exists, the promotion of tourism can be a great encouragement to economic development and, especially, employment.

However at this point it is, necessary to consider the seasonal nature of the tourism industry. Where general diversification alternatives are scarce, a combination of heavy dependence on tourism and highly marked seasonality calls for measures to develop off -season traffic. Employment multiplier: This multiplier is similar to the Income Multiplier except that in this case a multiplier impact on employment is observed.

Employment Multiplier can be expressed in the following two ways:

- As a ratio of the combination of direct employment. At the destination, the jobs are directly created in the industry there.
- As a ratio of secondary employment generated per additional unit of tourist expenditure to direct employment. The workers and their families require their own goods and services giving rise to further indirectly created employment in shops, schools, health care institutions, etc.

OTHER DIMENSIONS

The World Tourism conference which was held at Manila, Philippines in October 1980, considered the nature of tourism phenomenon in all its aspects. The role tourism is bound to play in a dynamic and vastly changing world was also identified. Convened by the World Tourism Organization the conference also considered the responsibility of various states for the development and enhancement as more than a purely economic activity of nations and peoples.

The significance of tourism was discussed in during the conference. The participants in the World Tourism Conference attached particular importance to its effects on the developing countries. It stated its conviction "that the world tourism can contribute to the establishment of a new international economic order that will help to eliminate the widening economic gap between developed and developing countries and ensure the steady acceleration of economic and social development and progress in particular of the developing countries."

THE ENVIRONMENTAL IMPACTS OF TOURISM

This section of the chapter discusses the environmental impacts of tourism. As will be illustrated tourism will have either negative or positive impacts upon the environment; rarely, if ever, will it have a neutral relationship with the environment.

Although the discussion will attempt to be as holistic as possible, our knowledge of the impacts of much of human action upon the environment, and subsequently the amount we know about the effects of tourism, is limited.

The limitations of the discussion that need to be taken into account can be summarised as follows:

- Research into impact studies is relatively immature and a true multidisciplinary approach to invest-igation has yet to be developed.
- Research into the environmental consequences of tourism tends to be reactive and therefore it is not always easy to establish a baseline against which to monitor changes.
- It is not always easy to separate out the environm-ental impacts attributable to tourism from the effects of other economic activities or anthropogenic factors, such as human habitation, and non-anthropogenic causes, such as natural environmental change.
- It is not always possible to separate the source of impacts upon the environment between local residents and tourists.
- The consequences of tourism are difficult to assess because tourism development is often incremental and the effects are cumulative.
- Spatial discontinuities are inherent to tourism. For example, the effects of air pollution caused by air and car emissions associated with tourism may contribute to acid rain which destroys forests hundreds of kilometres away.

The impacts of tourism upon the environment can be separated into two broad categories of negative and positive changes. To provide a structure to the discussion, the first part of the following section deals with the negative consequences of tourism and the second part with the positive effects for the environment.

This ordering is reflective of much of the observation and commentary that has been expounded on the impacts of tourism, which has raised awareness of the negative environmental aspects that can result from tourism development, whilst the positive environmental aspects are less well defined. This imbalance in the literature is also a reflection of the fact that any change to the natural environment by human action is likely to be viewed as harmful, involving at the very minimum damage to individual flora and fauna, and sometimes threatening the existence of species and whole ecosystems.

However, it should be realised that within the context of the discussion on impacts, the extent to which we determine impacts to be either positive or negative ultimately relies on value judgements. From an anthropocentric viewpoint, these judgements need to be balanced with the consideration that through the usage of natural resources for development, the standard of living for humans can be improved.

This is a particularly relevant consideration for societies that live in material poverty and struggle to meet their basic needs for food, clean water and shelter. Nevertheless, this is not to condone the negative effects of tourism upon the environment, as in many situations these result from a mixture of human ignorance and greed, rather than from a philanthropic desire to improve the living conditions of human beings.

THE NEGATIVE IMPACTS

There are a broad range of negative physical and cultural environmental impacts resulting from tourism development, which can be categorised into three major types of concern: resource usage; behavioural considerations; and pollution.

RESOURCE ISSUES AND TOURISM

The development of tourism requires physical resources to facilitate its expansion. One of the most noticeable developmental aspects of tourism in generating and destination areas is airport construction. Airports are an essential part of the international tourism system and can generate major employment opportunities for local people. The expansion and development of airports is also beneficial to the tourist by offering easier access to a wider choice of destinations.

However, the resultant effects for the environment, including the people who live near to airports, are not always as beneficial. For instance, airport development and expansion often involves the transformation of agricultural and recreational land which is covered by runways and terminal buildings. According to Friends of the Earth (1997), major international airports, like Heathrow in London, have paved areas equivalent to 320 kilometres of three-lane highways or motorways. In destination areas the extensive amount of land used for both airport and seaport development can also be problematic.

For example, in 'small island developing states' (SIDS), the loss of agricultural land for airport and seaport development can lead to an increased reliance upon food imports to meet local needs.

The development of an airport also requires additional infrastructure, such as new roads and railways, which again necessitates land-use changes and adds to the pollution of surrounding areas. As the demand for international tourism increases, the demand for the expansion of airports is likely to grow.

According to Whitelegg (1999), air transport demonstrates the biggest growth rate of any form of transport and the International Air Transport Authority (IATA) estimate that the rate of growth in air passengers will continue at 5 per cent per annum until the year 2010.

Within destinations, the development of the tourism superstructure, such as hotels and attractions, and its associated infrastructure, also requires land. Tourism is often a competitor for land use with other economic activities, such as agriculture, and in some cases extractive industries like logging and mining.

Subsequently, the use of land for tourism development is at the denial of other forms of economic activity, thereby incurring what economists refer to as 'opportunity costs', that is the potential economic benefits resulting from another type of development other than tourism are denied. The danger of unplanned and unregulated tourism development, in response to market conditions in which there is a high demand for tourism, can mean there is an overuse of resources for tourism and a lack of development of other forms of economic activity.

This can lead to an economic overdependence upon tourism and a lack of diversification of the economic base. The danger of this situation is that if tourism demand to a destination decreases, there is a lack of development of other economic sectors to support the local economy. This is likely to lead to high levels of unemployment and associated social problems.

Another key natural resource that is essential for tourism is water. The addition of hundreds or thousands of bed spaces in a destination, combined with the lifestyle demands of western tourists, such as a daily requirement for showering, clean sheets and bath towels, means that tourism is responsible in some destinations for the consumption of copious amounts of water compared to the needs of the local population.

Salem (1995) remarks that 15,000 cubic metres of water will supply 100 luxury hotel guests for 55 days, whilst the same amount will supply 100 nomads or 100 rural farmers for three years, and 100 urban families for two years. The effects of the development of tourism in areas where water resources are limited can mean that local people are denied the access to the water resources they previously used, for example to irrigate crops.

They may find that streams previously used for irrigation have been diverted further upstream to service tourism development, or that the water-table level has been lowered by overextraction to service tourism establishments, rendering their wells useless. Where it is impossible to continue to extract enough fresh water locally, hotels can pay to have the water imported, whilst local people suffer water shortages. Unsurprisingly, access to water resources has sometimes led to conflict over tourism development between the developers and the local community.

CONFRONTATION OVER WATER RESOURCES

In Tepotzlan in Mexico, the place from which Zapata led the peasant army in the Mexican Revolution of the early twentieth century, the residents who are mostly Nahua Indians protested against plans to build a golf course, five-star hotel and 800 tourist villas. Apart from the fact that such a development will be exclusive of local people in terms of employment opportunities, it is calculated that the development will use up to 525,000 gallons of water a day, threatening shortages in the town. Using slogans of 'Zapata lives' and 'Land and Liberty', the locals took over the town hall periodically, and barricaded the streets with barbed wire and boulders in protest against the scheme.

In Goa, in India, tourism development has also caused discord over resource issues between developers and local people. This has resulted in local people organising protest groups against tourism development and open antagonism towards tourists.

CLASHES OVER RESOURCES IN GOA, INDIA

The development of tourism in Goa raises many issues over the interaction between local people and tourism. Goa is a state in western India facing the Indian Ocean. It possesses the typical 'exotic' image of paradise for westerners with over 65 kilometres of sandy beaches and coconut palms. The area began to develop its international tourism (it was already very popular for domestic tourism) potential in the 1980s with the first German charter arriving in 1987.

The development of tourism has been characterised by investment from outside the region and the building of large four- or five-star hotels. Unfortunately, this style of development has meant that tourism has excluded some local people from the resources that they need for their livelihoods. Nicholson-Lord (1993) gives examples of the 'Cidade de Goa Hotel' which built a 2.4-metre wall around a beach to deny local people access, and the Taj holiday village and Fort Aguada beach resort hotels, where guests are guaranteed water twenty-four hours a day whilst nearby villagers are denied access to the pipeline for even one to two hours a day. Many villagers face electricity and water shortages, with one five-star hotel consuming as much water as five villages, and one fivestar tourist consuming twenty-eight times more electricity than a Goan. Many of the hotels were also built directly on the beach, damaging the dunes, and human sewage was put directly into the water without being treated. The extent of the feeling of exclusion of local people from the benefits of tourism has led to the growth of protest groups against tourism development, notably the Jagrut Goenkaranchi Fauz (Vigilant Goan's Army) and the 'Goa Foundation', an environmental group.

Occasionally there has been open aggression towards tourists, such as the pelting of German tourist buses with rotten fish in the late 1980s, and ten tourists were beaten up by a group of villagers in Nuven village after knocking down two pedestrians.

Besides possibly having restricted access to water resources, local people may also find that they are excluded from other areas that they used to use for natural resources and recreation, such as beach areas. A typical sign on beaches that have been privatised to accompany up-market hotel development, especially in less developed countries, taken on the island of Langkawi in Malaysia.

Tourism development can also lead to the displacement of people from their homes, particularly of poorer people in less developed countries, many of whom possess no rights of land ownership and have limited or no access to legal representation. One of the most notable examples of the displacement of indigenous people associated with tourism was the exclusion of the Maasai people from their traditional lands, when the Maasai Mara reserve in Kenya was established. However, the exclusion and displacement of local people from lands for tourism development is not something that is specific to Kenya.

The development of the Chitwan National Game Reserve in the Terai area of Nepal was also achieved by the exclusion of local people, and on the island of Langkawi in Malaysia, the compulsory reclamation of land by the state government led to the splitting up of a long established community and a loss of livelihood for many villagers. Displacement of people from the land for the development of 'golf villages' in South-East Asia has also occurred.

The development of these golf villages usually involves the transformation of agricultural land, the development of condominiums, conference centres and other leisure facilities. Their size can be up to 80 times the size of a typical European golf course. It is difficult to have a global perspective on the numbers of people that may be displaced from the land for tourism development. However, it is evident that tourism development can be an exclusive process, and as landowners and entrepreneurs become aware of the financial opportunities to be gained from tourism, then the pressure on local tenants to leave their land is likely to increase.

THE SOCIO-CULTURAL IMPACT OF TOURISM PROMOTION

If, as we have argued earlier, tourism promotion by a single organisation is rarely exposed to a very wide international audience, except on Internet, there is another sense in which tourism as an aggregate network of representations, is becoming a major element of globalisation. Tourism with its the images of escape, fantasy, far-away exotica, dream-worlds and otherness, is now a ubiquitous presence internationally, not just in promotion specifically selling tourism, but as an element in many other kinds of promotion and publicity. It is thus part of a global consumption ethic:

The new consumption ethic which was taken over by the advertising industry by the late 1920s celebrated living for the moment, hedonism, self-expression, the body beautiful, paganism, freedom from social obligations, the exotica of far-away places, the cultivation of style and the stylization of life.

Tourism is now synergistically associated, through visual imaging, with the selling of numerous other commodities such as cars and petrol (advertisements always reflect the leisure use, not the work use, of cars), pop music and fashion, and is thus an overt constituent of 'lifestyle', the 'aestheticisation of life' and the 'promotional culture' (Wernick 1991), that postmodern commentators have been diagnosing. Visual images of multinational promotion, particularly in metropolitan cities and urban conurbations, centralise the idea that travel is good, glamorous and high status.

The central idea is that postmodern cities have become centres of consumption, play and entertainment, saturated with signs and images to the extent that anything can become represented, thematised and made an object of interest, an object of the tourist gaze. Dann has demonstrated how tourism is now explicitly linked, in lifestyle magazines like Conde Nast *Traveller*, to the sale of other luxury items which depict a placeless, global consumption ethic. These cross-product advertising presentations are anchored in the multi-referentiality of travel and tourism as a tie-concept that brings together an international hedonism of food, jewellery, clothes, cars, entertainment, etc. - Lafant's 'tourist neoculture' (Dann 1998). However, this may not be completely new. Travel has always been a status badge, associated through the life styles of the classes that could afford it, with privileged access to other goods. Indeed, tourism choice may be seen as an important, hierarchically derived, form of taste discrimination to add to those other kinds of consumer decision and aesthetic choice that Bourdieu (1984) has so brilliantly shown to be related to social position, occupation and family status (Seaton 1999a). However, as we have argued earlier, this tendency towards a world consumer culture does not mean that a homogenised global market has emerged for tourism. As Warhurst, Nickson and Shaw have concluded:

Even within a global culture of consumerism, consumer needs, wants and demands across the globe may continue to vary. In short, it is one thing to argue that the world's economic activity is becoming dominated by consumerism and market transactions and quite another to then insist that this market and its consumers are homogenized. The two phenomena should not be conflated: a domineering ideology of consumerism does not equate with a single world market.

It has distinguished five different dimensions of globalisation (locational, consumer, promotional, competitive and cultural) and suggested that there are differences in the extent to which tourism is associated with each. The main effect of globalisation on tourism marketing has not been the visible homogenisation of promotional campaigns directed to world markets by tourism organisations, but in converging approaches to strategic planning, and the gradual emergence of state-of-the-art managerial techniques which include: refinements in market segmentation, use of consumer research, and the application of benchmarking to the tourism sector. One of the most significant effects of tourism promotion and publicity worldwide has been to contribute to the evolution of a global ethos of consumption, through the aggregate and cumulative dispersion of tourism and destination imagery, alongside other kinds of luxury commodities in media representations of placeless, postmodern life-styles.

Finally, the chapter has identified the potential consequences of globalisation for SMEs as an antidote to more usual focus on globalisation and MNEs.

ECONOMIC IMPACT ANALYSIS

A variety of economic analyses are carried out to support tourism decisions. As these different kinds of economic analysis are frequently confused, let's begin by positioning economic impact studies within the broader set of economic problems and techniques relevant to tourism. These same techniques may be applied to any policy or action, but we will define them here in the context of tourism. Each type of analysis is identified by the basic question(s) it answers and the types of methods and models that are appropriate. Benefit cost analysis and economic impact analysis are frequently confused as both discuss economic "benefits".

There are two clear distinctions between the two techniques. B/C analysis addresses the benefits from economic efficiency while economic impact analysis focuses on the regional distribution of economic activity. The income received from tourism by a destination region is largely off-set by corresponding losses in the origin regions, yielding only modest contributions to net social welfare and efficiency. B/C analysis includes market and non-market values (consumer surplus), while economic impact analysis is restricted to actual flows of money from market transactions. While each type of economic analysis is somewhat distinct, a given problem often calls for several different kinds of economic analysis. An economic impact study will frequently involve a demand analysis to project levels of tourism activity.

In other cases demand is treated as exogenous and the analysis simply estimates impacts if a given number of visitors are attracted to the area. A comprehensive impact assessment will also examine fiscal impacts, as well as social and environmental impacts. Be aware that an economic impact analysis, by itself, provides a rather narrow and often one-sided perspective on the impacts of tourism.

Studies of the economic impacts of tourism tend to emphasize the positive benefits of tourism. On the other hand environmental, social, cultural and fiscal impact studies tend to focus more on negative impacts of tourism. This is in spite of the fact that there are negative economic impacts of tourism (*e.g.*, seasonality and lower wage jobs) and in many cases positive environmental and social impacts (*e.g.*, protection of natural and cultural resources in the area and education of both tourists and local residents). An economic impact assessment (EIA) traces changes in economic activity resulting from some action.

An EIA will identify which economic sectors benefit from tourism and estimate resulting changes in income and employment in the region. Economic impact assessment procedures do not assess economic efficiency and also do not generally produce estimates of the fiscal costs of an action. For many problems economic impact analysis will be part of a broader analysis. Environmental, social, and fiscal impacts are often equally important concerns in a balanced assessment of impacts. An economic impact analysis will assess the contribution of tourism activity to a region's economy.

The basic questions an economic impact study usually addresses are:

- How many jobs in the area does tourism support?
- How much tax revenue is generated from tourism?
- How much do tourists spend in the area?
- What portion of sales by local businesses is due to tourism?
- How much income does tourism generate for households and businesses in the area?

An economic impact analysis also reveals the interrelationships among economic sectors and provides estimates of the changes that take place in an economy due to some existing or proposed action.

The most common applications of economic impact analysis to tourism are:

1. To evaluate the economic impacts of changes in the supply of recreation and tourism opportunities. Supply changes may involve a change in quantity, such as the opening of new facilities, closing of existing ones, or expansions and contraction in capacity. Supply changes may also involve changes in quality, including changes in,
   - The quality of the environment,

- The local infrastructure and public services to support tourism, or
- The nature of the tourism products and services that are provided in an area.

2. To evaluate the economic impacts of changes in tourism demand. Population changes, changes in the competitive position of the region, marketing activity or changing consumer tastes and preferences can alter levels of tourism activity, spending, and associated economic activity. An economic impact study can estimate the magnitude and nature of these impacts.
3. To evaluate the effects of policies and actions which affect tourism activity either directly or indirectly. Tourism depends on many factors at both origins and destinations that are frequently outside the direct control of the tourism industry itself. Economic impact studies provide information to help decision makers better understand the consequences of various actions on the tourism industry as well as on other sectors of the economy. For example, increased air pollution standards have been opposed in some regions due to the predicted economic consequences of the closing of plants that cannot meet the new standards. Tourism interests counter these arguments with estimates of the potential gains in income and jobs in tourism industries that depend on good air quality and visibility.
4. To understand the economic structure and interdependencies of different sectors of the economy. Economic studies help us better understand the size and structure of the tourism industry in a given region and its linkages to other sectors of the economy. Such understandings are helpful in identifying potential partners for the tourism industry as well as in targeting industries as part of regional economic development strategies. Issues such as economic growth, stability, and seasonality may be addressed as part of these studies.
5. To argue for favourable treatment in allocation of resources or local tax, zoning or other policy decisions. By showing that tourism has significant economic impacts, tourism interests can often convince decision-makers to allocate more resources for tourism or to establish policies that encourage tourism. Tax abatements and other incentives frequently given to manufacturing firms have also been granted to hotels, marinas and other tourism businesses based on demonstrated economic impacts in the local area.
6. To compare the economic impacts of alternative resource allocation, policy, management or development proposals. Economic impact analyses are commonly used to assess the relative merits of distinct alternatives. The economic contribution of expanded tourism offerings

may be compared for example with alternatives such as resource extraction activities (mining, timber harvesting) or manufacturing. Impacts of alternative tourism development proposals may also be evaluated, *e.g.*, tourism strategies that emphasize outdoor recreation, camping development, a convention facility, or a factory outlet mall.

Tourism has a variety of economic impacts. Tourists contribute to sales, profits, jobs, tax revenues, and income in an area. The most direct effects occur within the primary tourism sectors—lodging, restaurants, transportation, amusements, and retail trade. Through secondary effects, tourism affects most sectors of the economy. An economic impact analysis of tourism activity normally focuses on changes in sales, income, and employment in a region resulting from tourism activity.

A simple tourism impact scenario illustrates. Let's say a region attracts an additional 100 tourists, each spending $100 per day. That's $10,000 in new spending per day in the area. If sustained over a 100 day season, the region would accumulate a million dollars in new sales. The million dollars in spending would be distributed to lodging, restaurant, amusement and retail trade sectors in proportion to how the visitor spends the $100. Perhaps 30% of the million dollars would leak out of the region immediately to cover the costs of goods purchased by tourists that are not made in the local area (only the retail margins for such items should normally be included as direct sales effects). The remaining $700,000 in direct sales might yield $350,000 in income within tourism industries and support 20 direct tourism jobs. Tourism industries are labour and income intensive, translating a high proportion of sales into income and corresponding jobs.

The tourism industry, in turn, buys goods and services from other businesses in the area, and pays out most of the $350,000 in income as wages and salaries to its employees. This creates secondary economic effects in the region. The study might use a sales multiplier of 2.0 to indicate that each dollar of direct sales generates another dollar in secondary sales in this region. Through multiplier effects, the $700,000 in direct sales produces $1.4 million in total sales. These secondary sales create additional income and employment, resulting in a total impact on the region of $1.4 million in sales, $650,000 in income and 35 jobs.

While hypothetical, the numbers used here are fairly typical of what one might find in a tourism economic impact study. A more complete study might identify which sectors receive the direct and secondary effects and possibly identify differences in spending and impacts of distinct subgroups of tourists (market segments). One can also estimate the tax effects of this spending by applying local tax rates to the appropriate changes in sales or income. Instead of focusing on visitor spending, one could also estimate impacts of construction or government activity associated with tourism. There are several other categories of economic impacts that are not typically covered in economic impact assessments, at least not directly.

For example:

- *Changes in prices*: Tourism can sometimes inflate the cost of housing and retail prices in the area, frequently on a seasonal basis.
- *Changes in the quality and quantity of goods and services*: Tourism may lead to a wider array of goods and services available in an area (of either higher or lower quality than without tourism).
- *Changes in property and other taxes*: Taxes to cover the cost of local services may be higher or lower in the presence of tourism activity. In some cases, taxes collected directly or indirectly from tourists may yield reduced local taxes for schools, roads, etc. In other cases, locals may be taxed more heavily to cover the added infrastructure and service costs. The impacts of tourism on local government costs and revenues are addressed more fully in a fiscal impact analysis.
- *Economic dimensions of "social" and "environmental" impacts*: There are also economic consequences of most social and environmental impacts that are not usually addressed in an economic impact analysis. These can be positive or negative. For example, traffic congestion will increase costs of moving around for both households and businesses. Improved amenities that attract tourists may also encourage retirees or other kinds of businesses to locate in the area.

INDUCED EFFECTS

A standard economic impact analysis traces flows of money from tourism spending, first to businesses and government agencies where tourists spend their money and then to:

- *Other businesses*: Supplying goods and services to tourist businesses,
- *Households*: Earning income by working in tourism or supporting industries, and
- *Government*: Through various taxes and charges on tourists, businesses and households

Formally, regional economists distinguish direct, indirect, and induced economic effects. Indirect and induced effects are sometimes collectively called secondary effects. The total economic impact of tourism is the sum of direct, indirect, and induced effects within a region. Any of these impacts may be measured as gross output or sales, income, employment, or value added. Direct effects are production changes associated with the immediate effects of changes in tourism expenditures. For example, an increase in the number of tourists staying overnight in hotels would directly yield increased sales in the hotel sector. The additional hotel sales and associated changes in hotel payments for wages and salaries, taxes, and supplies and services are direct effects of the tourist spending. Indirect effects are the production changes resulting from various rounds of re-spending of the hotel industry's receipts in other backward-linked industries (*i.e.*, industries supplying products and services to hotels). Changes in sales, jobs, and income in the linen supply industry, for example, represent indirect effects of changes in hotel sales. Businesses supplying products and services to the linen supply industry represent another round of indirect effects, eventually linking hotels to varying degrees to many other economic sectors in the region. Induced effects are the changes in economic activity resulting from household spending of income earned directly or indirectly as a result of tourism spending. For example, hotel and linen supply employees supported directly or indirectly by tourism, spend their income in the local region for housing, food, transportation, and the usual array of household product and service needs. The sales, income, and jobs that result from household spending of added wage, salary, or proprietor's income are induced effects.

By means of indirect and induced effects, changes in tourist spending can impact virtually every sector of the economy in one way or another. The magnitude of secondary effects depends on the propensity of businesses and households in the region to purchase goods and services from local suppliers. Induced effects are particularly noticed when a large employer in a region closes a plant. Not only are supporting industries (indirect effects) hurt, but the entire local economy suffers due to the reduction in household income within the region.

Retail stores close and leakages of money from the region increase as consumers go outside the region for more and more goods and services. Similar effects in the opposite direction are observed when there is a significant increase in jobs and household income. Final demand is the term used by economists for sales to the final consumers of goods and services. In almost all cases, the final consumers of tourism goods and services are households. Government spending is also considered as final demand. The same methods for estimating impacts of visitor spending can be applied to estimate the economic impacts of government spending, for example, to operate and maintain a park or visitor centre.

REGIONAL MODELS

An input-output model (I-O model) is a mathematical model that describes the flows of money between sectors within a region's economy. Flows are predicted by knowing what each industry must buy from every other industry to produce a dollar's worth of output. Using each industry's production function, I-O models also determine the proportions of sales that go to wage and salary income, proprietor's income, and taxes. Multipliers can be estimated from input-output models based on the estimated re-circulation of spending within the region. Exports and imports are determined based upon estimates of the propensity of households and firms within the region to purchase goods and services from local sources (often called RPC's or regional purchase coefficients). The more a region is self-sufficient and purchases goods and services from within the region, the higher the multipliers for the region. Input-output models make a number of assumptions.

The basic ones are that:

- All firms in a given industry employ the same production technology (usually assumed to be the national average for that industry), and produce identical products.
- There are no economies or diseconomies of scale in production or factor substitution. I-O models are essentially linear—double the level of tourism activity/production and you double all of the inputs, the number of jobs, etc.
- The model doesn't explicitly keep track of time, but analysts generally report the impact estimates as if they represent activity within a single year.
- One must assume that the various model parameters are accurate and represent the current year.

I-O models are firmly grounded in the national system of accounts, which relies on a standard industrial classification system (SIC codes) and various federal government economic censuses, in which individual firms report sales, wage and salary payments and employment. I-O models will generally be at least a few years out-of-date, although this isn't usually a major problem unless the region's economy has changed significantly. An I-O model represents the region's economy at a particular point in time. Tourist spending estimates are generally price adjusted to the year of the model.

Multiplier computations for induced effects generally assume that jobs created by additional spending are new jobs, involving new households in the area. Induced effects are computed assuming linear changes in household spending with changes in income. Estimates of induced effects may be inflated due to the violation of these assumptions. Induced effects tend to account for the vast majority of the secondary effects of tourism, and therefore should be used with caution.

MULTIPLIERS EFFECTS OF TOURISM

Multipliers capture the secondary economic effects (indirect and induced) of tourism activity. Multipliers have been frequently misused and misinterpreted in tourism studies and are a considerable source of confusion among non-economists. Multipliers represent the economic interdependencies between sectors within a particular region's economy. They vary considerably from region to region and sector to sector. There are many different kinds of multipliers reflecting which secondary effects are included and which measure of economic activity is used (sales, income, or employment).

For example,

- The Type I sales multiplier = direct sales + indirect sales direct sales.
- The Type II or III sales multiplier[1] = direct sales + indirect sales + induced sales direct sales.

Multiplying a Type I sales multiplier times the direct sales gives direct plus indirect sales. Multiplying a Type II or III sales multiplier times the direct sales gives total sales impacts including direct, indirect and induced effects. The multipliers defined above are called ratio type multipliers as they measure the ratio of a total impact measure to the corresponding direct impact. Comparable income and employment ratio type multipliers may be defined by replacing sales with measures of income or employment in the above equations. Ratio multipliers should be used with caution.

A common error is to multiply a sales multiplier times tourist spending to get total sales effects. This will generate an inflated estimate of tourism impacts. The problem is that tourism spending or sales is not exactly the same as the "direct effects", appearing in the multiplier formula. Tourist purchases of goods (vs. services) are the primary source of the problem. To properly apply tourist purchases of goods to an input-output model (or corresponding multipliers), various margins (retail, wholesale and transportation) must be deducted from the "purchaser price" of the good to separate out the "producer price".

In an I-O model, retail margins accrue to the retail trade sector, wholesale margins to wholesale trade, transportation margins to transportation sectors (trucking, rail, air etc.) and the producer prices of goods are assigned to the sector that produces the good. In most cases the factory that produces the good bought by a tourist lies outside of the local region, creating an immediate "leakage" in the first round of spending and therefore no local impact from production of the good. Before applying a multiplier to tourist spending, one must first deduct the producer prices of all imported goods that tourists buy (*i.e.* only include the local retail margins and possibly wholesale and transportation margins if these firms lie within the region). Generally, only 60 to 70% of tourist spending appears as final demand in a local region. While all tourist purchases of services will accrue to the local region as final demand, only the margins on goods purchased at retail stores should be counted as local final demand. The ratio of local final demand to tourist spending is called the capture rate.

Capture rate = local final demand/tourism spending in local area. Capture rates, like multipliers, will vary with the size and nature of the region as well as the kind of tourist spending included. One must therefore be cautious in taking a multiplier or capture rate cited in one study and using it in another.

Another way of calculating a multiplier (generally the preferred approach among economists) is as a ratio of income or employment to sales. This kind of multiplier is sometimes called a Keynesian multiplier or response coefficient.

- Type III Income multiplier = Total direct, indirect, and induced income direct sales
- Type III Employment multiplier = Total direct, indirect, and induced employment direct sales

This income (employment) multiplier produces total income (employment) impacts when multiplied by the direct sales. One must still be careful in distinguishing between tourism spending/sales and direct sales effects. Some studies may embed the capture rate in the multiplier, expressing the ratio in terms of tourism spending rather than direct sales.

The economic impacts of tourism are typically estimated by some variation of the following simple formula:

Economic Impact of Tourism = Number of Tourists × Average Spending per Visitor × Multiplier

The formula suggests three distinct steps and corresponding measurements or models:

1. Estimate the change in the number and types of tourists to the region due to the proposed policy or action. Estimates or projections of tourist activity generally come from a demand model or some system for measuring levels of tourism activity in an area. Economic impact estimates will rest heavily on good estimates of the numbers and types of visitors. These must come from carefully designed measurements of tourist activity, a good demand model, or good judgement. This step is usually the weakest link in most tourism impact studies, as few regions have accurate counts of tourists, let alone good models for predicting changes in tourism activity or separating local visitors from visitors from outside the region.
2. Estimate average levels of spending (often within specific market segments) of tourists in the local area. Spending averages come from sample surveys or are sometimes borrowed or adapted from other studies. Spending estimates must be based on a representative sample of the population of tourists taking into account variations across seasons, types of tourists, and locations within the study area. As spending can vary widely across different kinds of tourists, we recommend estimating average spending for a set of key tourist segments based on samples of at least 50-100 visitors within each tourism segment. Segments should be defined to capture differences in spending between local residents vs. tourists, day users vs. overnight visitors, type of accommodation (motel, campground, seasonal home, with friends and relatives), and type of transportation

(car, RV, air, rail, etc.). In broadly based tourism impact studies, it is useful to identify unique spending patterns of important activity segments such as downhill skiers, boaters, and convention and business travellers. Multiplying the number of tourists by the average spending per visitor (be careful the units are consistent) gives an estimate of total tourist spending in the area. Estimates of tourist spending will generally be more accurate if distinct spending profiles and use estimates are made for key tourism segments. The use and spending estimates are the two most important parts of an economic impact assessment. When combined, they capture the amount of money brought into the region by tourists. Multipliers are needed only if one is interested in the secondary effects of tourism spending.

3. Apply the change in spending to a regional economic model or set of multipliers to determine secondary effects. Secondary effects of tourism are estimated using multipliers or a model of the region's economy. Multipliers generally come from an economic base or input-output model of the region's economy. In many cases multipliers are borrowed (often improperly) or adjusted from published multipliers or other studies. One should not take a multiplier estimated for one region and apply it in a region with a quite different economic structure. Generally, multipliers are higher for larger regions with more diversified economies and lower for smaller regions with more limited economic development. A common error is to apply a statewide multiplier (since these are more widely published) to a local region. This will yield inflated estimates of local multiplier effects. Multipliers can also be used to convert estimates of spending or sales to income and employment. Simple ratios can be used to capture how much income or jobs are generated per dollar of sales. These ratios will vary from region to region and across individual economic sectors due to the relative importance of labour inputs in each industry and different wage and salary rates in different regions of the country. Be aware that job estimates are generally not full time equivalents, making them difficult to compare across industries with different proportions of seasonal and part time jobs. Income or value added are generally the preferred measures of the contribution of tourism to a region's economy.

THE TYPICAL APPROACHES FOR AN ECONOMIC ASSESSMENT

At the simple, "quick and dirty" end of the spectrum are highly aggregate approaches that rely mostly on judgement to determine tourism activity, spending and multipliers. Such estimates can be completed in a couple hours at little cost and rest largely on the expertise and judgement of the analyst. At the other extreme are studies that gather primary data from visitor spending studies and apply the spending estimates to formal regional economic models for the area in question. In between are a wide range of options that employ varying degrees of judgement, secondary data, primary data, and formal models.

Different levels of detail and corresponding expense (time and money) and accuracy are possible for each of the three steps—estimating tourist volume, spending, and multiplier effects. Four typical approaches illustrate the levels of detail that are possible and the associated methods to sales estimates. With sound judgement in choosing the parameters, the MGM model can yield reasonable ballpark estimates of economic impacts at minimal cost. This approach, however, provides little detail on spending categories or which sectors of the economy benefit from either direct or secondary effects. The aggregate nature of the approach also makes it difficult to adjust recommended spending rates or multipliers to different applications. The Bureau of Economic Analysis's (BEA) RIMS II user handbook illustrates how to apply published multipliers to estimate economic impacts. This approach starts with visitor spending (from survey or secondary sources) divided into a number of spending categories and makes use of sector specific multipliers to estimate the direct and total sales, income and employment effects. Multipliers from the BEA's RIMS II models are used to estimate secondary effects. Multipliers are reported for 39 sectors for each state in the second edition of their report.

This method uses margins to properly account for retail purchases of goods and makes use of disaggregate sector-specific multipliers for each state. Multipliers for sub-state regions are not as readily available, but can be acquired from BEA or other sources. Secondary effects cannot be disaggregated to individual sectors using the BEA approach.

The MI-REC/IMPLAN System: Stynes and Propst have developed a fairly complete micro-computer-based system for estimating economic impacts of recreation and tourism. The system combines spreadsheets for estimating spending with the IMPLAN input-output modeling system. IMPLAN uses county level data to estimate 528 sector input-output models for regions down to account level. IMPLAN generates a complete set of economic accounts for the region including multipliers and trade flows. MI-REC spreadsheets estimate visitor spending within up to 33categories based on the number and types of visitors attracted to an area. Spending is then bridged to the IMPLAN model sectors to estimate direct, indirect and induced effects in terms of sales, income and employment. Users may estimate spending via visitor surveys or use the MI-REC database of spending profiles, compiled from previous studies. The system also includes price indices to easily update spending data to a current year.

Two other systems for estimating economic impacts of tourism should be noted. The TEIM or Travel Economic Impact Model developed by the U.S.

Travel Data Centre has been widely used to estimate tourism and travel impacts at state and national levels. A more recent development is the satellite accounting approach developed by the World Travel and Tourism Council. Both of these systems are primarily designed for estimating the overall economic significance of tourism at national or state levels. They are not readily applied to estimate the impacts of particular policies and actions at the local level.

The TEIM relies on national travel surveys to estimate trip volume and spending on a state-by-state basis. Local estimates of impacts are obtained using simple allocation formulas to distribute statewide impacts to counties and cities within the state. These local estimates do not account very well for the distinct types of tourism activity or spending patterns in different sub-regions of a state. The WTTC effort also focuses on national and statewide accounting of tourism's economic significance. Their satellite tourism account identifies the contribution of travel and tourism to gross national product (GNP) or gross state product (GSP). Using the standard national system of accounts, they identify the portion of sales, taxes and investment attributable directly to travel and tourism. The WTTC system does not use multipliers or attempt to estimate secondary effects. It does, however, capture a great deal of travel-related economic activity, not covered by visitor trip spending, such as durable goods purchases (boats and RV's), construction and investment in tourism, and government expenditures.

An economic impact study involves four basic:

1. Define the problem
2. Estimate the change in final demand (tourism spending).
3. Estimate the regional economic effects of this change
4. Interpret, apply, and communicate the results

The most important part of any study is the first step—clarifying the nature of the problem being addressed and intended uses of the results. Before launching an economic impact study, be sure this is the kind of study that is needed rather than one or more of the other kinds of economic analyses. Stynes and Propst (1996) identify seven factors that should be specified as part of defining a problem for an economic impact assessment:

- Define the action to be evaluated. Begin by clarifying the action or actions involved in the problem. Actions may include construction, government investment, changes in marketing, management, or policies, or changes in the quality or quantity of tourist facilities. If evaluating impacts of existing tourism activity, be sure to define what is to be included as "tourism".
- Identify the change in the amount and kinds of recreation/tourism activity resulting from the action. The action must be defined precisely enough in step one to be able to estimate the changes in the number and types of visitors to the area and/or their spending patterns. As a

general rule, the analysis should be with vs. without the action rather than simply before vs. after. Thus, if tourism has been growing by 5% per year and a new promotional programme increases this to 10% this year, only half of the 10% growth can likely be attributed to the promotional programme. Identifying the net changes in activity that are attributable to an action can be a complex and difficult task. Assessments of economic impact, however, rest firmly on such estimates, so attention to these details is very important. In situations of some uncertainty, we recommend evaluating impacts using a range of estimates in order to establish rough confidence intervals around your estimates. Evaluating a range of alternatives also helps to evaluate the sensitivity of the results to your initial estimates of changes in activity levels.

- Identify the kinds of spending to be included. Tourism may impact the local economy through visitor trip spending, durable goods purchases, government spending, or investment and construction. Which to include in a given analysis depends on how the problem is defined, and again, on attributing given spending changes to the proposed action.
- Identify the study region. Perhaps the most important, yet often neglected part of a recreation and tourism impact assessment is the definition of a study region. The region defines the area for which impacts are desired, as well as the portions of visitor spending that are relevant. An impact assessment evaluates the impacts on households, businesses, and organizations within the given region. Spending that visitors make outside of a study region either at home or en route are not included in assessing impacts of spending on the designated region. For an economic impact analysis, the study region should be large enough to constitute a viable economic region. Since little economic data exists below the county level, the county is generally the smallest region one should consider for a tourism impact assessment.
- Identify key economic sectors and desired sectoral detail. The proposed action and anticipated uses/users of the results should suggest the key sectors that will be impacted. Recreation and tourism activity typically impact the lodging, restaurant, amusements, retail, transportation and government sectors most directly. In the problem definition stage consideration of impacted sectors helps to identify relevant categories of spending. The desired sectoral detail plays an important role in structuring the presentation of results. In some cases only an aggregate measure of impacts may be desired. In other cases, clients may be interested in which particular sectors are most

heavily affected and will want estimates of sales and jobs broken down by sector. If formal input-output models are used, impacts may be estimated in considerable sectoral detail. This is not possible if an aggregate spending estimate or multiplier is used.

- Identify the most important measures of economic activity. Tourism impacts may be reported in terms of visitor spending, business receipts/sales/production, wage and salary income, proprietors income and profits, value added, and employment. The direct effects are the most important and are captured well by estimates of visitor spending. Simple ratios can be used to convert direct spending or sales to the associated income and jobs. Input-output models and multipliers are needed only if one is interested in secondary effects.
- Identify the tolerable levels of error in the results. Although confidence intervals and estimates of error are rare in economic impact studies, this doesn't mean they are not important. You should have at least a ballpark idea of how much error you can tolerate in the analysis, as this will dictate how much effort and expense you must put into it. The more accuracy you demand, the greater the requirements to gather up-to-date local data on visitation, spending and economic activity. These data allow you to fine tune the spending estimates and input-output models or multipliers. Such fine tuning will require time, knowledge, and money that must be weighed against the benefits of the improved estimates. Estimates of impacts are based on three components: visits, spending, and multipliers. You should try to balance the errors across these components.
- What are some questions to ask when evaluating or interpreting a tourism economic impact study? Evaluating, interpreting and applying an economic impact study requires a clear understanding of the findings and at least some knowledge of the underlying concepts and methods. Judging the accuracy or quality of a study can be based on the reputation of the author or the quality of presentation, although a careful evaluation of the methods that were used is the best approach. Here's some questions to ask when reading or evaluating a tourism economic impact study.
- *Impact of what?* The report should identify the action being evaluated. An economic impact assessment is most useful when evaluating the effects of a particular action or policy. If so, the action and assumptions about alternatives should be spelled out in presenting a with vs. without scenario. If the study reports impacts of existing tourism activity, identify how tourism is defined (if at all). What kinds of tourism activity and spending are included? Which trip expenses are included? Does the study include all visitor spending or only spending

of tourists who live outside the local region? Does the study address impacts of visitor trip spending, durable goods purchases, operational expenses of a programme, or construction and investment?

- *On what region?* The study region should be defined (preferably with a map). It should be viable both economically and as a distinct tourism destination area. Spending that is included should be restricted to spending in this region and multipliers should represent the given region of interest. A short profile of tourism and economic activity in the region provides useful background for an economic impact study.
- *Sources and quality of the data:* The report should identify the sources of the data for estimating visits, spending, and regional economic multipliers/models. The methods that were used to estimate impacts should be clear. Judgements of the quality of the estimates must be based largely on an understanding of the data and methods that were used. A more disaggregate analysis reporting spending within at least six categories, visitors for two or more distinct segments, and multipliers and results broken down by sector will generally be more accurate and meaningful than a study that only uses aggregate data. Disaggregation is particularly helpful when adjusting secondary data taken from government reports or other studies to a new situation. The fundamental question is whether the visit estimates, spending profiles and multipliers adequately represent the intended population and study area.
- *Quality of methods:* There are a number of issues to watch for in evaluating methods.
- *Visits:* Has the study clearly defined which visits/visitors will be affected by the proposed action, separated local visitors from tourists, and identified which visitors would be lost or gained due to the action (with vs. without the action)? Are secondary sources of visitation reliable? If models are used, how good are they and do the assumptions hold for the intended application? Has the study handled potential double counting problems in estimating visits?
- *Spending:* How accurate are the spending estimates? Do the spending averages or totals seem reasonable? If spending averages are taken from a secondary source, evaluate the source, as well as how well these averages may apply to the intended application. What year does the spending represent? Has the data been price adjusted to the current (or model) year? If spending data come from a visitor survey, evaluate the survey methods-how was spending measured, what was the sample size, the response rate, soundness of the analysis? Are variances and confidence intervals reported for the spending estimates? Are visitors divided into distinct segments to reduce

variances? Also make sure the units for which spending is reported match the units for visits, *i.e.*, the study doesn't multiply a per party spending average times the number of person visits. If adjustments are made in units of analysis, evaluate the assumed or estimated average length of stay or party size assumptions.

- *Multipliers:* If "off-the-shelf" or borrowed multipliers are used, investigate the source. Does the study clearly define what type of multiplier is being used (Type I, Type III, income, sales or employment, ratio or Keynesian) and use the multiplier appropriately? In particular, watch for studies that multiply tourism spending by a multiplier taken from an input-output model. They should adjust for the capture rate either by reducing spending, only using retail margins on goods purchased by tourists, or using a "tourist spending" multiplier that takes the capture rate into account. If an input-output model is used, the report should summarize where it came from, what year it represents, the levels of sectoral aggregation, and the basic assumptions of the model.
- *Communication and reporting of results:* The study should communicate the study results in terms that are understandable to the intended audience. For most audiences, a summary and glossary of economic terms is helpful. Most readers will not fully understand terms like indirect and induced effects, Type I and Type III multipliers, and input-output models. Formal definitions of the measures of sales, income, and jobs that are reported are also needed to clarify what each of these terms include and the measurement units. For example, is income only wage and salary income or does it also include proprietors income, rents and profits? Study limitations and errors should be indicated.

ENVIRONMENTAL MANAGEMENT OF TOURISM DEVELOPMENT

Tourism plays an important role in economic development at community, national, regional and global levels by using natural resources and environments as key physical inputs. In making use of the environment and natural resources, the negative impacts have to be minimized to assure sustainable use, as well as generate enough tourism revenue to reinvest a certain portion of funds. The reinvestment should aim at enhancing the quality of the resources and build the management capacity at various levels.

There is a complex relationship between tourism and the environment, such that tourism has inevitable and important environmental impacts, including: resource use, consumption, waste, pollution and effects from tourism-related transport. At the same time, beaches, mountains, rivers, forests and diverse flora and fauna make the environment a basic resource that the tourism industry needs in order to thrive and grow. While the viability of tourism could be threatened by negative environmental impacts, tourism could also contribute significantly to environmental protection.

This shows that tourism and the environment are interrelated and interdependent in complex ways, and together they could provide a sustainable economic base for development. In light of these observations, tourism policy-makers, managers and planners must address the issues of environmental management of tourism development in a sustainable manner. The adverse impact of tourism on the environment relates to pressure on natural resources, harm to wildlife and habitats, creation of pollution and waste and related social and cultural pressures.

Among the environmental issues that need to be addressed are:

- Deterioration of natural resources (fresh water, land and landscape, marine resources, atmosphere and local resources), which may be resilient, but can deteriorate rapidly if impact exceeds tolerable limits;
- Disruption of wildlife and habitats, including vegetation, endangered species, use of forest resources, intrusion into fragile areas with sensitive ecosystems;
- Creation of pollution and waste contaminating the land, fresh water sources, marine resources, as well as causing air and noise pollution.

There has been growing recognition that traditional tourism management practices have led to such undesirable social and environmental impacts, thus threatening the tourism industry's prospects for continued prosperity. The Environment Committee of the World Tourism Organization (WTO) has taken action through its Tourism and Environment Task Force by developing indicators of sustainability that are relevant to the tourism industry and accepted internationally. Tourism managers and planners can use these indicators to address concerns about sustainability. The ecological aspects of environments that become tourist destinations should be seen as ecosystems that are life-creating natural networks. Ecosystems temper climate, purify and store water, recycle wastes, produce food and support all other living things.

There are five categories of ecosystem, of which four are natural:

1. Coastal and marine,
2. Fresh water
3. Grasslands and
4. Forests; plus
5. Man-made ecosystems based on agriculture or aquaculture.

All five ecosystems can be viewed as tourism resources. The main issue for all categories is whether they can absorb negative impacts and remain sustainable. The notion of carrying capacity can indicate whether an ecosystem can sustain itself or whether it has become irreparably damaged. At the international level, attention to ecosystems and environmental threats to tourism has come from the World Tourism Organization through its ten-point Global Code of Ethics for Tourism approved in 1999, Agenda 21 agreed at the United Nation's Conference on Environment and Development, and the 1992 Rio Declaration on the Environment and Development.

Major environmental threats to the tourism industry have been identified as:

- Global warming,
- Loss of biological diversity and
- Deterioration of the abiotic environment (climate, soil, water and air) that nurture biotic components of ecosystems.

All of these issues make it evident that formulating policies to preserve the environment are decisive and must be made while meeting economic development goals, especially eradicating poverty, at the community, national, regional and global levels.

Making effective policies require that the roles of different stakeholders be considered. The major stakeholders involved with issues of sound environmental management are: the community, the tourism industry, non-governmental organizations (NGOs), the government and international communities.

Each type of stakeholder should be actively involved and aware in managing the sustainable development of tourism, and they must also work in partnership. If all stakeholders work in partnership to sustain tourism development plus protect the environment, then the present generation will provide a meaningful legacy for future generations. Understanding the limits to economic growth, the carrying capacity of natural resources and the need for sustainable action should be the guiding forces in the management of tourism development.

COMMUNITY-BASED SUSTAINABLE TOURISM

Thailand's rich historical, cultural and natural attractions have contributed to the development of mass tourism, which has had both positive and negative effects on development. Small-scale tourism development projects that are community-based, focus on an ethnic group at a remote location and involve NGOs are less well known. For three years, a community-based sustainable tourism project has been implemented at the ethnic Karen village of Baan Huay Hee in the northwestern Thai province of Mae Hong Son. The project has been carried out with the help of a small NGO, the Project for Recovery of Life and Culture (PRLC).

The aims have been to:

- Improve the overall quality of village people's lives,:
- Preserve and reinforce the importance of Karen culture,
- Empower villagers to make their own decisions about their way of life and

- Contribute to the conservation of natural resources and the environment.

Tourism development in Thailand has spead from Bangkok to almost all parts of the country. Since the 1970s, the natural, cultural and historical attractions and friendly people of northern Thailand have made it a popular destination, first with trekking tourism followed by hilltribe tourism. Six major hilltribe groups make their home in the North: Akha, Hmong, Karen, Lahu, Lisu, Shan, Mien and Haw Chinese. By the 1990s, hilltribe tourism had become highly organized.

However, the number of visitors has not been monitored systematically by the Tourism Authority of Thailand. Over the past ten years, the northern province of Mae Hong Son has become a major tourist destination due to its mist-covered mountains, dense forest areas and the cultural and ethnic diversity. While most hilltribe communities have maintained their way of life, some have become vulnerable to the negative aspects of tourism, especially giving a false image of the people as exotic and primitive based on lack of knowledge and communication among the tourists and the local people. Uncontrolled access to many remote areas has caused problems with waste management and has threatened the ecology in general.

The concept of community-based sustainable tourism (CBST) was developed as a way to overcome or minimize negative effects of tourism in a remote, rural area. CBST was developed as a form of tourism aimed at empowering local communities to be self-reliant, use a group process for local decision-making, support people's human rights and capabilities and help people raise incomes and improve standards of living on their own terms. Local knowledge, community participation, support for local capabilities and cultural exchange with tourists would help to sustain both cultural and natural resources. The NGO (PRLC) helped the Karen village at Huay Hee become the first site for CBST. The village became a successful model for over 60 villages and communities. The project for CBST became holistic in its approach and included natural resource management, sustainable tourism development, strengthened civil society, prevention of HIV/AIDS and drug abuse and youth leadership development. The people of Huay Hee developed a land classification system and cooperation model to work with government agencies responsible for a nearby national park in order to prevent deforestation and degradation of watersheds.

The village has been receiving tourists for about three years with the help of PRLC and another Thai NGO, Thai Volunteer Service-Responsible Ecological Social Tours (TVS-REST). Villagers could explain how they protect the forest and follow their own traditions, while adding to their incomes and improving their standard of living. Villagers became more aware of environmental issues, especially when tourists left garbage behind and picked rare orchids as they trekked on the mountains.

Men in the village received guide training and increased their understanding about how tourists should behave during treks. Women in the village provide meals, sell items made with traditional Karen weaving and take care of tourists during home stays. Home stays and guiding were shared among the families on a rotation basis, which meant both responsibility and income were shared.

Some of the earnings from tourism activities were saved in a village fund that was used to conserve the forest, grow orchids, buy equipment for hosting tourists and support education and travel related to their tourism training. Well-informed exchanges with tourists helped prevent cultural degradation and created more respect for Karen traditions. Equally important, the people at Huay Hee were empowered to see that tourism should provide supplementary income, especially since it was a seasonal activity. With training and support from the CBST project, people used their knowledge of traditional agricultural methods of subsistence farming to be self-reliant in food and to show tourists the role of agriculture in their everyday way of life.

The community-based sustainable tourism project implemented by Karen villagers at Baan Huay Hee in Mae Hong Son Province can serve as a model for other communities. They can be empowered to control the impact of tourism, avoid degrading the environment and create a stronger, empowered community. NGOs can help spread the concept and provide training, but then they must step back as villagers work together to find ways to make the CBST project succeed. The most sustainable form of tourism will be achieved when local people take control of their lives and determine to live according to their traditions on their own terms.

TOURISM CONTRIBUTION TO ECONOMIC CONSERVATION

The main positive economic impacts of tourism relate to foreign exchange earnings, contributions to government revenues, and generation of employment and business opportunities. These are discussed briefly here; further information on economic contributions from tourism can be found at the World Travel & Tourism Council's home page.

FOREIGN EXCHANGE EARNINGS

Tourism expenditures and the export and import of related goods and services generate income to the host economy and can stimulate the investment necessary to finance growth in other economic sectors. Some countries seek to accelerate this growth by requiring visitors to bring in a certain amount of foreign currency for each day of their stay and do not allow them to take it out of the country again at the end of the trip.

An important indicator of the role of international tourism is its generation of foreign exchange earnings.

Tourism is one of the top five export categories for as many as 83% of countries and is a main source of foreign exchange earnings for at least 38% of countries.

Contribution to Government Revenues

Government revenues from the tourism sector can be categorized as direct and indirect contributions. Direct contributions are generated by taxes on incomes from tourism employment and tourism businesses, and by direct levies on tourists such as departure taxes. Indirect contributions are those originated from taxes and duties levied on goods and services supplied to tourists.

The United States National Park Service estimates that the 273 million visits to American national parks in 1993 generated direct and indirect expenditures of US$ 10 billion and 200,000 jobs. When visits to land managed by other agencies, and to state, local, and privately-managed parks, are added, parks were estimated to bring around US$ 22 billion annually to the US economy. These expenditures also generate significant tax revenues for the government.

The World Travel and Tourism Council estimates that travel and tourism's direct, indirect, and personal tax contribution worldwide was over US$ 800 billion in 1998-a figure it expects to double by 2010. (Source: WTTC/Michigan State University Tax Policy Centre)

Employment Generation

The rapid expansion of international tourism has led to significant employment creation. For example, the hotel accommodation sector alone provided around 11.3 million jobs worldwide in 1995. Tourism can generate jobs directly through hotels, restaurants, nightclubs, taxis, and souvenir sales, and indirectly through the supply of goods and services needed by tourism-related businesses. According to the WTO, tourism supports some 7% of the world's workers.

Stimulation of Infrastructure Investment

Tourism can induce the local government to make infrastructure improvements such as better water and sewage systems, roads, electricity, telephone and public transport networks, all of which can improve the quality of life for residents as well as facilitate tourism.

Contribution to Local Economies

Tourism can be a significant, even essential, part of the local economy. As the environment is a basic component of the tourism industry's assets, tourism revenues are often used to measure the economic value of protected areas. For example, Dorrigo National Park in New South Wales, Australia, has been estimated to contribute 7% of gross regional output and 8.4% of regional employment. The importance of tourism to local economies can also be illustrated by the impacts when it is disrupted: the catastrophic 1997 floods that closed Yosemite National Park in California cause locally severe economic losses to the areas around the park. In the most heavily impacted county, Mariposa County, 1997 personal income was reduced by an estimated US$1,159 per capita (US$18 million for the entire county)-a 6.6% decline. The county was also estimated to have lost US$1.67 million in county occupancy and sales tax revenues, and 956 jobs, a significant number in a county of fewer than 16,000 residents. There are other local revenues that are not easily quantified, as not all tourist expenditures are formally registered in the macro-economic statistics. Money is earned from tourism through informal employment such as street vendors, informal guides, rickshaw drivers, etc. The positive side of informal or unreported employment is that the money is returned to the local economy, and has a great multiplier effect as it is spent over and over again. The World Travel and Tourism Council estimates that tourism generates an indirect contribution equal to 100% of direct tourism expenditures.

INVESTMENT IN TOURISM INFRASTRUCTURE

A variety of strategies and measures can be implemented to ensure a favourable atmosphere for investment in tourism infrastructure. In this chapter, the range of measures is presented for consideration by member economies as well as regional organizations and agencies.

NATIONAL LEVEL

Create a Clear Picture of the Role of Tourism in Solving Social, Economic and Environmental Problems

There is an urgent need for countries to emphasize, both to their own population as well as to the external community, the important role that tourism can play in solving a range of social, economic and environmental problems. This will require detailed studies of existing problems and the role that sustainable tourism development can play in achieving societal objectives such as the alleviation of poverty and the improvement of the quality of life of women.

It is only with this kind of information that government departments as well as aid agencies will understand that tourism is an essential development tool. Even more importantly, emphasis should be placed on the fact that if economic and social issues are to be dealt with, investment decisions in overall infrastructure development must support tourism initiatives.

Creation of Tourism Investment Information Centres

Within an increasingly competitive global market there is an urgent need to provide investors with relevant information on infrastructure possibilities.

Countries could therefore consider the establishment of tourism investment information centres to assist national as well as foreign investors. The centres would provide a one-stop service for tourism investment by providing information on investment opportunities and regulations in the tourism industry.

Encourage Cooperation and Integrated Tourism Development Planning

Given the fragmented nature of the public sector as well as private sector aspects of the industry, there is an urgent need for cooperation among all relevant stakeholders.

Specific steps could include:

- The encouragement of other governmental agencies in addition to tourism departments to become involved in tourism investment;
- Increased cooperation between various organizations including the international community, the private sector and relevant government agencies, in order that tourism infrastructure investment is seen as a legitimate development tool for country economies;
- The development of investment programmes and policies in consensus with all the stakeholders. This cooperation will ensure that various government departments as well as the private sector will be more likely to work with one another;
- Involvement of the town and country planning agencies in integrating area development plans with tourism development.

Creation of a Positive Investment Climate

Evidence now suggests that investors are looking for stable and transparent economies in which to invest. In order to achieve this condition, the following strategies could be considered:

- The creation of official procedures that will encourage investment in all aspects of infrastructure and remove the need for corruption as a means of getting things done;
- The development of a comprehensive and transparent legal system and framework as well as legislation that will allow effective implementation and support of infrastructure investment;
- Improvement of the investment environment on a continuous basis, *e.g.*, by alleviating administrative regulations and providing efficient support for information distribution;
- Making incentives more flexible, through consultation or negotiation if necessary, with individual foreign investors rather than by the uniform criterion that may not recognize specific needs and local conditions;
- Increasing lease periods on land and reviewing land rents on a regular basis in an open and transparent manner;

- The provision of strong protection for foreign investment, backed by the force of law;
- Making revolving lines of credit available to the private sector for tourism projects that support strategic societal objectives.

Creation of Special Tourism Investment Zones

Consideration should be given to establishing special zones where investment incentives and clearly understood procedures are in place for tourism development. Within the zones there could be support for infrastructure development, especially in key environmental and public sector areas such as water supply, electricity and telephone. Within those areas there must also be special interest bank loans for infrastructure investment.

Support Human Resource Development

Attracting investment requires that governments as well as private sector stakeholders are aware of the investment procedures and conditions of the global market. In addition, investors must be assured that there is a reliable source of trained personnel in all aspects of tourism activity. Governments and the private sector should therefore consider the establishment of tourism institutes in order to supply the required work force. It is important to stress that training and capacity-building must address actual demands.

Create Opportunities for Strategic Product Development

Given the definition of infrastructure adopted in this study, it is vital that all aspects of the tourism environment be considered. This requires strategic investment in infrastructure that will support local as well as national development.

Specific strategies can include:

- Increased accessibility for existing and potential tourist markets by investing in various forms of transportation facilities and modes;
- Investment in cultural as well as natural heritage sites and attractions, given the importance of these aspects of a destination in meeting overall tourism needs;
- Development of places of pilgrimage by providing the requisite infrastructure facilities;
- Development of the attraction of tourism destinations based on several themes including: islands and beaches, highland resorts, eco-tourism, historical places, cultural attractions and technical parks.

Adopt Innovative Means of Delivering Quality Infrastructure Development

Countries should assess the adoption of build-operate-transfer arrangements to attract foreign investment in tourism infrastructure development. This will require that careful study be undertaken of the costs and benefits of such arrangements, and that public officials are well trained in the development of contracts and arrangements that will benefit all stakeholders. In addition, very careful analysis should be made of the feasibility of such arrangements before any contractual commitments are made.

Other Measures

Other measures that could be implemented in order to create favourable conditions for investing in tourism infrastructure include:

- Increasing local autonomy. Special consideration should be given to ensuring that the autonomy of local government is further enhanced thereby providing local authorities with the incentive to develop policies and approaches to attract and support foreign investment in infrastructure;
- Investing portions of the results of taxation in tourism infrastructure development. Mechanisms should be put into place to tax those benefiting from the tourism economy. One way to ensure that tourism strategies are supported is to direct portions of the tax receipts directly back into investment in tourism infrastructure. This will convince taxpayers that their money are being used in an open and productive manner;
- Development and use of appropriate applications of new technologies for promoting tourism products. Development of the information technology aspects of tourism is essential if the full benefits of tourism infrastructure investment are to be realised;
- Stopping income leakages at the local level. One of the major issues in trying to encourage local investors to contribute to the infrastructure development relates to the significant leakages that often occur from tourism activity. Stopping such leakages also has the added advantage of ensuring that the economic and social needs of local people are enhanced through tourism development. Specific actions can include:
  - Involving local communities at all levels in all aspects of the policy-making, planning, and management decisionmaking process;
  - Training and the provision of financial as well as technical assistance that will support the creation of locally owned and operated small and medium-sized enterprises. This will help to maintain tourism incomes within the community;
  - Encouraging tourism development that makes use of local agricultural products and materials. This may require some investment, but the long-term benefits are that the local

community will have the capacity to benefit directly from tourism development;

- Creating taxes that stay within the local community to help to support infrastructure development;
- Ensuring that capacity-building initiatives are designed to develop trained local workers to assume both managerial as well as lower-level positions within the tourism industry. Local governments may wish to give preference to tourism developments that employ local labour and help to build capacity of local people.

Monitoring the Effectiveness of Investment in Tourism Infrastructure

It is essential that governments at all levels effectively monitor the benefits as well as the costs of investment in tourism infrastructure. This information is vital not only to guiding national as well as local level public sector investments, it is also an essential area of information for encouraging investment by the private sector at the national or and international levels.

REGIONAL LEVEL

A great deal can be done at the regional level to ensure that there are sufficient resources to expand opportunities for investment in tourism infrastructure at all levels. Some of this effort can occur through cooperation between countries, and some initiatives can be taken by organizations such as ESCAP to achieve these objectives.

Specific strategies could include:

- A review of current initiatives and existing strategies to assess their effectiveness in encouraging tourism investment;
- The Asian Development Bank (ADB) and the World Bank could ensure that their existing policies view investment in tourism infrastructure as an essential dimension of their social and environmental programmes;
- Multilateral agencies and institutions should assist governments in recognizing the economic and social contribution of tourism, and they should include tourism in mainstream programmes for job creation, export promotion and investment stimulation;
- ESCAP could take initiatives to establish an information technology network through which the member countries could provide and use information related to investment in tourism infrastructure;
- ESCAP could provide consultative services on investment in the member countries.

LEAKAGES FROM TOURISM IN DEVELOPING COUNTRIES

As a modality of international commerce, tourism involves not only inflows of foreign financial resources but also outflows, referred to herein as "leakages".

When they exceed specific levels, these outflows can significantly neutralize the positive financial effect of international tourism. Leakage is the process whereby part of the foreign exchange earnings generated by tourism, rather than being retained by tourist-receiving countries, is either retained by tourist-generating countries or repatriated to them in the form of profits, income and royalty remittances, repayment of foreign loans, and imports of equipment, materials, capital and consumer goods to cater for the needs of international tourist and overseas promotional expenditures. Leakages can be divided into three categories: internal leakage or the "import-coefficient" of tourism activities; external leakage or pre-leakage, depending on the commercialization mode of the tourism package and the choice of airline; and invisible leakage or foreign exchange costs associated with resource damage or deterioration.

Internal leakages can be measured by establishing "satellite accounts" within national accounting and survey procedures to detail all tourism-related economic activities. It is a normal effect present in both developed and developing countries. In principle, import-related leakages are highest where the local economies are weakest owing to sparse factor endowment or inadequate quality of goods and services. The average leakage for most developing countries today is between 40 and 50 per cent of gross tourism earnings for small economies and between 10 and 20 per cent for most advanced and diversified developing countries. Importantly for LDCs, tourism import-related leakages are often inferior to other economic activity leakages, including manufacturing and, in some cases, agriculture, thus confirming tourism as a choice sector of development for which they possess comparative advantages in many areas.

A first step in reducing internal leakage is to identify what levels are appropriate given the economic structure of a country and then to ensure that effective leakage remains near this objective range while strategies to build up the local supply capacity are put in place. Although restrictive trade policies can reduce the size of the market, it is important to note that import openness tends to facilitate the leakage effect unless the economy has already in place a structure capable of reacting to the competitive stimulus of imports, which is usually not the case in LDCs.

External leakage or pre-leakage is much more difficult to measure and relates to the proportion of the total value added of tourism of services actually captured by the servicing country. To the extent that developing countries have limited access to commercialization channels in their target markets, they can only offer base prices to intermediaries that capture the mark-up on those services. Observed differences between paid and received prices for developing country tourism services (lodging, food, entertainment, etc.) suggest external leakage or pre-leakage levels of up to 75 per cent. In some cases, base prices do not allow for the economic sustainability of projects, and normally do not contemplate replacement costs associated with resource depletion. This leads to problems of infrastructure and environmental sustainability, which tend to be overlooked in view of the short-term importance of crucial foreign exchange inflows.

As a flow variable, leakage levels do not have a static effect. They vary in time depending on:

1. The stage or cycle point of the tourism industry. For example, a nascent tourism industry tends to require large amounts of one-time imports, whereas loan grace periods may allow for a decrease in leakage during the first few years of operation. During a maturity phase leakage may increase as large sums are invested in marketing, rehabilitation of facilities and upgrading of products provided, etc.
2. The evolution of the economy to provide new services and products resulting from demand from the tourism sector. The import of products and services initially not available should trigger enough entrepreneurial response to enable these to be provided locally, thus allowing for a lessening of leakage. It is therefore a main objective of leakage limitation to provide and promote these links between domestic industry and tourism. For example, in the Dominican Republic leakages diminished between 1990 and 1995 as local industry became increasingly interested in servicing the tourism market. The largest companies have now created subsidiaries specifically for this purpose.

Another factor to be evaluated in identifying appropriate leakage levels is the type of tourism being promoted. High-income tourism, because it requires the provision of very high quality and high priced goods, may actually result in increased leakage in some cases despite of the higher income it may generate. Mass tourism could have higher potential for leakage than ecological or adventure tourism because the latter value and consume local resources as part of the tourism experience. However, low-leakage tourism can also equate to low-income tourism, resulting in lower total income and therefore limiting the possibilities for expansion and development by other sectors of the receiving country's economy. In order to correctly evaluate the return on investments it is necessary to carry out a cost-of-opportunity study that will establish a "leakage break-even point" as a function of the country's economic capacity to serve different types of tourism and choose the type most suitable for a project or country.

Leakage effects on tourism net income levels are nonetheless offset by increased value added or volume. As an example of the positive outlook for LDCs, value added in tourism, measured as tourism income per tourist arrival (Yt/At) has grown by over 100 per cent in 21 (almost half) of the LDCs surveyed between 2000 and 2005.

Interestingly, growth in income per tourist appears to bear no clear relationship to the level of or growth in arrivals. This suggests that growth in income per tourist is not a function of volume, and has therefore grown basically because of a favourable quality/price ratio. This also confirms the enormous diversity of situations present in LDCs and their tourism industries; but, in general, as value added grows, the *potential* for leakage lessens.

Tourism policy should therefore be based on the premise that although leakage is an intrinsic element of international tourism, and increased value added will also benefit the economy, leakage-containment measures have multiplicative effects that will allow developing countries to maximize the financial benefits to be derived from an expansion of tourism. A study on Indonesia showed that the tourism multiplier (1.59) was the highest of all categories, including final demand, and exhibited strong links to the agricultural sector, on which it had no direct effect at all.

To the extent that leakages lead to a definition of economic opportunities it can be useful as a strategic blueprint for further economic development. Domestic policies in developing countries against leakages from international tourism should include (i) the provision of incentives to reinvest profits and potential cash transfers that otherwise would be invested abroad; (ii) the enhancement of the capacity of tourist destinations for intensifying the production of goods and services required by the tourism sector; (iii) the provision of incentives to domestic investors to expand their participation in tourism and iv) the enforcement of domestic competition policy against anti-competitive practices by tour operators.

As regards external leakages, most issues address points of discussion under the GATS Annex on tourism in the WTO, such as (i) local and international competition policy, particularly with regard to market access issues and best business practices in relation to regulations on contractual practices; and (ii) ecological and economic sustainability and the valuation and use of non-tradable resources.

As such, a policy to reduce leakages and thus to improve the chances for a more viable tourism sector, should be based on the premise that leakages can be managed and need to be reduced from its present levels, where combined visible internal and external leakage can easily reach 75 per cent of the market value of paid services. Management of leakages, should allow countries to profit as best as they can from the market expansion and competitive factor that tourism demand represents for local industry and the local economic structure in all fairness to least developed and developing countries, without engaging in anti-competitive practices that contradict other WTO principles, and reduce the contribution of tourism to sound economic development.

4

Sustainable Tourism Future in a 'Green Economy'

'Green economy' is a new euphemistic term that has been widely used in the corporate world of tourism. But so far, there is no agreed definition or an international consensus on what green economy means, and it remains unclear how people and nations, particularly in the developing world, can benefit from it. The idea, which was first introduced by UNEP in late 2008, is to develop a system of green economic activities "that result in improved human well-being over the long term, while not exposing future generations to significant environmental risks and ecological scarcities". Discussions on the green economy concept and related policies have gained much in importance as one of the two key themes at the UN Rio+20 conference in 2012 is: 'Green economy in the context of sustainable development and poverty reduction'.

Under immense pressure to respond to the challenges posed by the 2008 economic recession, poverty, environmental degradation and climate change, the UNWTO and the European Travel Commission (ETC) jointly organized in September 2009 the 'Gothenburg Symposium on Tourism and Travel in the Green Economy' with considerable input from the private sector, *e.g.* the WTTC, the World Economic Forum and the aviation industry. Basically, the purpose of the Symposium was to justify the contemporary tourism model by promoting the vision of profound change towards "a sustainable tourism marketplace in a global green economy".

The conference statement, known as the 'Gothenburg Symposium Conclusions' was primarily aimed at lobbying climate change negotiators at the 2009 UN Conference of Parties (COP15) in Copenhagen to 'seal a deal' that protects the economic, environmental and social base of the tourism industry and to allow its unrestricted growth. The statement said the tourism sector should be considered "as a key contributor to a green economy approach that promotes economic recovery and also assists poor countries in reaching the MDGs and greening their economies. By participating in the green economy, tourism can play a positive catalytic cross-cultural role to improve the sustainability of several related sectors such as agriculture, energy, transport and construction, as well as contributing to its own sustainable sectoral development".

In February 2011, UNEP published a 600-page Green Economy Report (GER) that covers 10 key economic sectors, including a 40-page chapter on tourism developed in cooperation with the UNWTO. The GER, a comprehensive study conducted as part of the UNEP-led 'Green Economy Initiative' (GEI), uses economic analyses and modelling approaches to demonstrate that investment in greening a range of sectors – natural sectors: agriculture, fisheries, forests, water; and built capital sectors: energy, manufacturing, waste, construction, transportation, tourism – can drive economic growth, while at the same time it addresses social and environmental challenges.

As for tourism, the GER assumes that an investment of 0.2% of global GDP – or US$135 billion at current levels of GDP – per year between 2011 and 2050 would allow the sector to continue to grow steadily while enhancing its sustainability and ensuring significant environmental benefits such as reductions in water consumption by 18%, energy use by 44% and CO2 emissions by 52%, compared with a 'business-as-usual' scenario.

Surely, few would object to a green economy – an economy that is environmentally-friendly, sensitive to the need to conserve natural resources, minimize pollution and emissions during the production process and promotes environmentally-friendly lifestyles and consumption patterns. But serious concerns have been raised by developing countries' delegates, civil society and Indigenous Peoples' organizations that the green economy concept is prone to abuse and could give rise to harmful developments that particularly affect poor countries and people. Participants of a side event

held during a UNCSD meeting in New York asked 'whose green economy' is this and why did the topic of green economy suddenly emerge in all kinds of dialogue mechanisms after 2008.

The fact that UNEP's GEI has been spearheaded by Pavan Sukhdev, an investment banker on sabbatical from Deutsche Bank and chairman of the World Economic Forum's Global Agenda Council on Biodiversity, added to the suspicion that the green economy idea was brought up to push big business interests and to dominate the global agenda in the run-up to Rio+20. As Thomas comments, "the most vocal cheerleaders are the Davos crowd of Fortune 500 companies and G8 diplomats. Most alarmingly, some of these voices are positioning the 'green economy' as an upgrade or replacement to the 'outmoded' concept of 'sustainable development' that was agreed on 20 years ago. They seem content to throw out Rio's 'baby' of sustainable development for new green bathwater just as the baby reaches the age of maturity" (2011).

Discussing the role of the green economy in the context of sustainable development, poverty and equity, Khor warned that the green economy will be defined or operationalized in a one-dimensional manner, taken out of the context of UNCED's sustainable development framework, the Rio Declaration principles and Agenda 21. The focus may be narrowed to environmental management issues, without fully considering the development and equity aspects as well as international dimensions. "In such a situation, if the green economy concept gains prominence, while the sustainable development concept recedes, there may be a loss of the use of the holistic sustainable development approach, with imbalances between the three pillars [environmental protection, economic development and social development]." Khor also stressed the importance of adhering to the principle of 'common but differentiated responsibility', arguing that a 'one-size-fits-all' approach to the green economy that treats all countries in the same manner was bound to fail. "The levels and stages of development of countries must be fully considered, and the priorities and conditions of developing countries taken into account."

Quintos pointed out the danger of the "green growth" agenda, saying that while giving monetary incentives to generate 'green behaviour', 'greed behaviour' will continue to thrive because the green economy is premised on the accelerated commodification of nature and ecosystem services and allows continued exploitation for profit-making. The treatment of natural resources as tradable assets will just exacerbate "private expropriation, appropriation and accumulation in the hands of the few". Quintos strongly criticized carbon trading and off-setting – market-based mechanisms on which particularly the travel and tourism industry rely to reduce their carbon footprint. These activities "merely allow the large polluting countries and corporations to continue business-as-usual as long as they can afford to pay for the offsets and profit from trading carbon emission permits, which is becoming a subject of speculative activities as well for financial investors who are responsible for the global financial crisis".

The focus on 'green technologies' is also regarded as problematic. As it is mainly big companies from developed countries that have the resources and technological know-how to promote the green economy, critics call to carefully examine whether the people on the ground really benefit.

Developing countries may be disadvantaged because they may not have the capacity to develop new green technologies themselves and become dependent on importing these more expensive technologies from more advanced industrial countries to comply with international standards. There is also the danger that the new imported technologies are not appropriate or sustainable in the local context.

There are also concerns that big hydroelectric dams, nuclear power plants, and other highly controversial and risky energy technologies will find approval as 'clean and green'. "If RIO+20 is not to become a handy loophole for every technological wolf to assume green clothing (and funds), governments are going to need to get specific about what is and what isn't a 'green and just' technology and to resurrect the precautionary principle first agreed at Rio 20 years ago," warns Thomas (2011).

UNEP's GER also promotes biofuels, even though it has been well documented that the rapid expansion of oil palm, sugar cane and jatropha monoculture plantations for the production of biofuels leads to land grabs, environmental degradation, less land available for food crops, destruction of small-scale farming and skyrocketing food prices.

The director general of the International Air Transport Association (IATA), Tony Tyler, confirmed at the September 2011 'Greener Skies' conference in Hong Kong that the global aviation industry's objective to slash air travel's carbon emissions by half until 2050 primarily depends on new biofuel technologies.

Policies and programmes that promise 'low carbon' or 'carbon-neutral' travel and tourism need to be closely scrutinized and monitored as many of them offer 'false solutions' that are unhelpful and may obstruct pathways and innovations towards a genuinely non-polluting and sustainable future. In a World Bank publication, for example, Fernandes and Romo hail Costa Rica, a renowned 'ecotourism' destination, for launching a 'National Strategy for Climate Change' that aims at achieving carbon neutrality by 2021.

The authors suggest that Costa Rica's policies make good business sense and motivate a number of tourism enterprises to participate in the country's greening efforts as part of their GHG emissions offsetting programmes. Costa Rica's Nature Air, which claims to be the world's first carbon-neutral airline and represents the travel sector in UNEP's task force to devise regulations for aviation, is portrayed as a success story for balancing profitability and corporate social responsibility, even though Nature Air heavily relies on controversial carbon offset mechanisms and the use of biofuels to improve its emissions record.

Moreover, Fernandes and Romo see new trends toward renewable energy in 'non-traditional' or 'niche' tourism, describing the activities of the company 'Blue Energy' that has begun to develop energy solutions based on hydro, wind and solar sources in partnership with some small eco-lodges along the Caribbean coast of Nicaragua. In the conclusion, however, the authors admit that positive green measures such as alternative energy production are like drops in the ocean because conventional grid-connected tourist accommodation catering to mass and luxury tourists still "typically operate with few energy supply concerns and end-use restrictions".

Evidently, not much progress has been made in changing unsustainable consumption patterns – an important issue that has been sidelined in tourism and green economy discourses. Yet, one has to bear in mind that much of tourism and related goods and services produced are luxuries that only affluent people can afford, while the vast majority of the world's population is struggling hard to fulfill their basic needs. In addition, the globalization of the tourist lifestyle has resulted in excessive demands and promoted wasteful and unsustainable consumption, which poses enormous stress on the environment and climate. There is also exploitation involved, the victims being urban middle and upper-class people who are unswervingly enticed by industry and the media to spend their surplus on dreams and illusions. "There is a danger throughout the global economy, and not least tourism, of locking in a self-defeating spiral of over-consumption by those who are already wealthy, justified against achieving marginal increases in wealth among poorest members of society." 'Green consumerism' does nothing to solve the problem.

As Paul Hawken, an American author and environmental activist, once commented in the *New York Times*, "Green consumerism is an oxymoronic phrase" that distracts from other more serious issues. "We turn toward the consumption part because that's where the money is. We tend not to look at the 'less' part."

As it stands, the slogan 'the consumer – the only person who matters', coined by the Pacific Asia Travel Association (PATA) in 1977, remains valid in the green economy.

The tourism chapter of UNEP's GER considers 'customer expectations', 'customer satisfaction' and 'tourist preferences', but cuts short on the development needs, expectations and preferences from the perspective of local communities in tourist destinations.

Will people's voices and rights be heeded in the green economy as they should be? Deeply concerned about the substance of and processes related to the green economy, Indigenous Peoples have called on the United Nations to reaffirm the ecosystem and human-rights-based approach to development. "We cannot separate development from the protection and respect of our rights to self-determination, to our lands, territories and resources, our cultural rights, rights, right to free, prior and informed consent and our traditional knowledge, among others. These rights are contained in the UN Declaration on the Rights of Indigenous Peoples. If States and the UN promote and respect this Declaration, sustainable development can become a reality." At the Manaus global preparatory meeting on Rio+20 in August 2011, Indigenous Peoples representatives agreed to create adequate opportunities to critique the concepts of the green economy and institutional framework for sustainable development. "We continue to challenge this development model which promotes domination of nature, incessant economic growth, limitless resource extraction, profit-seeking, unsustainable consumption and production and the unregulated commodity and financial markets."

A growing number of NGOs and people's organizations understand that it is hardly possible to safeguard people's rights and work for economic, social and environmental justice in a green economic system that will be financed and dominated by corporate powers-that-be. At the 64th Annual UN Department of Public Information/ NGO Conference, held in Bonn, Germany in September 2011 as part of the preparation process towards Rio+20, NGO delegates called for a replacement of the current unsustainable, inequitable and unjust economic model and for placing people and the environment above profit. Their Declaration states among other things: "We propose that where the current economy aids inequity, destruction and greed, it should be replaced by an economy that cares for the human-earth community."

THE GROWTH OF 'GREEN' CONSUMERISM

The late 1980s in the developed countries of the world marked the beginnings of a change in consumer behaviour, with concerns over the environmental effects of products being expressed in the buying patterns of a significant market segment of consumers. Cairncross (1991) takes the view that the extensive media coverage of environmental concerns, such as climatic change, the burning of rainforests and the vanishing ozone layer, was highly influential in getting people to think about the environmental effects of what they were buying.

Martin (1997) takes the view that the rapid economic growth experienced in Britain during the early 1980s was influential in moving people's concerns on from basic economic needs to wider ethical considerations of consumerism. Generally, levels of public concern over the environment tend to reflect economic cycles, that is, when the economy is buoyant environmental concern is at its highest (Martin, 1997).

Evidence of this shift in concern of consumerism towards environmental issues was demonstrated by the *Green Consumer Guide* becoming top of the list of best-selling books in Britain in September 1988. This publication was a seminal consumer guide, in that for the first time, ratings of the performance of companies and products were provided based upon environmental criteria.

Concern over the environment manifested itself in consumer behaviour, in various ways, in different countries. In Britain, there was a virtual consumer boycott of aerosols that contained chloro-fluorocarbons (CFCs), after the media and environmental pressure groups alerted consumers to the role of CFCs in ozone depletion. In America, consumers' primary concern was with waste and excessive packaging on products, and German consumers' concerns also rested with packaging and the plastics used to make drink bottles.

Market research at the end of the 1980s supported the observation that concern over the environment was high. Martin (1997) comments on the results of a survey conducted in 1989, of a representation of the British public by the Market Opinion Research Institute (MORI), a leading British market research company.

When asked the question: 'What would you say is the most important issue facing Britain today?', 35 per cent of the respondents identified environmental issues, a higher percentage than for health care, unemployment, and inflation. However, as Martin points out, just sixteen months later when the survey was repeated, only 10 per cent of the sample identified the environment as being the most important issue and in subsequent surveys this would seem to be a consistent rating. This 'outbreak' of green consumerism forced companies to begin to respond to the environmental concerns of an affluent and sizeable minority of the market.

Not only did this influence the retail side of the market but also the supply side of the market as a few retailers began to check the environmental practices of their suppliers. For instance, B&Q a British hardware chain, questioned their suppliers about the quality of their environmental management of the peat bogs from which the peat sold as fertilizer in their shops came from, and one supplier was subsequently discontinued for having insufficient environmental standards.

In America, the three leading tuna canners, controlling 70 per cent of the market, decided to ensure that their fish were caught only in 'friendly ways' which were not harmful to other types of fish.

Other new companies emerged into the consumer market, based upon a philosophy of selling ethically sound and environmentally friendly products. One of the most notable business success stories in the British market was the Body Shop, which now has hundreds of stores worldwide. The Body Shop's primary concerns are with skin and hair care, and it has emphasised from its foundation that environmental and social considerations have been at the forefront of its decision making.

The view of the Body Shop is made clear in their policy document: 'The Body Shop has always had a clear, top-level commitment to environmental and social excellence. Because of this, we make sure we include environmental issues in every area of our operations'. As part of this policy, the company does not carry out any animal experiments to test its cosmetics and also emphasises 'fair trade' practices with its suppliers, based upon buying from businesses who wish to protect their culture and practise traditional and sustainable land use.

There was also a growing consumer demand for ethical investment funds, which can be traced to the early 1980s and the desire of the universities and churches in America not to put money into companies trading with South Africa, whose government supported the system of apartheid at that time.

The consequences for companies that ignore consumers' environmental concerns are illustrated by the case of Royal Dutch Shell, the world's biggest oil company. In 1995, Shell intended to bury an obsolete oil rig called the Brent Spar, at the bottom of the North Sea. Concerns raised by Greenpeace, the non-governmental organisation, over the possibilities that toxic sludge released from the rig would contaminate the sea floor, led to a great deal of controversy over the plan. Activists encouraged boycotts of Shell service stations in Germany and motorists also began to shun Shell garages in Denmark and Holland. In Germany, service station income fell 30 per cent and the financial losses and adverse publicity led Shell to cancel the sinking of the oil rig.

At the beginning of the twenty-first century, 'green consumerism' seems to have established itself as an integral part of the consumer market. Although it is difficult to define exactly what green consumerism is, and therefore measure it, consumer surveys of behaviour patterns, based upon environmental attitudes, lend support to the feeling that environmental concern will play an increasing part in consumer behaviour in the future.

For instance, when a sample of 2,000 people in Britain were asked if they had 'Selected one product over another because of environmentally friendly packaging/ formulation/ advertising', 36 per cent said they had in 1996 compared to 19 per cent in 1988. Market research results in America also support evidence of a trend towards green consumerism. A survey by Michael Peters (MPG) of Americans in the summer of 1989, found that 53 per cent of the public had decided not to buy a product during the previous year, owing to concerns over the effects of the product or the packaging upon the environment.

A survey carried out by the same firm in Canada found that approximately 66 per cent of the Canadian public would be more likely to buy a product that is recyclable or biodegradable, and approximately 60 per cent said they would be willing to pay more for such products. The growth in demand for organic farm products since the mid-1990s in Britain, associated with scares over salmonella poisoning in chickens and bovine spongiform encephalopathy (BSE) in cattle, also support the notion that people want to consume in a healthier, less environmentally damaging and more ethical way. The relatively high prices charged for organic farm produce in comparison to other produce reflect the willingness of a sizeable part of the consumer market, to pay premium prices for 'environmentally sound' produce.

The willingness of people to pay more for products and services that are advertised as being environmentally sensitive does, however, offer the opportunity for consumer exploitation by companies. Claims that a company operates in an 'environmentally friendly way' are often difficult to substantiate, and many people remain sceptical that a company's claim of employing green practices and acting in an environmentally conscious way, is little more than a public relations exercise.

According to Cairncross (1991), a market survey carried out by Environmental Research Associates of Princeton, New Jersey, found that 47 per cent of consumers thought that environmental claims made by many companies were 'mere gimmickry'. Consumers may often be confused about which products are genuinely environmentally friendly, given the lack of, or misleading, information that is sometimes presented. There is a necessity for the regulation of environmental claims made by companies through independent bodies.

For example, organisations such as the Organic Soil Association in Britain who verify farmer's claims of organic farming have been influential in implementing standards set by the European Commission on organic farming and reassuring the public that claims are genuine. Thus, although certification by the association is voluntary, it has become virtually necessary for any UK farmer wishing to sell organic produce to have certification, especially to sell their produce in supermarket chains.

In the tourism sector, besides the 'International Standards Organisation' (ISO) logo that is available to companies who implement 'environmental management systems', other green labels emphasising green credibility have appeared over recent years. One such scheme is the 'Green Globe', which was originally launched by the World Travel and Tourism Council (WTTC) in 1994.

The WTTC is a trade association which incorporates many of the leading multinational travel and tourism corporations. In 1999, 'Green Globe 21 Certification' became established as an organisation independent of the WTTC, concerned with verifying the environmental standards of companies and destinations operating in the tourism market.

The Green Globe 21 logo is applicable to many of the different elements of the tourism system, including tour operators, transport services, visitor attractions, hotels, local communities and destinations. Any travel and tourism company can apply to become a Green Globe 21 member as long as they want to be involved in sustainable tourism development. Green Globe 21 provide information and advice on the ways companies can modify their business practices to improve the environmental quality of their operations.

After six months the company must decide whether to pursue formal certification from Green Globe 21, which involves establishing environmental management systems (EMS), necessitating the formulation of an environmental policy for the company, and environmental auditing of their business practices. Once the company decides to pursue certification they must pay a fee to Green Globe 21, which in 2000 varied from US $750 for local companies to US $15,000 for companies operating internationally, after which they can use the Green Globe 21 logo.

The verification that standards are being met is undertaken by Societe Generale de Surveillance (SGS), an international verification body, and an International Advisory Council of industry, government, and NGO experts. This is a direct attempt to overcome the earlier criticism of the scheme, which was that as environmental monitoring was carried out on a self-assessment basis by the company rather than by independent verifiers, there was no real guarantee of standards and it was open to bias. However, a major criticism of the present scheme is that a company can use the logo after electing to follow the certification scheme, without having actually put an environmental management system into place.

Once the company has implemented an EMS system and met the necessary criteria, a new logo is given to the company with a tick in it, though the ability of the consumer to understand the difference is very uncertain. Indeed, at present the level of awareness of the logo in the consumer market is probably low, and its meaning uncertain.

Consequently, the scheme remains open to criticism about its standards, and to suspicion over the degree to which it represents a true desire to improve the environmental standards of the tourism industry, or an attempt to make money on the premise of voluntary environmental regulation.

Consumers are also encouraged to become members of Green Globe 21 by registering on their web page, for which there is no charge, but customers will find environmental information about companies and destinations. The third part of the system is the inclusion of communities into the award scheme. The basic cost of membership for communities is US $50,000 and thereafter the fee will be adjusted to reflect the complexity and scale of the EMS.

The scheme is innovative, both in the idea of certifying the operations of the tourism sector, and in its holistic approach which recognises tourism as a system, incorporating consumers, the industry, and the destination community. However, the scheme is very market-driven and its success will be dependent upon a growing number of consumers being interested in the green credentials of tourism companies and destinations, and having faith in the environmental integrity of the logo.

Another symbol of environmental standards in the tourism sector is the kitemark awarded by the 'Campaign for Environmentally Responsible Tourism' (CERT). Established in 1994, CERT is currently located in the United Kingdom and unfortunately is currently only accessible to UK tour-operating companies, although there are plans to expand the scheme into other countries and other companies in the sector.

Tour operators can be awarded the CERT logo if they make a commitment to:

- Develop and publish an environmental policy statement which is relevant to the business needs and destinations of operation;
- Ensure that staff are aware of this environmental policy and trained in its implementation;
- Distribute a lively, upbeat leaflet to clients which provides advice about how they can reduce the environmental impact of their holiday;
- Include some questions about their environmental performance in their customer evaluation form. These are passed on to CERT and provide independent verification of the status and effectiveness of their environmental programme;

- Help raise funds for environmental projects which will bring benefits to the environment, local people and the travel industry.

The effectiveness of the company in meeting the above criteria is verified by a CERT specialist who also gives specialist advice to help the company. However, as for Green Globe 21, the success of this scheme will be dependent upon its recognition by consumers, and an understanding of and belief in the environmental quality that is portrayed in the logo.

CONSUMER TRENDS AND GREEN TOURISM

The influence of green consumerism upon the tourism market is not easy to discern. As Swarbrooke and Horner (1999:198) comment: 'One thing is clear - as the debate has developed, the term "green tourist" has not achieved the acceptance that the phrase "green consumer" has in general.' This does not mean that consumers do not have concerns about the activities of the tourism industry.

The interests of consumers in the environmental aspects of tourism were reflected as early as 1991 with the publishing of the book, *The Good Tourist*, which advised tourists how to act in a more environmentally responsible way. As Wood and House (1991) comment on the back cover:

Thankfully now, the mistakes of the past are being recognised and a new breed of tourist is emerging. Travelling independently or in small groups, living as locals caring for the country they are visiting and its peoples, the Good Tourists take a long-term look at travelling and the world we live in.

Empirical research also supports the view that consumers are aware of the environmental impacts of the tourism industry. Martin (1997) cites a survey carried out by MORI in the summer of 1995 in Britain, in which when asked 'how much damage to the environment do you think travel and tourism causes?', 64 per cent of the respondents were found to think that tourism caused some degree of damage to the environment. However, in the same survey, when asked about the damage to the environment caused by tourism in comparison to other industries, tourism ranked fourteenth out of seventeen possible choices behind other services such as road transport and domestic waste disposal.

The opinion of the public about the efforts of the tourism industry to mitigate any of the harmful environmental impacts caused by it, in comparison to the efforts of other industries to reduce the negative environmental impacts their operations may be causing, is not reassuring for the sector. When presented with the statement, 'I'd like you to tell me how much you feel each industry is doing to reduce any harmful effects its activities might have on the environment', tourism ranked sixteenth out of seventeen industries behind 'nuclear fuel manufacturing and reprocessing' and 'oil exploration and production'. Yet, as for other consumer goods and services, there does seem to be a market opportunity for tourism companies to increase their revenues through environmental improvements. In the 1995 MORI survey, 30 per cent of the respondents stated they would be prepared to pay an extra premium on top of their holiday price, to ensure that tourism companies were committed to environmental protection.

In reality, there is always a difference between people's willingness to say they would pay more for environmental care, and the likelihood of them actually doing it, as was discussed within the context of charging admission fees to visit national parks. Nevertheless, the results suggest that a sizeable minority of the market is willing to pay more for environmental quality.

Although concerns over the environmental effects of tourism are unlikely to stop the vast majority of people taking some kind of holiday, for a part of the market, the type of holiday they choose may be increasingly influenced by their environmental attitudes.

The development of green consumerism in the 1980s coincided with the development of a range of holiday types that inferred a greater level of awareness of the environment than is associated with mass tourism.

Many terms have subsequently been used, often interchangeably, to describe these new forms of tourism including 'alternative', 'green', 'nature', 'sustainable', 'responsible', and 'ecotourism'. Mowforth and Munt (1998) extend this list to include other forms of new tourism such as academic tourism, agro-tourism, appropriate tourism, contact tourism, and wildlife tourism. A common theme of these labels is that they are indicative of a more caring approach to how tourism should be developed in the future.

As Shackley (1996:12) comments on new approaches to tourism: 'Terms such as environmentally friendly tourism, sustainable tourism, ecotourism, responsible tourism, low impact tourism are just a few among many in common use.... These designate low impact tourism programmes which might result in some form of sustainable benefits to the destination area.'

Certainly, the idea of alternative types of tourism to mass tourism seems to have found favour with a significant segment of the tourist market. Besides the growth in environmental consciousness since the late 1980s, the development of alternative forms of tourism can also be associated with consumer over familiarity with mass tourism, and a subsequent desire for new types of holidays. This latter point means that the concept of 'alternative tourism' can be interpreted in at least two ways: alternative tourism as a form of more environmentally aware tourism; or alternative tourism as types of tourism that are different to mainstream tourism without necessarily being any less environmentally damaging. For example, 'activity holidays' have become a segment of the tourism market that is growing, attracts high income groups, and is a component of a healthy lifestyle for many. Concerning changes in the market and the growth of the activity holiday market in Scotland, Scottish Enterprise (1995:2) comment:

Changes in consumer behaviour and values are a driving force for tourism. Today's tourist is becoming more experienced, more quality conscious, more independent, more discerning, and is therefore more difficult to please.... However, not only is the tourist becoming more sophisticated, experienced and quality conscious but also more active on holiday, reflecting the general growing awareness of healthy lifestyles and the increasing importance of active relaxation.

Yet it would be mistaken to think that a sports-based activity holiday would necessarily be compatible with the surrounding environment. For example, mountain biking, downhill skiing, and even hiking have all caused soil erosion, disturbance of wildlife, and problems of aesthetic pollution in mountain areas.

So what are the criteria of alternative tourism? Whilst there is no universal agreement on a definition of what alternative tourism actually is, the differences of alternative tourism to mass tourism are highlighted by Cater (1993:85) as follows: 'Activities are likely to be small scale, locally owned with consequentially low impact, leakages and a high proportion of profits retained locally.

These contrast with large-scale multinational concerns typified by high leakages which characterise mass tourism.' Utilising this definition it is possible to highlight the characteristics of alternative tourism which differentiate it from mainstream tourism.

Characteristics of alternative tourism:

- Small scale of development with high rates of local ownership
- Minimised negative environmental and social impacts
- Maximised linkages to other sectors of the local economy, such as agriculture, reducing a reliance upon imports
- Retention of the majority of the economic expenditure from tourism by local people
- Localised power sharing and involvement of people in the decision-making process
- Pace of development directed and controlled by local people rather than external influences

Using these criteria, alternative tourism surpasses purely a concern for the physical environment which typifies green tourism, to include economic, social, and cultural considerations. If the physical, environmental and cultural dimensions of the environment are considered in an integrated fashion, and tourism is developed with the characteristics displayed, then alternative tourism can be viewed as being synonymous with the concept of sustainable tourism development.

A kind of tourism that is often associated with the characteristics of alternative tourism outlined above is 'ecotourism'. According to Shackley (1996) it is a term invented by conservationists in the 1970s, whilst according to Fennell

(1999) the term can be traced back as far as 1965 to the work of Hetzer, who used it to explain the interaction between tourists and the environments that they come into contact with.

However, like the concept of alternative tourism, there is no consensus about the meaning of ecotourism. The difficulty of trying to define ecotourism is referred to by Cater (1994:3) thus: 'In particular, the term ecotourism is surrounded by confusion. Is it a form of 'alternative tourism' (furthermore, what is "alternative tourism?")? Is it responsible (defined in terms of environmental, socio-cultural, moral or practical terms)? Is it sustainable (however defined)?' Waldeback (1995) recognises different dimensions and interpretations of what ecotourism can be.

Dimensions of ecotourism:

- *Activity*: Tourism which is based upon experiencing natural and cultural resources
- *Business*: Tour operators who provide ecotourism tours
- *Philosophy*: A respect for land, nature, people and cultures
- *Strategy*- a tool for conservation, economic development and cultural revival
- *Marketing device*: For promoting tourism products with an environmental emphasis
- *Handle*: Convenient umbrella name for a number of tourism related concepts such as 'responsible or ethical travel', 'low-impact tourism', 'educational travel', 'green tourism' and so on
- *Symbol*: Of the debate about the relationship between tourism and the environment
- *Principles and goals*: Defining the symbiotic and sustainable relationship between tourism and the environment

Evidence of the confusion over the term can be seen in the continued attempts to define what it is. For example, McLaren (1998:97) comments:

Ecotravel involves activities in the great outdoors - nature tourism, adventure travel, birding, camping, skiing, whale watching, and archeological digs that take place in marine, mountain, island and desert ecosystems. Much of the travel is now called ecotourism, although critics argue that the definition of 'ecotourism' is so broad that almost any travel would qualify, as long as something green was seen along the way.

The danger of ecotourism being used as a marketing term in a disingenuous fashion to promote unsustainable forms of tourism is highlighted by Goodwin (1996), who comments upon its opportunist usage by the tourism industry, where the tag 'eco' has become synonymous with responsible consumerism. Hall and Kinnaird (1994) also make the point about the problematic nature of defining ecotourism, stating that there is no consistent definition. They comment that: this term [author's note: ecotourism] is used in a generic sense to cover tourism development which is sympathetic to, complements and/or is employed as a vehicle for, conserving and sustaining natural and cultural environments and their resources and which may encompass the domain of such terms as 'sustainable', 'green', 'soft', and 'alternative' tourism.

Holden and Kealy (1996:60) add an explicit economic component in their definition:

Implicit in all the definitions is respect or friendliness for the physical and cultural environment, *i.e.,* developing a form of tourism that is non-damaging and non-degrading; subject to adequate and appropriate management controls; and that offers financial contributions for the protection of indigenous cultures and environments. Goodwin (1996:288) links this economic dimension directly to conservation of resources in his definition of ecotourism as: Low impact nature tourism which contributes to the maintenance of species and habitats either directly through a contribution to conservation and/or indirectly by providing revenue to the local community sufficient for local people to value, and therefore protect, their wildlife heritage area as a source of income.

Both these latter definitions emphasise the economic aspect of ecotourism in conservation, and the involvement, instead of the exclusion of local communities in the conservation process. A comprehensive list of guiding principles for the development of ecotourism is set out from Wight (1994:40).The direct relevance of ecotourism to sustainability following the principles of Wight (1994) is highlighted by Shackley (1996:13) stating: Ecotourism projects should meet the following criteria.

They must:

- Be sustainable (defined as meeting present needs without compromising the ability to meet future needs)
- Give the visitor a unique and outstanding experience
- Maintain the quality of the environment.

Guiding principles for ecotourism:

- It should not degrade the resource and should be developed in an environmentally sound manner
- It should provide long-term benefits to the resource, to the local community and industry (benefits may be conservation, scientific, social, cultural, or economic)
- It should provide first-hand, participatory and enlightening experiences
- It should involve education amongst all parties - local communities, government, non-governmental organisations, industry and tourists (before, during and after the trip)
- It should encourage all-party recognition of the intrinsic values of the resource
- It should involve acceptance of the resource on its own terms, and in recognition of its limits, which involves supply-oriented management

- It should promote understanding and involve partnerships between many players, which could include government, non-governmental organisa-tions, industry, scientists and locals (both before and during operations)
- It should promote moral and ethical responsibilities and behaviour towards the natural and cultural environment by all players
- sustainable use
- Resource conservation
- Cultural revival and decolonisation
- Economic development and diversification
- Life enhancement and personal growth
- Maximum benefits and minimal costs/impacts
- Learning about the natural culture and environment.
- Who are the 'ecotourists'?

Based upon the principles and goals of ecotourism described by Wight (1994), Waldeback (1995) and Shackley (1996), it is evident that ecotourism places a much heavier emphasis upon conservation, education and ethics than mass tourism. The emergence of a form of tourism that is based upon the premise of an ethical relationship with the environment is reflective of changes that are occurring in the consumer market for tourism. Poon's (1993) concept of the 'new tourist' was referred.

According to Poon 'new tourists' display a 'see and enjoy but do not destroy' attitude and do not assert that the 'west is best'. Other labels have also been given to the tourists who constitute this emerging environmentally conscious market segment, including the 'ethical tourist', 'environmentally responsible tourist', 'good tourist' and 'ecotourist'.

So who are the ecotourists? Just as there is no definitive definition of ecotourism, similarly there are different opinions on the characteristics of ecotourists, and who ecotourists actually are. Given the difficulty in defining ecotourism, it is unsurprising that it is subsequently difficult to categorise the 'ecotourist', which leads to confusion over the type of behaviour that ecotourists could be expected to display.

As Cater comments: 'There is an inherent risk in assuming that the ecotourist is automatically an environmentally sensitive breed. Although small, specialist, guided groups of ecotourists may attempt to conform to this identity, the net has now been cast sufficiently wide to include less responsible behaviour.'

It would therefore be mistaken to think that being labelled an 'ecotourist' will necessarily mean that a tourist will particularly desire to be environmentally educated and have a minimal impact upon the environment. According to Mackay (1994), the tourist industry divides ecotourists into three distinct categories, of the big 'E', little 'E' and soft adventure types.

The most popular group is the little 'E', in which tourists' environmental concerns are characterised by a wish to know that the hotel, airline or tour operator they intend to use has acceptable environmental standards. Big 'E' travellers are willing to travel into new, 'undiscovered' areas, and accept the standards of accommodation and services offered by local people or camp in the wilderness.

The 'soft adventurer' also wishes to visit wilderness areas, but wishes to visit them in comfort, however, without a sense of feeling that the nature or culture of the area they are visiting is being 'exploited' through tourism.

A further categorisation of tourists into different types relating to their level of interest in the environment, based upon the work of Cleverdon (1999).The level of demand for each typology is reflected in the width of the base of each segment, that is, demand decreases upwards from the base of the pyramid to its apex. The model suggests that the largest segment of the tourist market, the 'loungers', has a low level of interest in the environment beyond its providing pleasant surroundings.

The focus of the holiday of this typology is likely to be based upon relaxing and enjoyment. The second typology of tourist, 'the users', is interested in the environment having the special features that are required for the type of holiday they wish to pursue. The types of environment required for this typology are therefore specialised and limited. For example, typical activities associated with this group would include wildlife watching and downhill skiing, each of which need environments that possess specialised features.

The next typology, the 'eco-aware' show an increasing interest in the environment, not for how they can use it but for its own sake. They have an interest in environmental issues connected with tourism, and would look for evidence of environmental commitment, and perhaps certification of a high level of environmental practice from the tourism companies and suppliers they use.

Typical types of holiday activity will reflect an interest in knowing more about the nature and the culture of the destination they are visiting. The last group, the 'specialist ecotourist' has a high level of commitment to the environment, to the extent that they want to actively protect it. This is reflected in the kinds of holiday they participate in, such as conservation holidays or scientific research.

Just as it as incorrect to talk about tourists as being one homogeneous group, Swarbrooke and Horner (1999) suggest that it is not possible to talk about the 'green tourist' as if they were one homogeneous group, preferring to refer to 'shades of green'.

They suggest that the environmental commitment of tourists will be influenced by an amalgam of different factors, including: their awareness and knowledge of the issues associated with tourism and the environment; attitudes towards the environment in general; and the degree of fulfilment of other commitments in their life such as employment, housing and family needs. The different categories of green tourist and their associated environmental attitudes and actions are shown.

Empirical studies of ecotourists are limited, however research based upon demographic (age, gender, occupation, income) characteristics and psychographic (values, attitudes and motivation) characteristics has been attempted. According to Wearing and Neil (1999) research conducted in the USA suggests that ecotourists have higher than average incomes and levels of education, and are also willing to spend more than the normal tourists. In terms of their psychographic characteristics, Wearing and Neil report that they possess an environmental ethic, and are biocentric rather than anthropocentric in orientation.

APPROACH OF SUSTAINABLE TOURISM

Many destinations are now pursuing strategies that aim to ensure a sensitive approach when dealing with tourism. Many of these strategies are based on a formal expression of principles for sustainable tourism. Planners and others can use these principles as basic guidelines when attempting to incorporate the broad vision of sustainability into local policies and practices.

The list of principles provided below are important for destinations and organizations that wish to be guided by the ethic of sustainable and responsible tourism. Residents of a community must maintain control of tourism development by being involved in setting a community tourism vision, identifying the resources to be maintained and enhanced, and developing goals and strategies for tourism development and management. Equally important, community residents must participate in the implementation of strategies as well as the operation of the tourism infrastructure, services, and facilities. A tourism initiative should be developed with the help of broad-based stakeholder input. Tourism development must provide quality employment.

The provision of fulfilling jobs has to be seen as an integral part of any tourism development. Part of the process of achieving quality employment is to ensure that, as much as possible, the tourism infrastructure (hotels, restaurants, shops, etc.) is developed and managed by local people. Experience has demonstrated that the provision of education and training for local residents and access to financing for local businesses and entrepreneurs are central to this type of policy. Broad-based distribution of the benefits of tourism must occur at the tourism destination. Local linkages and resident participation in the planning, development, and operation of tourism resources and services will help to ensure that a more equitable distribution of benefits will occur among residents, visitors, and other service providers. Sustainable tourism development has to provide for inter generational equity. Equitable distribution of the costs and benefits of tourism development must take place among present and future generations. To be fair to future generations of tourists and the travel industry, society should strive to leave a resource base no less than the one we have inherited. Sustainable tourism development must, therefore, avoid resource allocation actions that are irreversible. A long-tend planning horizon needs to be adopted by businesses and destination tourism organizations to ensure that destinations are not used for short-tend gain and then abandoned as visitor tastes and business interests move elsewhere. A longer-tend horizon encourages the use of proactive strategies to ensure destination sustainability and the establishment of local linkages over time.

Hannony is required between the needs of a visitor, the place, and the community. This is facilitated by broad stakeholder support with a proper balance between economic, social, cultural, and human objectives, and a recognition of the importance of cooperation among government, the host communities, and the tourism industry, and the non-profit organizations involved in community development and environmental protection. Tourism strategies and plans must be linked with a broader set of initiatives and economic development plans.

A need exists for more coordination at both policy and action levels among the various agencies involved and among different levels of government. This is particularly relevant to tourism and environmental policies. Service provisions such as transportation, parking, and water and sewer capacities must also be considered in conjunction with tourism plans and developments. Cooperation among attractions, businesses, and tourism operators is essential given that one business or operation can be directly affected by the performance or quality of another. There is a definite need for impact assessment of tourism development proposals. The capacity of sites must be considered, including physical, natural, social, and cultural limits and development should be compatible with local and environmental limits. Plans and operations should be evaluated regularly with adjustments as required. Guidelines have to be established for tourism operations, including requirements for impact assessment. There should be codes of practice established for tourism at all levels -national, regional and local. There is also a need to develop indicators and threshold limits for measuring the impacts and success of local tourism ventures. Protection and monitoring strategies are essential if communities are to protect the resources that form the basis of their tourism product.

Tourism planning must move away from a traditional growth-oriented model to one that focuses on opportunities for employment, income and improved local wellbeing while ensuring that development decisions reflect the full value of the natural and cultural environments. The management and use of public goods such as water, air, and common lands should include accountability on behalf of the users to ensure that these resources are not abused. Sustainable tourism development requires the establishment of education and training programmes to improve public understanding and enhance business, vocational and professional skills.

Sustainable tourism development involves promoting appropriate uses and activities that draw from and reinforce landscape character, sense of place, community identity and site opportunity. These activities and uses should aim to provide a quality tourism experience that satisfies visitors while adhering to the other principles of sustainable tourism.

The scale and type of tourism facilities must reflect the limits of acceptable use that resources can tolerate. Small-scale, low impact facilitiec and services should be encouraged, for example, through financing and other incentives. The tourism process must also ensure that heritage and natural resources are maintained and enhanced using internationally acceptable criteria and standards.

Sustainable tourism marketing should include the provision of a high quality tourist experience which adheres to the other principles outlined above, and whose promotion should be a responsible and an ethical reflection of the destination's tourism attractions and services. These principles are ambitious, and it is fair to say very difficult to achieve so that tourism developments that will always adhere to all of these principles. However, these principles must be seen as targets for all tourism planning.

Crategic integrated sustainable tourism planning The nature of sustainable tourism development requires a process of planning and management that brings together a series of interests and concerns in a sustainable and strategic form of planning and development. Tourism planning continues to be contentious and somewhat nebulous, because most government officials and tourism industry practitioners harbour their own definitions and parameters of the task. By its very nature, planning is multidimensional and is purposely integrative. Even in the less complex circumstances of some Asian and Pacific countries at early phases of tourism development, it is necessary for those with the responsibility to oversee- or administer tourism planning in the public interest to be cognizant of two special dimensions: strategic planning and integrated planning.

Need for integrated tourism planning Although there is evidence that some tourism destinations have been developed without conscious, strategic and integrated planning, many of them have experienced unforeseen consequences that have led to their deterioration.

THE NEED FOR PLANNING

Some managers and decision-makers argue that we are overwhelmed with plans and planning processes. Others argue that we require more regulation and planning in order to ensure that the goals of sustainable tourism can be met. There are others who maintain that we require less planning and possibly less regulation. There is no right answer to the level of planning that a particular situation calls for and clearly every society context will determine what is appropriate. Similarly, though sustainable tourism calls for a high level of local involvement in planning and developing tourism, the amount and quality of resident participation will vary depending on the cultural and political factors in the destination. It is obviously useless to develop a sophisticated planning system if there is no political or community support for it. In these cases, one might first have to create an appropriate setting or structure for a planning process that avoids the failures of past planning practices.

THE FAILURES OF TRADITIONAL PLANNING

Many people are sceptical about the effectiveness of planning. They see it as a waste of time since most plans never see the light of day and end up on a shelf. In many cases, planning in the past has tended to be very much based on developing regulatory procedures as opposed to creating suitable mechanisms for achieving the goals and objectives developed within the planning process. The failure of traditional and rational approaches to planning can be attributed to a number of factors as discussed below.

Lack of Flexibility

The logical, rational approach to planning, it has been argued, has made plans far too rigorous and unable to adapt to changing conditions. Unless the external environment is perceived to be quite static, a detailed step wise approach that is rigorously adhered to could make it very difficult for the organization or destination to create an optimal fit between its resources and the forces influencing tourism in its setting. A dynamic approach as provided through strategic planning principles enables a dynamic planning process, better able to adapt to changes.

Lack of Strategic Thinking and Vision

A major criticism has been launched against traditional, rational planning approaches by some researchers who argue that such plans lack leadership vision in the process of formulating strategies. The inclusion of "strategic vision" by leaders and decision-makers (not technical planning experts) ensures that the plan is not merely an operational plan, but provides direction and concepts for achieving the organizations broad goals and interests.

Ineffective top-down planning

Planning by the destination's planning officials or by retaining planning experts from outside the destination results in a plan which is unable to effectively represent the diverse opinions, needs and attitudes of a range of tourism stakeholders. The chances of successful implementation of such a top-down plan is further inhibited by the lack of community support and involvement in the process, particularly inpolitical systems where residents seek greater participation in the decision- making of their community direction.

Poor Linking of Formulation and Implementation

Another major impediment to planning has been the inability to link formulation of the plan to the outcomes of implementation so as to ensure accountability and to measure the success of the planning exercise. The lack of clear, easy to implement actions and responsibilities to ensure accountability for carrying out the actions, has been a deterrent to effective implementation. A clearly defmed relationship between the planning and implementation of action steps must be present to ensure effective delivery of both the tourism experience and the sustainability of the destination's assets and resources. Strategic tourism planning -an action planning approach

A strategic planning approach is essential for sustainable tourism, where by the disparate planning and development activities related to tourism are linked to an overall, broad strategic tourism plan to provide an integrated framework for directing tourism. Strategic planning seeks an optimal fit between the system and its environment. Hence, it: is long-term; contains vision; specifies goals (ends); specifies major actions (means) to achieve goals; specifies the major resource allocations to arrive at (ways); is dynamic, flexible and adaptable; ensures that formulation and implementation of the strategic plan are not discrete, but linked closely through constant monitoring, environmental scanning, evaluation and adjustment; and is not a linear process (*e.g.*, constant environmental scanning occurs throughout the process to enable proactive response and adjustment; monitoring can start as soon as target indicators and levels are established to provide base line information). A strategic approach to a sustainable community tourism plan alsorequires: close coordination with local and regional legislative and political structures; community participation and support; a new role for planners as educators and providers of technical expertise, but not solely plan designers; the plan is designed primarily by those who have a stake in the outcome; an innovative and inclusive organizational structure for joint planning; a learning community that is informed, educated and aware; applying the principles of sustainable tourism development to ensure the long-term sustainability of the ecology, the local economy and the socio-cultural values of the host community, while distributing the benefits equitably among the stakeholders.

LOCAL AUTHENTICITY AND ECONOMIC SUSTAINABILITY

Unlike theme parks, which are synthetic and totally engineered for leisure, thematic zones are supposed to remain fundamentally embedded in local cultural and societal activities. Several of the thematic zones identified by the STB, such as Chinatown and Little India, carry within their landscape traditions a rich history of buildings dating back to the colonial era, indigenous retail activities, local festivals, ethnic foods and places of worship.

By demarcating a thematic zone, it is hoped that the landscape and its activities are not only authentically conserved, but will successfully attract both local and foreign visitors for generations to come, thereby generating its own economic sustainability.

Whether the redeveloped Singapore River is locally authentic, however, is debatable. If we define 'authenticity' as the ability of a place to sustain both traditional 'hardware' (architecture) and 'software' (activities and people), the revamped thematic zone is only partially successful. The three river quays have been totally refurbished, and many of their shophouses and warehouses have been restored for contemporary use. For example, the Clarke Quay Festival Marketplace involved a wholesale conservation of five blocks of warehouses dating back to the early twentieth century; instead of trading-related services the warehouses today contain classy restaurants, curio-shops and pubs. At Robertson Quay, warehouses have been converted to discos and lifestyle shops.

The development of new condominiums and hotels has further led to the demise of traditional lighterage and related activities such as boatbuilding, boat repairs, entrepot and storage functions, and trading (import/export) establishments (Plate 1). The massive 'ecological clean-up' in the 1970/80s, urban restoration in the early 1990s, and thematic enhancement from 1998 have therefore entirely altered the social and spatial fabric of the Singapore River.

The preservation of 'hardware' in the form of architecturally and historically significant buildings, in contrast to the obliteration of indigenous 'software' in the form of traditional activities, lies at the heart of the authenticity debate. Most of our interviewees lamented the loss of the traditional activities that were historically intrinsic to the area and which distinguished the riverscape as uniquely Singaporean. Instead, as epitomized in the following quote by a restaurateur, many feel that the River today evokes the ambience of festival marketplaces and waterfronts of many other cities:

Sydney, London, America, they all belong to the same cultural background. But when people come from all these countries to Singapore, and see the same thing that they see at home, they don't appreciate it at all. They say, 'Why should we travel all the way to the East to experience the East and see something that we have right at our backyard?' Personal communication, November 2000

This view is not without merit as both the URA and STB have looked to successful urban waterfronts, primarily in Western cities, as models for Singapore. For example, the URA referred to the Seine (Paris) and Paseo del Rio (San Antonio) (URA 1992), while the STB studied the plans for Darling Harbourplace (Sydney) for their development plans (personal communication with STB).

STB also depended on foreign consultants, such as the Australia-based Cox Group (responsible for the King Street Wharf at Darling Harbour, Sydney) to propose marketing and enhancement plans for the River in 2001. By emulating other cities, the River runs the risk of becoming what Page and Hall (2003, 340) describe as a 'nonplace urban realm'.

Devoid of local authenticity, there is no reason why international tourists would visit the site. We would, however, like to forward the notion that 'authenticity' can and should be defined more flexibly.

Rather than delineating local authenticity as embracing only traditional architecture and activities, the thematic zone can also be regarded as authentic if locals continue to identify with the area.

Certainly, theme districts must appeal to tourists and locals in order to be economically viable. On the one hand, if locals feel that theme districts are only for tourists, such districts will end up becoming tourist traps and will be avoided by Singaporeans; on the other hand, when the resident population patronizes a place, tourists are also more likely to visit it as well, believing the site to be authentic and locally relevant.

In this light, the Singapore River thematic zone may be considered 'authentic' because our survey and research interviews consistently reveal that many Singaporeans are drawn to the area because of its restaurants and pubs.

Our survey established that while almost every commercial establishment has been able to tap into the tourist market at the River, only a quarter (26.1 per cent) of the businesses has tourists comprising at least half of their clientele. For most (50.7 per cent), however, tourists make up no more than 20 per cent of their clients, and although expatriates form part of the clientele of almost every establishment, they constitute the majority of clients (more than half) for only one in five (18.8 per cent) of the businesses.

Instead, for most businesses (63.6 per cent) at the Singapore River, the majority of their customers are Singaporeans.

Interviews with younger Singaporeans reveal that many do identify with the River, particularly because the pubs, restaurants and entertainment outlets cater to their lifestyle. Three frequent visitors in their twenties described how they feel about the waterfront transformations (personal communication, August 2000):

I think that every society must progress and transform, so it's a pretty good idea for Singapore River to transform Margaret, age 20. There are always changes and it depends on whether it's good or not. In this case, I think it's okay because in Singapore, there are so few places that you can go and enjoy yourself, so the more you have the better Wai Peng, age 25

Yes, it shows the higher standard of living and [that] people are getting wealthier and better off Jeremy, age 21. Certainly, more Singaporeans visit the River today than ever in the past when it was a 'working place'. Thematic development thus appears to provide the Singapore River local viability and economic sustenance, as younger Singaporeans and visitors (re)discover the area with its wide array of food and entertainment outlets.

This apparent success, however, needs to be measured against the fact that its attraction is predicated on its ability to maintain change and an upmarket profile reflective of Singapore's progress.

Continuing this line of development into the future may raise issues of place uniqueness, and ultimately mar the Singapore River as a 'one of a kind' attraction for tourists. The implications for theme zones as a means to economic sustainability thus need to be monitored over time.

LIVED EXPERIENCES AND SOCIAL SUSTAINABILITY

As thematic zones such as the Singapore River or Chinatown represent natural outcomes of historical and cultural inertia, the phenomenological experiences of their residents must be embodied in the landscape for the place to be attractive to tourists yet socially relevant to locals. It is the residential population after all that defines a place's identity, through sentiments for their neighbourhood and by their everyday activities in their social space.

Without them, thematic zones become purely tourist attractions and empty social statements. Thus, another issue that needs consideration pertains to the lived experience of former residents at the River. The loss of this residential population raises doubts about issues of social sustainability.

As a thematic zone, the Singapore River has been both successful and unsuccessful in sustaining a lived population. As mentioned, most of the old buildings in the area have undergone refurbishment and residents and workers have been relocated.

The historic conservation and adaptive reuse of shophouses (Boat Quay) and warehouses (Clarke and Robertson Quays) have meant that only economically sustainable businesses (and residents) have been able to rent/own the refurbished building spaces. In addition, with the demolition of fairly recent residential buildings housing lower-middle income residents at the River, and their replacement by upmarket service condominiums in the 1990s, thematic development has resulted not only in the dislocation of existing residents, but the introduction of new residents as well.

A public housing complex at Clarke Quay—comprising two blocks of flats, a wet-market, food stalls and shops selling basic necessities and sundry goods built by the government in 1974 to house lower-middle income families relocated from the shophouses in the vicinity—was demolished in 2000-1 to make way for an underground public transit station and retail development. Before the buildings were demolished, many ex-residents (who were relocated in the late 1990s) continued to return to the area, upholding a time cherished tradition of the River serving as a popular social site for elderly residents who lived and worked nearby. Today, the River throbs with nocturnal life but the patronage has changed to comprise mainly local youths and yuppies, tourists and expatriates. As Dobbs puts it, 'the new face of the river is young' (2002, 306).

Our interviews with ex-residents reveal that many hold fond memories of the River. When asked why they persisted in returning to the River everyday, two former residents spoke passionately about their social and spatial bonds (personal communication, May 2000):

The old people who used to live here [Clarke Quay] have no place to go anymore. When we moved to our new house [away from the River], we had no friends anymore. Do you want us to become senile and stay at home everyday? It is better if we come back here... We miss our old home, we were born here. Tan, age 67

We talk about many things. We hope the government will allocate a place to us here [at the River], that they will give us a place to sit and drink tea... All the old people are disappearing but we are not dead because we talk every day. We will not fall sick. If we are not together, we will fall sick. That is what will happen when you grow old. Lee, age 68

However, the riverbank's once free-access public spaces have increasingly become privatized with the proliferation of condominiums and restaurants fronting the river, alienating those who are neither clients nor residents. The informality of lived experiences at the River appears to be irreparably lost:

In the past, you can do anything you like. Now, you can't do that, they'll fine you for everything, from smoking to spitting. Everything requires money, so it's not so good in our eyes. The only good point is that it is cleaner now... Then, there was free trade [at the River]. The area was bustling with life. You can do anything. If there's anything you want to sell; you just display it there and sell.

Now, they will fine you if you do that. Everything now goes according to the law, down to the smallest thing. Thus, life is very hard. If you park your cars there, they'll fine. In the past, you can do business in anyway you like... Now, it is not so free. They say that it's a free country but nothing is free now. Lee, ex-resident, personal communication, May 2000

A testament to this lifestyle change is exemplified by the flea market at Clarke Quay. Flea markets of the past were informally organized and used goods were sold through bargaining. Today, the flea markets at Singapore River are staged by the Clarke Quay management on weekends; tenants (not necessarily residents at the River) pay a stipulated sum to the management, and many sell brand new items sold at prices pegged to cover the cost of renting prime retail space.

We argue that a new social sensibility pervades the area. Four new condominiums and five hotels built in the 1990s have modified the residential profile at the site. The wave of alfresco cafes, pubs and entertainment joints following in their wake has given the River a cosmopolitan image.

The new upmarket population attracted by the commercial developments has been at the expense of the community that once lived at the River since the 1970s, and even earlier. Place attachment is a curious mix of materiality, primordial attachments and location, and the character of an area is the product of local residents living their normal lives in their existential landscapes. Without them, theme districts may lose their local appeal, something we fear for the revamped Singapore River. A diverse population adds character to the site, as acknowledged in the following quote by a pub manager. When we enquired whether the old residential buildings should be conserved, she replied Absolutely! Not only [do the buildings add] character but characters... Why not let people keep their lives on the river? A river is not just about pubs and restaurants. It's about people! The old characters that live there can only colour, not take it away Personal communication, November 2000

Thematic development runs the risk of creating landscapes that are vibrant by night but a ghost town throughout the day. Of course, it would be inaccurate to say that the River does not have a residential community today. However, we argue that the authorities' refusal to retain original residents at the River over the years undermines the rationale for sustainable tourism and negates the possibility for social sustainability.

COMMEMORATING HISTORY AND CULTURAL SUSTAINABILITY

Related to social sustainability is the issue of cultural sustainability, or the ability to retain and adapt cultural elements to distinguish oneself from others. Under the government's vision to develop Singapore as a 'Global City of the Arts' unveiled in 1996, a number of downtown precincts have been designated as arts and cultural districts. These districts comprise key institutions (museums, theatres and performing spaces) and public works of art (sculptures and monuments).

The Singapore River has been identified as a potentially rich cultural district because it is home to three important arts venues/institutions: the Asian Civilizations Museum (at Boat Quay); Victoria Theatre and Concert Hall, adjacent to the museum; and the Singapore Repertory Theatre (at Robertson Quay). Close to the River are also the headquarters of the Ministry of Information and the Arts (responsible for Singapore's arts and cultural policies) and the newly constructed Esplanade—Theatres by the Bay near to the river mouth.

The concentration of cultural institutions and activities at the River does not, however, guarantee cultural sustainability. This is because the museums and theatre spaces showcase various aspects of Asian cultures, rather than the 'artefacts' and 'sociofacts' specifically associated with Singapore and the

Singapore River. For example, the Asian Civilizations Museum houses cultural artefacts from its Southeast Asian, East Asian and South Asian collections, whilst the concert halls and theatre spaces are 'free to rent' venues for all local and foreign performing groups. The Singapore River cultural district is thus aimed more generally at providing artistic and cultural amenities than at promoting the River's cultural legacies.

The question remains as to how the thematic zone might offer opportunities for cultural sustenance. In 2000, the STB unveiled plans for a new 'museum'—the Singapore River Outdoor Interpretive Centre. Unlike the 'elite cultures' on display in the Asian Civilizations Museum, the Interpretive Centre is aimed at showcasing 'history from below', specific to the Singapore River (Warren 2003, 324). The Centre is an alfresco museum commemorating the life of the River through select depictions of historical figures, people and events.

To date, five life-sized tableaux, all sculptured by Singaporeans, have been installed. Called 'People of the River', the series of historical figures feature a mix of the powerful and everyday including business leaders, colonial officers, traders and merchants, as well as coolies and children. Sponsored by commercial organizations like banks and hotels, the STB hopes to install more sculptures.

Respondents in our survey clearly endorse the alfresco museum concept. Many feel that the sculptures will not only distinguish the River as a unique attraction, but afford important and interesting historical lessons for present and future generations of Singaporeans.

As one noted, What Singaporeans are lacking today is [knowledge of] local history. It is something that the new generation is unsure of.

So, I think it is better to have sculptures that are local. Singaporeans will come and bring their children along, otherwise children will have no chance to see anything local; they have the chance to see something global [instead]... I think we should stick to our local theme, concentrate on local traditions. The trouble is that we look too much to the outside and forget what we have within. Personal communication, November 2000 Despite their popularity with school children and tourists, the outdoor museum may not be fully able to convey the historical depths and cultural complexities of the site.

For example, the descriptive plaque on the 'River Merchants' tableau simply describes the sculpture as a business transaction between the colonial government officer Alexander Johnston and Chinese and Malay traders. The tableau is silent, however, on issues such as the power relations and exploitative relations of the colonial period, which is only slightly hinted at by the depiction of two coolies toiling away shirtless while the business merchants discuss the price of their wares in elaborate garb. The depiction of the colonial officer (Johnston) seated talking to the unnamed standing Chinese and Malay merchants also alludes to colonial relations, but the plaque (and accompanying tourist brochures) are silent on this as well.

The hard life of the coolies, many of whom committed suicide in the River, is never told anywhere on stone or paper. In the case of another tableau, 'Celebration', the descriptive plaque was missing until 2004 and visitors were left to negotiate the meaning of the sculpture on their own, wondering why it is the boys (and not girls) who are jumping into the River, and for what purpose. Without proper signage and comprehensive narratives, visitor interaction with the environment is necessarily superficial.

One reason for the well-edited plaques is that visitors are seldom interested in a surfeit of information. In a survey of 230 Singaporeans conducted by Low (2001), she revealed that the majority of Singaporeans are apathetic towards public art. A total of 75 per cent of respondents said they would 'casually look at sculptures and walk away'; another 21 per cent will 'read inscriptions of the sculptures' while only 4 per cent will 'interact with the sculptures by touching and photographing it'. This view is confirmed by our interviewees working at the River. According to one respondent,

I would say the majority do not [look at sculptures]. I myself have been to UOB a few times but I did not see the 'Bird' [by sculptor Fernand Botero]. I could be taking it for granted... I would not differentiate, this is European art, this is Asian art, [nor] be too particular about it.Personal communication, November 2000

Another commented that Singaporeans are not culturally enlightened and the outdoor museum is of no interest to them:

It's one of those things that after you've seen it once, that's it. You won't re-visit the place because of [the sculptures]. You go there maybe because you like the river or something. If you can make it like Southbank Centre in Melbourne, where you have a little market on Sunday that would be nice. To make a place interesting you need more than [sculptures]. By and large, Singaporeans at this particular point in time, are still a relatively uncultured lot. Things like that don't attract them. Personal communication, July 2001

Public works of art, however, are successful in ensuring cultural sustainability in at least one respect. The sculptures provide a rare window into many quaint cultural activities and practices that were once common to the River, but have since been effaced by development. For example, the Indian chettiers (money changers) that used to ply their trade near to the River, the copra merchants and their distinctive weighing scales called the daching, the bullock carts that served as a form of transport, and the frolicking naked children swimming in the River have all been sensitively and accurately captured in stone or bronze.

The sculptors we interviewed agreed that permanent works of art are effective reminders of Singaporeans' cultural origins and heritage. Elsie Yu, whose work 'Joyous River' was one of the earliest sculptures to be installed, opined that young Singaporeans are the main beneficiaries of public art:

The STB has installed sculptures all over the place, more for pedestrians. It's very good for educational excursions for school children and kindergarten—little boy and girls can go and see how their great great great grandparents used to live, and how they made a living... You want thirty pieces of work, that's fine. I still think the thirty sculptures along the Singapore River are an excellent idea for locals. Personal communication, 9 June 2003

A critical mass of sculptures is necessary if we hope to offer tangible reminders of a place legacy. The existing five tableaux are insufficient. The lack of appropriate sites by the River and the difficulty in enticing corporate sponsors to fund the art works must be overcome. Corporate sponsors like Far East Organization and Malayan Bank (MayBank) have funded sculptures directly outside their property. The authors of this paper had worked as historical consultants to the STB in 2000 and had proposed a comprehensive list of 30 sculptures to be located throughout the River. Leaving the fate of the Interpretive Centre largely on the availability of private corporations able and willing to sponsor the installation of sculptures along the River appears to be a fallacious act of reasoning. Given its important role in securing cultural sustainability for the River, public funds should be made available for the purpose.

Singapore's dizzy urban (re)development in the last three decades (1960-90) has eliminated or modified many of its distinctive functional areas through the 'politics of re-invention'. The original character of areas, such as the Singapore River, has been replaced by modern symbolic landscapes of 'colours and contrast, culture and cuisines' and they have been promoted as thematic zones within Singapore's 'instant Asia' and 'new Asia' tourist promotion strategies.

This paper has examined the viability of thematic zones as a strategy of 'sustainability' to an urban tourism environment, focusing on the case study of the Singapore River, and emphasized the need to incorporate a comprehensive range of dimensions in considering sustainable urban tourism.

Sustainable urban tourism is a multifaceted issue and different criteria apply when we consider its ecological, economic, social and cultural dimensions. From a theoretical standpoint, the paper has demonstrated that sustainable tourism—even managed on the relatively small scale of a thematic zone—is difficult to attain because success in one area may be offset by tradeoffs in another.

The ecological goal of maintaining the Singapore River as a clean waterway has been attained only at the price of overlooking the very social, cultural and economic life of riverine activity that was once the defining characteristic of the River.

Similarly, continued economic growth at the River, achieved through the development of a new retail economy in the form of restaurants, hotels and entertainment outlets, has had mixed effects on social sustainability, as it has led to a gradual displacement of traditional cultural activities and social communities. It is therefore difficult to gauge the 'sustainability' of urban tourism development unless we take a holistic view on the subject.

It is also important to note that the issue of sustainability requires continual reassessment, and there is no one point in time when sustainability can be said to have been achieved. As Teo notes, 'Sustainability, is... an ongoing exercise of discovery. It is not about balancing the "good" with the "bad", the "negative" against the "positive". Rather, it is about the responsiveness of the tourism system to the multiple inputs that comprise its constitution' (2002, 471).

In terms of policy implications, the study has revealed that thematic zones can and do offer a viable strategy in urban tourism, catering to multiple interests. These thematic zones have been marketed at Singaporeans and tourists, as attractions that are authentic, distinctive and locally relevant. The Singapore River is not just a food, hotel and entertainment hub, but also a cultural district, residential enclave and a heritage site. However, we have also identified some problems that must be monitored over time.

They include fears that the Singapore River is becoming an elitist landscape and displacing the original vernacular landscapes and populations that used to live and work in the area. There are also concerns that modernization and tourism have erased the River's place uniqueness as it changes into a waterfront not unlike those found in many Western cities. It is vital that specific policies are put in place to ensure that indigenous (or 'local') landscape elements of thematic areas like Singapore River do not give way to the modern (often equated with the 'global') if Singapore is to have a sustainable urban tourism programme.

Ultimately, urban sustainable tourism is about preserving the historic continuity of urban places so that succeeding generations of residents, as well as travellers and tourists, can continue to experience and sample the environmental, economic, social and cultural aspects of these places. If the uniqueness of places is eroded, their appeal to both locals and tourists will be severely undermined and the tourist industry of nation-state or city will lose its goose that lays the golden eggs. More importantly, cities and countries owe it to their citizens to preserve the uniqueness of their cultural landscapes, to maintain the everyday way of life of their peoples, and to preserve the diversity of their natural habitats.

When societies have a sense of self-respect for their own cultural identity and heritage, the tourist attractiveness of place and people becomes automatically sustainable. In a world where globalization is rapidly degrading environments and homogenizing urban areas, thematic zones are a way of ensuring that the uniqueness of places, the biodiversity of nature, the pride of national identity, the jigsaw of ethnic districts and the curiosity of cultural heterogeneity will remain the fountainheads for a sustainable tourist industry and an inviting world for personal discovery. The typical images of paradise shown in travel brochures and on television are of lush green foliage, wild animals, smiling natives, and exotic food. These promises of unforgettable experiences lure people to the developing world. Pristine natural environments, abundant wildlife, and rich traditions in the least developed countries (LDCs) are irresistible attractions to tourists of the developed world. However, the creation of these paradises does not come without hidden costs to host populations.

David Harrison and the 16 contributors in Tourism and the Less Developed World: Issues and Case Studies examine the issues associated with the creation of tourist paradises in LDCs. Tourism claims to be the fastest-growing industry in the world; LDCs, rich in natural resources but short of capital, expertise, and trained personnel, tend to choose tourism as a development tool.

Although the definition of a LDC is a matter of debate, Harrison and the contributors use the term based on the countries' classification by the World Tourism Organization as "developing" or as economies "in transition."

Harrison discusses the issues of international tourism using a wide range of development paradigms. International tourism has historically been a movement of affluent tourists from "developed societies" to "less developed societies." Alongside multinational corporations that are involved in developing tourism in LDCs, international tourists today are knowingly or unknowingly creating a new form of colonialism. Yet under the development paradigm of "modernization," international tourism can also contribute to the transfer of capital, technology, and human resources to LDCs and the development of a free market in these countries. Inadequate infrastructure is one major obstacle in developing international tourism in LDCs. In Tourism and the Less Developed World, one contributor notes the inadequate telecommunication and transport facilities in the South American Common Market, while others observe similar problems in India and China.

In his contribution "Tourism and Development in Communist and Post-Communist Societies," Derek Hall identifies the disadvantages such countries face when introducing international tourism as poor infrastructure and the inability to transport and cater to large numbers of people. However, the construction and improvement of infrastructure in LDCs can be a double-edged sword; one contributor suggests that infrastructure-building for tourism purposes may consume resources that could be used to meet more fundamental needs.

International tourism also raises the issues of pleasure migration and labour migration. Pleasure migration is the ownership of second homes, time-share properties, or the retirement of people in areas they previously visited as tourists. Pleasure migration potentially introduces a variety of issues relevant to development, including land ownership, conflicts between migrants and local laws, and the enclosure and segregation of pleasure migrants (tourist ghetto). On the other hand, tourism development tends to have an impact on labour markets, attracting mainly unskilled laborers in direct and induced jobs. The migration of laborers causes not only a shift in human resources in the primary and secondary industries, but also the relocation of the population. Peter Dieke, in "Human Resources in Tourism Development: African Perspectives," examines the serious shortage of human resources in African tourism and describes current attempts to provide more training and education to local people.

The shortage of educated personnel is a problem for the tourism industry as well as for government agencies. Bureaucrats' lack of experience, expertise, and training means that the implementation of tourism as a means of socio-economic development is not always successful. Michael Hall notes that the Japanese government emphasizes outbound tourism as a means of balancing trade and improving diplomatic relations.

However, Harrison explains that LDC governments are usually uninterested or unable to support outbound tourism. Inherent problems in many LDCs, such as intragovernmental conflict, lack of horizontal and vertical cooperation within organizations, corruption, decentralization, and issues of privatization obstruct the development of tourism as an industry. LDC governments determine the effectiveness of tourism development through their intervention in and ownership of infrastructure and tourism facilities, along with their response to the involvement of multinational enterprises and foreign investors. Th e historical background of the country is another key factor in successful tourism development. A government's attempt to promote political stability and to maintain sustainable tourism development is not always understood or well received by locals.

Sustainability is a buzzword in the contemporary development discussion and the use of the term in the tourism industry is no exception. As national resources, including culture and heritage, are the main assets in tourism, it has been argued that economic well-being should not precede social and environmental well-being. Officials have debated whether alternative forms of tourism rather than mass tourism, which has been the mainstream product for quite some time, are more sustainable.

Ecotourism, particularly community-based ecotourism, is becoming the mainstay of alternative tourism development in LDCs. In Tourism and the Less Developed World, four out of six case studies illustrate examples of community-based ecotourism in the Caribbean, South Africa, Indonesia, and Fiji. In spite of the popularity of ecotourism, the exponential growth in the number of small-scale ecotourism operators and products is criticized as transforming ecotourism into another form of mass tourism. Particularly in LDCs, the concept and goals of ecotourism may not be fully understood, but they could be interpreted in ways to suit public agencies and private entrepreneurs. Some claim that cruise ships and enclave resorts, which restrict tourists' activities to within the resort premises, may be less detrimental in terms of environmental degradation and cultural contamination.

Harrison and the contributors provide an outline of the issues involving tourism as a development tool in LDCs. Harrison admits that the review is broad in scope and often brief in description, but it provides an important picture of international tourism and identifies the specific issues of the regions of the world reviewed. The case study section identifies several significant side-effects of tourism development, such as child prostitution. The case studies discuss at length the key issues of international tourism development in LDCs, namely infrastructure, human resources, state involvement, sustainability, and socio-cultural changes.

Unfortunately, Harrison's attempt to write about these issues in terms of development theories merely scratches the surface. In the essays, he and the contributors frequently allude to but do not directly address issues of tourism in terms of the political economy of international tourism. This book can be read as a sequel to Harrison 's earlier book Tourism and the Less Dev eloped Countries (John Wiley & Sons, 1992), with each theme in the 1992 book more deeply probed. Still, Tourism and the Less Developed World: Issues and Case Studies successfully offers a thought-provoking piece of work on the often unseen dilemmas and conflicts that arise "in pursuit of paradise."

SUSTAINABLE TOURISM IN THE CITY

Sustainable tourism has become the buzz concept for government and tourist agencies around the world. In 2002, the Pacific-Asia Tourism Association made sustainable tourism the cornerstone of its policies and actions. The practice of sustainable tourism underscores two important concerns of governments, NGOs and the informed public: a deteriorating environment and cultural erosion.

By emphasizing the need to minimize the impact on the global environment, to sustain the local environment and to cater to both the host community and visitors, the notion of sustainable tourism also implies a desire to seek a more productive and harmonious relationship among visitors, host communities and the environment, whether natural or built, in both urban and rural settings.

Thus, as Butler notes, the term 'sustainable tourism', often implies tourism that is 'appropriate and morally correct as well as being environmentally suitable' (1998, 27).

While sustainable tourism may be defined as the 'management of all resources in such a way that we can fulfil economic, social and aesthetic needs while maintaining cultural integrity, essential ecological processes, biological diversity and life support systems', it is often associated more narrowly with green tourism, ecotourism (1), environmental issues and 'fragile environments'. For example, in the 1992 Rio Summit's global action plan Agenda 21, which identified various avenues for sustainable development, tourism was highlighted as offering sustainability to 'mountain economies' and 'threatened areas' of wildlife, national parks and bio-diversity. The city, however, is not conventionally considered a fragile and endangered environment because urban areas are seen to be at the forefront of development, and urban transformations are often visible and premeditated.

Indeed, although there are several books and even a journal dedicated to sustainable tourism issues, the major concentration of the literature either deals with ecotourism sites or non-urban tourist attractions, often focusing on the negative environmental outcomes of tourism on nature reserves and rural areas. As Hinch states, it is paradoxical that while urban areas are recognized as the most important types of tourist destinations, 'they are generally excluded from discussions on sustainable tourism' (1998, 185).

The neglect is particularly ironic given that a major variable with regard to sustainable tourism is the growing impact of mass tourism, commonly equated to a form of mass consumption characterized by 'standardization of production and products', and of which cities are a major recipient. Mass tourism is often regarded as the antithesis of sustainable tourism.

SUSTAINABLE TOURISM BEYOND ECOLOGICAL ISSUES

Urban environments are certainly not immune to tourist presence and tourism planning. Tourism's diverse impacts include changes to the ecological and hydrological systems of cities, overloading of infrastructure, alteration of land use, as well as transformations in the visual, architectural and social-cultural fabric of cities. In historic sites, the effects of urban tourism developments are double-edged. On the one hand, tourism provides a rationale for the preservation of historically unique artefacts and buildings; on the other hand, tourism's commercializing influence introduces new retail activities and land uses, often irreparably changing the residential and community profile of urban zones.

Researchers such as Hvenegaard and Dearden (1998) and Williams (1998) assert that studies on sustainable tourism should include a focus on a broad range of aspects, including environmental issues, if tourism development is to be holistic. This also applies to urban areas. As Pugh contends, a sustainable city will organize its multiple institutions towards environmental friendliness. This will be expressed in policy making, in institutional reform, in the growth and appropriate information (and the reduction of distorted and asymmetrically biased information).

Thus we agree that sustainable tourism in the context of urban environments must consider both the 'green issues' and non-ecological resources, including the conservation of historical landscapes, the preservation of heritage buildings, and the keeping alive of cultures, traditions and customs. In this context, Mowforth and Munt (1998) note three other important dimensions of sustainable tourism beyond the ecological; these are economic, social and cultural sustainability.

Economic sustainability refers to the economic gains from tourism that are sufficient to cover the costs and inconveniences incurred by development. Social sustainability refers to the ability of a local community 'to absorb inputs, such as extra people, for short or long periods of time, and to continue functioning either without the creation of social disharmony as a result of these inputs or by adapting its functions and relationships so that the disharmony can be alleviated or mitigated'.

Cultural sustainability concerns the ability of a community to retain or adapt elements of their cultural activities which distinguish them from other communities. As is visible from the definitions, the role of the local community—their rights, the benefits they stand to gain from tourism and the enshrining of local customs—underline sustainable development. Jansen-Verbeke's (1997) 'interaction model' further explains the urban tourism-sustainability nexus. She argues that within urban tourism research, inordinate attention is focused on economic impacts.

She thus proposes a model that conceives of urban tourism and sustainability in terms of 'artefacts', 'sociofacts' and 'mentifacts'. While artefacts refer to buildings, monuments and key urban sites, sociofacts concern tourism's effects on social relations—how government, the private sector and the lay-people relate to each other through tourism projects, as well as local involvement and participation in tourism schemes.

The least researched aspect is mentifacts, or the effects of tourism on local communities' behaviour, attitudes and values. This tripartite schema is useful in reminding us that tourism's effects are multifaceted, and benefits arising from tourism, such as its economic impact, or the conservation of urban artefacts, might be off-set by negative issues, including the strain that tourism planning places on government-people relations, or the displeasure engendered towards foreigners.

FUNCTIONAL AREAS IN THE TOURIST CITY

Most cities have a small area—variously referred to as the 'recreational business district', 'tourism business district', or the 'Central Tourist District' which usually contains most of the attractions and facilities used by tourists, but which also caters to non-tourists. Such a concentration of tourism and non-tourism resources makes this a place appealing and attractive to both tourists and locals. However, over and above this key tourist zone, most cities also have an assemblage of other districts, enclaves and streets that appeal to tourists. Indeed, all urban areas, in particular large cities, have complex spatialities that lend themselves as tourist attractions over and above their roles as areas, facilities and activities enjoyed by the residents.

The greater the landscape texture (spaces devoted to work, consumption, leisure and entertainment) of a city, the greater its opportunity to attract and invite curiosity and experience from visitors and locals. The areas that often become the object of tourist fascination and consumption are the city's 'enclavic spaces'. These enclavic spaces offer a kaleidoscope of experiences and are often 'edgy' transitional neighbourhood zones (such as areas of ethnic minorities, immigrants, or poverty) that are appealing precisely because they are 'unconstructed'.

Burtenshaw et al. (1991, 206-7) identify three main categories of urban space that also function as tourist attractions (2): historic districts whose physical attractions are thematically promoted (such as Westminster/Covent Garden/Bloomsbury in London); cultural quarters which often contain a range of cultural and entertainment services such as theatres, museum, art galleries and the like (such as the Les Halles-Beaubourg quarter in Paris); and linear facilities such as specialized shopping streets, canal excursions, river embankments, as well as trails and routes through selected sections of the city.

While many of these areas may have evolved spontaneously during the city's earlier growth, their role as tourist zones has been reinforced over time through 'a degree of selection... exercised by both visitors and urban managers'.

The need for urban spaces to perform multiple roles is very clear for a small, space bound city-state like Singapore (682 k[m.sup.2]), where sustainable urban tourism offers a logical, sensible and effective policy direction. In a city-state like Singapore, the multiple competing uses of space and land areas to cater to a diverse range of people has made urban planning a difficult exercise. The balance of conserving historic buildings, cultural places and ethnic districts within competing economic and social demands is a perennial contestation between political leaders, urban planners, civil servants, NGO advocates and the public.

Tourism thematic zones like the Singapore River are therefore multi-purpose landscapes: tourist attractions, heritage sites, residential areas and retail/entertainment precincts. In the rest of the paper, we examine—through a case study of the Singapore River—how successfully (or otherwise) thematic zones are being used as a tool of sustainable urban tourism in Singapore.

THE SINGAPORE RIVER SITE

The Singapore River thematic zone is linear and defined by the meanders of the river from its mouth to Kim Seng Bridge, some 3.2 km inland. It covers around 82 ha. Both sides of the river were once lined with three- and four-storey shophouses, warehouses, as well as tenement housing and squatters that developed alongside the Singapore River's rise as the centre of the city's entrepot trading function.

The river itself was a hive of lighterage and related activities, and lighters formed a virtual blanket over the garbage-strewn polluted waters of the Singapore River. As the city developed, the older structures along the river were demolished to make way for the skyscrapers of the adjacent central business district, the lighterage activities were gradually relocated, and an official plan was put in place in 1969 to clean up the river and make it (along with the Rochor, Whampoa and Geylang Rivers) an ecologically viable system. By 1983, a new phase of redevelopment and restoration was embarked upon to turn the Singapore River into a zone of recreation and entertainment.

Today, the River can be divided into three planning zones: the Boat Quay area comprising pubs and restaurants; the Clarke Quay area comprising a festival marketplace; and the Robertson Quay area which has many service apartments, hotels and some retail outlets.

The two key government agencies responsible for developing the Singapore River are the URA and the STB. While the URA is concerned with the hardware of heritage conservation and preservation of buildings, the STB is more focused on the software, often defined as activities and land uses. The URA's vision for the Singapore River zone (3) is to create a river of 'excitement' by blending elements of urban history with contemporary land uses (URA 1992, 26).

The Thematic Development Strategic Business Unit of the Singapore Tourism Board spearheads the development of the Singapore River as one of 11 thematic zones identified in Tourism 21, the tourism master plan to reposition Singapore 'as a Tourism Capital in the 21st century'. The Singapore River falls under the theme of 'The Night Zone', underscoring the vision of a 'City that Never Sleeps'; the zone features alfresco dining, vibrant nightlife, ambient lighting, festivals and family-oriented entertainment amenities.

Most of the housing along the Singapore River features high-end condominiums and service apartments that have in recent years replaced the warehouses, lower-income flats and two-, three- and four-storey shophouses of the past. These new upmarket residential areas house mainly expatriate professionals and affluent Singaporeans wishing to live in the heart of the city. There are also nine hotels, ranging from super-deluxe to modest accommodation, along or adjacent to the River. The River is thus being developed as a popular leisure and entertainment belt for a diverse market comprising tourists, expatriates and a mixed group of locals.

Our study of the Singapore River zone, as an example of sustainable urban tourism, is informed by various research methodologies. First, we undertook a land use plot of all the establishments and businesses along the Singapore River in May 2000. Periodic fieldtrips to the site over the years, involvement in various festivals at the River, and photographing new developments (such as sculptures and conserved buildings) ensured that we constantly updated our information on land use and activities in the thematic zone. Second, a drop-off, mail back questionnaire survey of all the retail and commercial businesses in the area was undertaken in June 2000. Out of a total of 234 questionnaires distributed, we received 69 replies, *i.e.*, a response rate of 29.5 per cent. Here, we were concerned with eliciting general responses on business conditions and clientele profiles, as well as feedback on development issues and problems.

Finally, between May 2000 and July 2003, we conducted in-depth interviews with key personnel of planning agencies (STB and URA), business operators at the River (25 in total), property developers (two), representatives of business associations at the River (three), and sculptors who have created works of public art for the River (six). The goal was to elicit policy insights into the River's development, future plans for the area, as well as positive and negative feedback on the current situation at the River.

In addition, interviews were conducted with four ex-residents of the River and nine frequent local visitors to the site. These interviews explored how ex-residents feel about their relocation from the River, and how frequent visitors respond to the River's redevelopment. Our research data are supplemented with interviews we had conducted earlier, in 1998, as part of an historical research project on the River.

THEMATIC ZONES AS A STRATEGY FOR URBAN TOURISM SUSTAINABILITY

The thematic approach, based on the urban design plans already laid out under the Urban Redevelopment Authority's Guide Plans, will enable the visitor to fully appreciate the beauty and significance of what we have to offer not just aesthetically pleasing sights, interesting attractions or historical buildings, but more importantly, an idea of how and why the area came about, its cultural and historical significance and how it is part of the overall Singaporean psyche and way of life.

This quote encapsulates the STB's planning philosophy for thematic zones. The 'visitor' refers to both tourists and Singaporeans, because theme districts not only cater to tourists but fulfil domestic needs and administrative contestations for space and amenities. While city planners seek effective use of space, the conservationists want historic buildings, conserved as a heritage of the city, whereas private developers demand land for residential, office and retail development and the layperson is concerned with public accessibility.

In this section, we analyse the extent to which the Singapore River as a thematic zone fulfils the various facets of sustainable tourism, namely, environmental, economic, social, and cultural sustainability while catering to different groups of people. We show that while development has been sustainable in some respects, there are also drawbacks and limitations. The tradeoffs of environmental sustainability Despite its historical and cultural landscape (re)embodiment, the Singapore River remains essentially a natural ecosystem. This ecosystem, however, has changed, in keeping with urban expansion as the River's watershed has been gradually encased with a built-up area of trading houses, godowns and cottage industries as well as farm and poultry areas.

The Singapore River was certainly not a sustainable environment throughout its river port history, but the authorities were less concerned with this than the River's roles as an economic lifeline and waterway for the city's waste products. Indeed, the Singapore River in the 1950s and 1960s was well known for its' intense sediment and chemical pollution, its putrid smells, its floating jetsam of material waste and its lack of aquatic life, as these quotes from our respondents demonstrate:

In those days [1950s], the riverfront was not a place of enjoyment and relaxation... it had a very bad reputation for being very unhygienic. It was smelly, muddy brown and full of [human waste] and things like that. Allan, 55 years old, lived in the vicinity of the Singapore River in the mid-1950s; personal communication, May 1998.

As time went by, because up the river people used to dump things, the water became more brackish, the smell became worse and I used to call it 'The Aroma of the South Sea'. This is the aroma... you cannot get anywhere else! Milton, 78 years old, had an office along the Singapore River from 1949 to the 1980s; personal communication, May 1998 The question of the River's environmental sustainability became the focus of official concern only when the authorities had decided that the River no longer served its purpose as an economic centre of Singapore's lighterage industry. Government planners realized that if the River was to be turned into a tourist theme zone and an upmarket housing area, the solid waste and chemical pollution, filth and smells had to be eradicated.

During its ecological cleanup between 1977 and 1987, hundreds of boats—cargo lighters, motorized twakows, miniature sampans that served as taxis, and residential crafts—were removed and sent to Singapore's west coast.

Today, two of the larger boats remain permanently moored at Clarke Quay to serve as dining venues, while a handful of the smaller vessels provide leisure cruises and 'river taxi' services. Before the cleanup, tourists, school children and artists came to the River for the singular attraction of the boats, their haphazard arrangement on the river providing a fascinating and picturesque scene and the subject of many paintings and artworks. Attractive as they are to visitors, however, the demise of the boats is not something the government will soon rectify. Most boats continue to be banned because of the fears of pollution and danger to public safety. While respondents strongly support the environmental clean-up of the River, seeing it as 'an excellent decision as it ties in with tourist promotion' (in Allan's words), many argued that the government could afford to relax the stringent regulations on the use of boats and other activities on and in the river. Other than national-level events (such as the Great Singapore Duck Race, the Dragon Boat Race and River Hongbao festivities), most other activities are prohibited from using the river. Firdaus Wong, Deputy Director, Clarke Quay Management, questioned:

I think we would like to see... more events happening on the river... The river is there but on the river, we haven't exploited that. There obviously can be things happening on the river. Why can't we have a concert on the river? Why can't you dance on the river? Why can't you jump into the river? Why can't you swim across the river? Personal communication, June 2001 Francis Phun (Chairperson, Singapore River Business Association and Managing Director, Singapore Explorer, a river taxi service at the River) also lamented, We are restricted by the number of boats. Whatever you see, that is the maximum number—20 of them—because the Ministry of the Environment feels that this is the number the river can take; you got any more than that [and] it will pollute the river. The Maritime Port Authority says that the river is very narrow; that is the maximum number they can take, if not there will be an accident. Then [there is] the design [of the boats]. The Singapore Tourism Board says that the Singapore River should only have the bumboat and no other boats because this is the authentic historical design. No other types of boats are approved Personal communication, May 2001.

In an interview with Dr Tan Gee Paw, Permanent Secretary of the Ministry of the Environment (personal communication, June 1998), he noted that allowing 'riverside dining' (within strict guidelines such as the prohibition of cooking and washing outdoors, dumping of waste material into the river, and leaking engines) was a concession made to the STB to bring life to the River. At the same time, a mechanical system to drain flotsam has been put in place, regular dredging of the River is conducted, and water samples taken and tested to ensure that the waters of the River remain at an acceptable level of cleanliness.

According to Dr Tan, all future developments for tourism and leisure at the River must not conflict with Ministry of the Environment's larger objective of ensuring 'healthy waters' in Singapore's water bodies. Thus, while the River has become a more ecologically viable and sustainable environment, the motivation was not primarily environmental, but more to sustain a new economic lifeline for river tourism and as an alternative reservoir for water.

Keeping the River pollution free and aesthetically pleasing has meant that only a narrow slate of government-organized events and activities has been allowed to exploit the waters of the River (as opposed to its riverbanks).

Today, with alfresco dining and drinking outlets lining the riverbanks at Boat, Clarke and Robertson Quays, the River's aesthetics are critical ingredients to the economic sustainability of these retail outlets.

BROAD-BASED SUSTAINABLE DEVELOPMENT THROUGH TOURISM

The Travel & Tourism industry has a vested interest in protecting the natural and cultural resources that are the core of its business. Travel & Tourism has less impacts on natural resources and the environment than other sectors and it has already done much to address the issues arising from its activities.

There are examples, however, from around the world where the impact of Travel & Tourism has been damaging to the local environment and people. Some of the factors which contributes to the harmful impact of tourism are:

- A lack of awareness on the part of those making decisions about tourism development of the social, economic and environmental balance to be pursued in achieving sustainable development;
- A lack of commitment by tourism operators and travellers to contribute to the maintenance of the local environment and culture of the host destination;
- A weak institutional framework with inadequate controls can lead to tourism development which is both inappropriate and intrusive;
- Unfairly traded tourism, whereby local communities are unable to share in its benefits;
- Large flows of visitors in remote or sensitive locations can place considerable strains on local resources (particularly water) and supply systems. Travellers' expectations of the goods and services, which should be available, can lead to these items or services, being imported from outside or local supply chains, being distorted to meet demands; and
- Tourism can change a destination's cultural make-up and, if poorly developed, can increase crime, prostitution and other social problems.

In order for tourism to realise its potential to achieve broad-based sustainable development, an effective partnership between Government and all sectors of the industry will be required. The following illustrates what is being done:

International Co-operation

IH&RA and the United Nations Organisation for Education, Science and Culture (UNESCO) have signed a co-operation agreement to encourage world-wide hotel chains to sponsor UNESCO cultural heritage sites and attract tourism to them via their marketing campaigns.

National Governments

In India, the government is pump priming local "eco-tourism" activities, which are primarily driven by local women. In Mexico, the government is kick starting village development for "eco-tourism" lodges in the Chiapas region involving the whole community. In England, the government has recently held a national consultation on sustainable tourism and, as a result, is developing a new strategy for tourism, which incorporates the principles of sustainable development as a core component. The Caribbean Tourism Organisation has developed a comprehensive strategy to develop "eco-tourism" in the Caribbean region. This strategy is closely integrated with the goals of the Association for Caribbean States (ACE) for a green Caribbean.

"Green Globe" has developed a specific "Destinations" programme to recognise those tourist destinations where there is a concerted effort by all those involved in the local tourism industry to improve the quality of the environment. The Destinations process provides a framework to guide tourist locations towards achieving sustainable development based on the principles of Agenda 21. The Destinations programmes are tailor made to reflect local circumstances, such as the level of environmental awareness, action taken to date and available resources. Each programme is based on achieving progressive environmental improvements.

Targets are set within a realistic timetable and are developed by a steering group made up of key partners. The island of Jersey has become the first "Green Globe" Destination. Vilamoura in Portugal, Dominica in the Caribbean and 3 destinations in the Philippines have also entered the Destination programme.

For example, in 1996 Luso tour SA, a tourism development company, enacted a management plan for Vilamoura whereby employees are given responsibility for individual environmental tasks. The company has invested money into rehabilitating the surrounding natural environment, which includes pine forests and a lake that has significance to local wetland areas. Guests are provided with a copy of the environmental policy and are encouraged to participate in the scheme through specialised brochures.

The campaign includes recycling; treating diseased pine areas; regular cleaning of the beaches and marinas; development of a sewage treatment plant and new buildings in the resort are designed to minimise visual and environmental impacts. For its work in Vilamoura, Lusotour SA is also a winner of the British Airways Tourism for Tomorrow Awards.

The "Africa tourism" brand has been developed by the Open Africa Foundation to encourage products, which embraces sustainable ecological, economic and social development based on Africa's unique cultural, natural and wildlife heritage. "Open Africa" is also developing a continuous network of "Africa tourism" routes from the Cape to Cairo, known as the "African Dream". The Dream helps to create awareness of the many rural and environmental projects, which exist throughout Africa. "Team Africa", a transcontinental alliance of governments, corporations, institutions, professionals and individuals, provides leadership and motivation in the development of the "African Dream".

Host Communities

"Whale Watch Kaikoura" is an initiative of local Maori people from a small town on the East Coast of New Zealand's South Island. Within a kilometre of the Kaikoura shore is an area ideal for whales, where visitors are guaranteed to see them all year round. The Whale Watch began 11 years ago and is now a booming tourist destination, run by indigenous people with a strong sense of heritage and a view of the future based on strong principles of sustainability.

Jordan Tourism Investments, has revitalised the traditional village of Taybeh, in Jordan, into a cultural tourist resort, with the help and agreement of villagers. With many of the younger generation moving to the cities, the village was losing its character. By restoring its 19th century buildings and reviving old crafts, the village is now thriving again. The village lies 9km south east of the historic city of Petra. Opened in July 1994, the village now accommodates around 60,000 guests each year.

Uluru and Kakadu National Parks are both owned by indigenous Australians, the local Aboriginal communities, and jointly run with the National Parks and Wildlife Service. They are both major tourism destinations and involve indigenous participation in planning, management, and ownership of tourism infrastructure, as well as interpretation for visitors. They bring significant economic, social and cultural benefits to the local indigenous communities. The Conservation Corporation in Africa has established a series of high quality game parks in which local communities are major stakeholders and beneficiaries of tourism. This initiative is also helping to re-invigorate local crafts.

Agents and Partnerships

The challenge facing the tourism industry in moving towards a more sustainable future is set out in "Agenda 21 for the Travel & Tourism Industry". To achieve the goals set out in this document will require a partnership between government departments, national tourism authorities, international and national trade organisations and Travel & Tourism companies. Working together in close co-operation such partnerships should aim to deliver the following:

- Close co-operation between the public and private sectors to deliver a regulatory regime, which encourages voluntary action but supplement, where necessary, with regulation in areas such as land-use and waste management.
- Agreed common standards and tools to enable the measurement of progress towards achieving sustainable development.
- Certification criteria developed and more widely applied to industry initiatives.
- A commitment to the controlled expansion, where appropriate, of infrastructure.
- Environmental taxes, where applied, should be fair and non-

discriminatory. They should be carefully thought out to minimise their impact on economic development, and revenues should be allocated to Travel & Tourism associated environment improvement programmes.

- International, national and local funding bodies should include sustainable development as apart of their criteria, so that in time, all funding would be dependent on sound environmental practice.
- Contemporary research into sustainable tourism needs to be funded and developed. Issues requiring attention include design, carrying capacity, tour operator activities, environmental reporting, auditing and environmental impact assessments.
- Environmental education and training should be increased, particularly in schools, for future hotel and tourism staff.
- Greater investment and commitment to the use of new technology.

5

The Marketing Mix and Business Tourism

INTRODUCTION

The marketing mix consists of those variables which are controllable or heavily influenced by an organization. They are divided into the 4 Ps, namely, product, price, place and promotion.

THE PRODUCT

The diversity of business travel and tourism makes it difficult to generalize about the nature of the product. For example, business travellers making individual business trips will see the 'product' as the transport and accommodation services they use primarily, as well as the general facilities provided by the destination. However, the convention delegate may see the convention centre itself as the most important element of the product. Like leisure tourism it could also be argued that business travel and tourism is not a product, but rather an experience. The nature of this experience will reflect, for example:

- The elements of the product
- The ambience of the destination and the venue
- The personality and experience of the business traveller.

The experience also includes three stages:

- Anticipation
- Consumption
- Remembrance.

Before the event – during the event – after the event.

Furthermore, the experience can also be divided into two sets of elements, as follows:

1 Those elements which are controlled or influenced by the supplier such as hotel meeting rooms.
2 Those elements which are not under the control or influence of suppliers, but which affect the experience, such as the weather and air road congestion.

Another area where great effort has been made to attract the business traveller is business-class services on airlines. A case study relating to this subject is to be found in Part Five of the book. All products, whether business tourism or not, have a range of factors which constitute the product. These can best be explained by using a convention centre as an example. Marketing of products such as this convention centre involves packaging all of these elements to create a satisfactory experience for the customer.

Price

Price is clearly a crucial issue in any market but it is a complex matter in business travel and tourism, for the following reasons:

1 There are direct and indirect costs for the traveller. Direct costs include, for example, fees for attending conferences or the price of an air ticket. There are also indirect costs such as the need to buy a visa when travelling to some destinations.

2 Prices for a similar product vary dramatically around the world. Some examples taken from *Business Traveller* magazine will illustrate this point as follows:

   (a) A non-residential one-day conference for 500 people including room hire, lunch, two tea/coffee breaks and taxes, would cost £9745 in Helsinki but £19 100 in Copenhagen (*Business Traveller*, May 2000).

   (b) A cocktail party for ten VIP guests in January 2000 including two-night suite hire, dinner and breakfast for one person included would have cost £2775 in Cyprus but £3350 in Rome (*Business Traveller*, January 2000).

   (c) A three-night full-board stay for thirty people in fifteen rooms in a leisure hotel with golf facilities in spring 2000, would have cost £9630 in Mauritius but £17 000 in Florida (*Business Traveller*, March 2000).

Even within one country prices can vary significantly. For example, the twenty-four hour delegate rate at the end of 2000 was £105 at the Britannia Adelphi Hotel, Liverpool, £195 at the Balmoral Hotel, Edinburgh, and £220 at the Grand Hotel, Eastbourne (*Conference and Incentive Travel, January 2001*).

For many purchasers/users, price is perhaps less important than perceived value for money. This term is concerned with the relationship between benefits received and price paid. For example, in January 2000 a survey published in *Business Traveller* found that 80 per cent of readers felt that conference delegates were offered better value for money from hotels in mainland Europe than in the UK. Of course, value for money is a wholly subjective concept. Most purchasers do not pay the published price, particularly for hotel accommodation and airline tickets. Negotiation is commonplace, which creates real challenges in terms of revenue planning and yield management. Discounting is also rife based on criteria such as seasonality, volume of business or whether the customer is a regular user of a particular product or service.

Some elements of the business tourism product are sold below their market value for various reasons. For example, many municipally owned conference venues are hired out to organizers at low, even no, cost to attract conferences because of the spin-off benefits they will bring to the area.

Destinations usually make no direct charge for entry to the resort, city or region or for use of its facilities such as beaches, parks and even the climate. Ye t these elements of the destination may be a major factor in the decision to locate a conference or incentive travel package in a particular location.

Some costs are compulsory, such as travel costs, while others are voluntary, like having a drink at the end of the working day.

Place

Place or distribution is concerned with how business travellers or tourists actually purchase the products they need. There are several dimensions to this:

1 Customers can buy whole packages such as an incentive travel package or individual elements such as air tickets, venues and accommodation.

2 Customers can purchase products directly or make use of the services of specialist intermediaries.

As with leisure travel and tourism, the Internet is beginning to play a big role in distribution in business travel and tourism.

By providing both information and an opportunity to purchase simultaneously it is blurring the distinction between two of the 4 Ps, namely, place and promotion. This leads us neatly on to the final P, promotion.

Promotion

To many people, promotion is synonymous with marketing; it is the visual face of marketing. However, promotion is simply one element of the marketing mix, fulfilling the function of making potential customers want to purchase a particular product.

ADVERTISING

Advertising, particularly in trade journals is a major weapon in the promotional armoury of many business travel and tourism organizations. As business travel and tourism is a high-spending activity, advertising tends to be glossy and colourful. To be successful, however, advertising has to:

- Be undertaken frequently to remind customers of brand names
- Be integrated with other promotional techniques.

The Internet

Just as in leisure travel, the Internet is beginning to play a growing role in business travel and tourism, both in terms of finding information and making reservations.

A readers' poll published in *Conference and Incentive Travel* in February 2000 found that:

- While 35 per cent of readers preferred to book travel and accommodation via the Internet, 60 per cent still preferred other means
- Only 15 per cent of readers felt that conference venue web sites offered the optimum of information for conference organizers.

It is clear, therefore, that more work needs to be done on developing this medium in the business travel and tourism field.

Trade Journals

Business travel and tourism is still a relatively small industry but it is a world in which buyers are always looking for information on new products or services. The trade journals therefore play a very important role in promoting products and allowing communication between buyers, suppliers and intermediaries. There are a large number of journals, most of which focus either on a sector (*e.g.* exhibitions) a region (*e.g.* the USA) or a particular angle (*e.g.* consumer advice for the business traveller). Furthermore, new journals are being launched all the time, around the world.

For example, a new journal, *CEI Asia Pacific*, was launched in September 2000 covering conferences, exhibitions and incentives. Focusing on this region where business tourism is a major phenomena this journal promised its readers, that it would 'publish industry news features, comments, and opinion from corporate buyers together with a regular series of interviews and corporate case studies. CEI Asia Pacific will be produced to the highest editorial standard' (*Conference and Incentive Travel*, June 2000).

Personal Selling

In an industry based so much on interpersonal skills and trust, it is not surprising that personal selling plays a major role in promotion in business travel and tourism. The main areas for personal selling are as follows:

- Venues selling their services to buyers
- Airlines and hotels selling to buyers and intermediaries.
- Incentive travel agencies and professional conference organisers selling their services to potential clients.

Telephone and face-to-face negotiation plays a vital role in marketing in this industry.

FAMILIARIZATION OR EDUCATIONAL VISITS

Decisions about the destination and venue of conferences, exhibitions, product launches and incentive travel packages involve purchases where the level of expenditure can run into millions of pounds. As one would expect, therefore, very few buyers make their decisions based on brochures, videos or advertisements. They must see the place and venue for themselves, check it out, ask questions and meet the people they will be working with before they decide to contract a particular venue or other service. The familiarization or educational visit, which is the name given to this process, is therefore very important in business travel and tourism.

The Market

It is now time briefly to turn our attention from the marketing mix to the market itself. Here we will simply consider the issues which are of greatest interest to marketers, namely, motivators, determinants and segmentation.

Motivators and Determinants

We discussed the motivators and focused on the different motivators between the customer (usually the employer) and the consumer (usually the business traveller). We also noted that motivators varied between different types of business tourism such as conferences, exhibitions and incentive travel.

It is important that marketing people should understand motivators so that they can design products and promote them effectively.

However, we also have to recognize that while motivators are important, determinants are the factors that influence what customers will actually be able to do in reality. These determinants can be either internal or external, both relating to the customer and/or the consumer.

Determinants affect whether any trip will be made at all and, if so, what kind of trip will be taken. To illustrate what we mean by determinants in concrete terms, let us imagine an employee who wishes to attend a professional conference in another country. First, he or she will have to persuade their employer that attendance will be worth the cost in terms of time and money. If the employer agrees the employee may not be able to attend if, for example:

- By the time the decision is made all flights and/or hotels and/or conference places are fully booked
- The financial situation of the travellers' organization deteriorates and a decision is taken to cut back on travel expenditure.

Even if this trip goes ahead, its characteristics will be determined by a wide variety of factors, including perhaps:

- What level of expenses the company has given our traveller for the trip
- The weather in the destination at the time of the conference

- Whether or not our traveller already knows some of the other delegates
- The quality of accommodation in which the delegate is staying
- The cost of living in the destination.

For individual business trips the main determinants of what kind of business trip will be taken is often where the company has business interests. Past experience and perceptions can also be a major determinant of behaviour. Business tourists travelling to new destinations may well like the security of using airlines and hotels with which they are already familiar and satisfied. Those readers wanting to read more about motivators and determinants, in general, might find *Consumer Behaviour in Tourism* by Swarbrooke and Horner, useful.

Market Segmentation

Until recently, marketers tended to view markets as single homogeneous entities. However, one must realize that every population or market is subdivided into segments – subgroups with shared buying characteristics.

It is important to recognize that segmentation is a very important technique for marketers today. The business travel and tourism market could be divided into a number of segments. Each of these segments should, according to marketing theory, require a different marketing mix.

Clearly some of these criteria can change, such as purpose of travel, while others will normally stay the same for each individual, for instance, sex.

DESTINATION MARKETING

The destination marketing is a difficult activity because:

1 Destinations exist at different geographical levels from individual towns to countries or even continents.
2 Tourist perceptions of destinations rarely match the official boundaries of the agencies set up to market destinations.
3 No direct charge is usually made to visit a destination unless there is a visa charge or tourist tax. Destination marketers therefore cannot directly use price as a demand management tool.
4 Most destination marketing is a public sector activity but most of the product is in the ownership of the private sector. Destination marketing, therefore, often focuses on promotion because it cannot control product or price.

THE RISE OF PARTNERSHIP MARKETING

There has been a growing recognition that the public sector cannot do everything itself and there needs to be partnership between key players in destinations. These partnerships can be of several types, notably:

- All organisations, both public and private, within a given geographical area

- Between sectors, for example, airlines and hotels or venues and hotels
- Within sectors, for example, convention centres.

The first type of partnership is now popular at local level through the rise of visitor and convention bureaux.

Visitor and Convention Bureaux

These organizations tend to be jointly funded by the public sector via a grant, and the private sector via membership fees and contributions to marketing campaigns. They usually have a number of roles, including brochure production, advertising, attending trade fairs, direct mail campaigns, organizing familiarization visits, preparing tenders for major events, public relations, and so on.

National Tourism Organizations

National tourism boards, recognizing the importance of business tourism are now becoming increasingly involved in promoting their respective countries as business tourism destinations.

Co-operation between Destinations

Some destinations are realizing that, if they can find partner destinations with complementary attractions, then co-operation can be better than competition. Recently, for example, a co-operative promotional campaign was mounted aimed at the incentive travel market by the Singapore Tourism Board and the Indonesian Department of Culture and Tourism, under the title, 'Start with a dry martini, then wet your pants' (white water rafting!)

The importance of destination image: Destination image is important in marketing business travel and tourism, in several ways:

1. Conference and exhibition organizers and incentive travel agencies choose destinations for their events, partly based on their perceptions of these destinations.
2. Conference delegates often choose to attend conferences partly based on the perceived attractions or otherwise of the place.
3. Partners choose to accompany business travellers visiting a destination only if they perceive it to be an attractive place.

The attraction of a destination is a function of a combination of factors, including climate, scenery or townscape, safety and security, the attitude of local people towards tourists, the quality of the infrastructure, price levels, and so on. But destination image is a subjective and abstract concept, where perceptions are more important that reality.

In recent years a number of destinations have succeeded in developing positive destination images, realistic or not. For example it is widely believed that:

- New York is safer than it once was
- Dublin is a lively, sociable, friendly city
- Singapore is an efficient, good value, high-quality service destination.

The above images bring real benefits for these destinations in terms of business travel and tourism.

KEY ISSUES IN THE DIFFERENT TYPES AND SECTORS OF BUSINESS TRAVEL AND TOURISM

Each type of business tourism and sector of the business travel industry has its own distinct characteristics and pattern of marketing activity. The key issues in marketing within the different sectors of the business travel and tourism industry. This is clearly a simplification of a very complex picture.

It is now time for us to move on to look at several key topical issues in business travel and tourism.

Topical Issues

Marketing in business travel and tourism, as in other industries, is going through a period of great change. Some of the most important issues and changes are briefly discussed in this section.

Quality and customer satisfaction: Everyone today believes in the importance of quality and customer satisfaction, even if they cannot actually define what it means. In business travel and tourism we need first to establish who the customer is, for, as we saw earlier in the book, there are customers and consumers in our industry.

Customers are generally the organizations which employ business travellers or organize business tourism events, while consumers are those who actually attend the events and use the services of the industry. And, of course, they both want different things. Quality and satisfaction to the customer will mean low price, while for the consumer it will mean comfort and status, as well as reliability which is of interest to both of them.

As frequent travellers, business tourists tend to be demanding, knowledgeable and able to compare the products of competing organizations.

We need to make the following points about the concept of quality and satisfaction in business travel and tourism:

1 The main criterion for judging quality and satisfaction is 'fitness for purpose', products and services which do what they are supposed to do. In other words quality means flights that operate on time and venues that enable conferences to take place efficiently. Reliability, again is the crucial issue here.

2 The concept of 'critical incidents' is important because there are many occasions in business travel and tourism when the overall experience hinges on a single incident, such as a delayed flight, a problem

with the audiovisual equipment at a venue or overbooking at a hotel. A customer may well be very satisfied if the organization turns the critical incident from a negative to a positive through its actions.

3 Quality has to be related to the price the customer or consumer is willing or able to afford. For example, a leisure traveller who has bought a £250 last-minute economy discount ticket from Paris to Singapore cannot expect to enjoy the same benefits as a

First Class passenger who has paid £3000 for the same journey. On the other hand, whatever price has been paid customers and consumers have a right to expect certain basic benefits such as safety. Organizations which serve business travellers are always trying to ensure that the quality they offer matches, or preferably exceeds, the expectations of their clients. Customer questionnaires are a crucial element of such activities. Exhibit 10.1 gives an example of one such questionnaire for the Hilton Hotel at Amsterdam Schipol Airport in the Netherlands. *Competition:* There is growing competition in most sectors of business travel and tourism. The ways in which competition is increasing. Let us now look at some of the ways in which the business travel and tourism industry has sought to respond to this more competitive situation.

Relationship Marketing and Brand Loyalty

It has often been said that it is easier to keep an existing customer than find a new one. Therefore, business tourism suppliers, in common with other industries, have started to focus on relationship marketing and brand loyalty. Airlines have led this trend and a case study of airline frequent flyer programmes is to be found in Part Five. However, hotels have also developed similar brand loyalty schemes.

However, some of these schemes can seem self-defeating because:

- Consumers often realize that they must accumulate many points to receive even modest benefits, and so they lose interest
- Consumers often join more than one scheme and use the one which offers the most benefits
- Employers - the customers - often object to schemes which benefit their employees rather than themselves.

Nevertheless brand loyalty schemes are a widely accepted aspect of modern marketing. However, they are, as yet, little used by destinations or many venues. This may be because they only work if the consumer can use them for visits to many different places. Nevertheless, for 'footloose' events, brand loyalty rewards could be a useful marketing tool.

Strategic Alliances

In an industry where capital costs are often great and barriers to entry generally high, takeovers and mergers can sometimes be impractical. In these cases, we have seen a growth in strategic alliances, often linked to brand loyalty programmes. Strategic alliances come in different forms, including:

- Alliances within sectors such as between airlines
- Alliances within geographical areas such as consortia of visitor attractions on hotels
- Alliances between sectors such as airlines and hotels.

Strategic alliances allow benefits for both organizations and consumers.

The former gain economies of scale and the ability to offer a wider range of products to their customers while consumers enjoy access to the broader range of products and a more 'seamless' transition from one service to another.

The airline sector has spearheaded this trend. The 'Qualiflyer' group for example includes:

- twenty-five airlines, including Sabena, Swissair, TAP Air Portugal, Austrian Airlines, All Nippon Airlines, Cathay Pacific, Qantas and US Airways - travellers gain points towards a 'consumer brand loyalty programme' by using the services of any of these airlines
- Nineteen hotel groups
- Five car hire companies
- Two credit card companies
- Duty-free shops at airports
- A telephone company.

In all, there are five major airline alliances, namely, Air France/Delta, One World, Qualiflyer, Wings and the Star Alliance, although these are changing all the time. These airline alliances are often criticized on the following grounds:

1. They lead to code-sharing where, to reduce costs, airline A may stop flying a route that is also flown by airline B. The flight will be operated under the separate codes of both airlines but will only be flown by airline As aircraft and crews. If airline A is lower in quality standards than airline B this could lead to dissatisfied customers who may feel cheated.
2. These mega-alliances make life difficult for small independent airlines, and could be seen as being anti-competitive. Ultimately this could lead to a reduction in choice for consumers as smaller airlines are squeezed out of the market.

Again, as yet, neither venues nor destinations have really begun to make use of strategic alliances, effectively. Furthermore, they are less used in the field of 'intermediaries' where 'barriers to entry' are fewer and acquisitions are a feasible option.

TOURISM MARKETING INFORMATION SYSTEM

The major aim of Tour MIS is an optimal information supply and decision support for the tourism industry. The first step is to provide aniline tourism survey data, as well as evaluation programmes to transform data into precious management information. Tour-MIS predominantly comprises:

1. A database containing tourism market research data (declarative knowledge),
2. Various programme modules (method-base, procedural knowledge) converting acknowledged methods/models into simple surfaces, and
3. Various administrative programmes which assist the maintenance of the data- base and track and control the information search behaviour of users.

The internet supports the transport and presentation of animated and unanimated pictures, sound and video recordings and text and numerical data and is expandable. ,A high- performance SQL-database and a functionally designed user interface for Tour MIS based on hypertext and Perl permits the development of interactive applications. The programme modules contained in the method-base are developed according to the specific requirements of tourism managers. The internet offers a number of advantages against the old PC-solution. Since changes in the database have immediate worldwide effect the speed of information transmission can be reduced to the availability of the information source.

For example, Tour MIS makes the monthly projections of Statistics Austria available within only a few seconds to all regional managers of the Austrian National Tourist Office regardless of whether they are located in New York, Sydney, Tokyo or Madrid. Anybody provided with access to the internet and entitled to use Tour MIS may access data and information, make calculations or simulations send or receive data – without tiresome postal procedures, danger of loss, delays and costs. All these advantages have led to a significan expansion in the number of users.

Conditions for the use of the System

In the beginning Tour MIS was provided with strict access control and used to be only accessible to certain users. In this respect the application did differ from traditional internet offers. However, the present concept is also not an Intranet. Unlike the Intranet which supports internal information management systems Tour MIS is not owned by a certain organization but is open to all authorized tourism organizations, societies, tourism consult- ants, companies, tourism training centres, pressure groups, etc. in Austria and abroad. By covering the maintenance costs, a consortium of 12 of the most important initiators of market research projects in Austria (Austrian National Tourist Office, nine provincial tour- ism organizations, the two special interest associations for Hotel Trade and Restaurant

Trade of the Federal Chamber of Commerce, Federal Ministry for Economic Affairs and Labour Tourism and Recreational Commerce Section)

guarantee the continuous updating of the comprehensive database. Since 2000 this initiative has provided the Austrian tourism industry with free access to overall data and functions (with some exceptions) of Tour MIS. The necessary hardware resources are situated at the Institute for Tourism and Leisure Studies at the University of Economics and Business Administration in Vienna where a major part of the necessary maintenance work is carried out.

The Tour MIS Database

In the beginning Tour MIS contained data that was strongly influenced by the internal interests of its commissioner, the Austrian National Tourist Office. In this respect international tourism statistical data, empirical tourism studies and economic indicators for the most important markets of origin for the Austrian tourism industry have been collected in Tour MIS. The PC-version, developed in the early nineties, contained more than 10,000 time series. The periodicity of information was generally based on annual data, however the most significant time series have also been recorded for periods of less than a year.

Over the years the database has continually expanded. Due to the increasing importance of overseas markets further information has been required. Unequal needs of provincial tour- ism organizations led to additional statistics regarding the federal provinces and Vienna, being city and federal province at the same time, acquired an exceptional position. Furthermore data on the Austrian and international city tourism has been added. This information was collected at the branch offices of the Austrian National Tourist Office, transmitted by fax and data was entered manually into the marketing information system in order to be available to users. Later based on international cooperation (European Cities' Tourism, European Travel Commission) the first online maintenance agreements with local tourism organizations were initiated. The most important available data sources of Tour MIS are indicated in. Besides the basic information search functions the method-base has also been continually upgraded. In this respect the system more and more meets the requirements of an efficient decision support tool. In the next paragraphs the most important data sources and the facilities for analysis and reporting are discussed.

National Tourism Statistics Austria

One of the first data sources which was installed in Tour MIS was the official tourism statistics in Austria. Data generated from the registration with accommodation suppliers is one of the fundamental supports of the official inbound tourism statistics in Austria. Accommodation statistics are divided into two different kinds of survey: the accommodation for inbound travel and the accommodation capacity. The data on arrivals and over nights are surveyed for 50 generating countries related to 13 different accommodation types and 1,600 municipalities (= report communities) on a monthly basis.

Thus the official travel survey offers 25 million data points per annum which can be transformed into precious information for tourism managers. From the data material important information on tourism development, trends in markets of origin and accommodation types, evaluation of the competing situation can be derived. For example, for each of the 1,600 municipalities the database allows the user to regularly monitor the development of the average duration of stay, the seasonality, market shares, guest-mix structure, and, in connection with the capacity statistics, the occupancy rate. Tour MIS presently offers official tourism statistics only at the provincial basis which nevertheless requires maintenance work of 11,700 data sets per month. The necessary data transfer from the host system of Statistic Austria (ISIS) to Tour MIS takes place automatically each time after the arrival of new data segments and in accordance with various maintenance routines.

The information supply of Tour MIS users takes place by means of predominate tables and reports created for the user in real time operations. The content and design of tables or reports plays an important role in the user's perception of the system's usefulness and usability. Only if the information supply meets the users' needs will the system achieve its aim of providing a high-performance usage of market data and improve the information supply in tourism management.

CHARACTERISTICS OF TOURISM INFORMATION SYSTEMS

There are three characteristics that all effective tourism information systems have:

Each channel in the system has its own function. Travellers use different channels to get different kinds of information. An example is deciding where to go on vacation. A person may consult a friend or family member for that decision, but in deciding what to do when he/she gets there, the person may talk with a repeat visitor or employee at the destination site.

All the information channels used in the system relate to each other. A tourism information system is like a novel because it has many different parts tied together by the theme. Even though a system's channels serve different functions in providing information, they are all tied together by the projected message.

All channels used in the system are interdependent. A tourism information system functions like a puzzle. The different pieces of the system, the channels, are used to communicate with tourists. If any of the puzzle pieces are missing, the puzzle's picture is incomplete. If one or more of the channels used is not dispersing information effectively, or if the information dispersed does not relate to the rest of the system, then the system will not effectively communicate its whole message. If one or more of these characteristics is missing from a tourism information system, then its message will be inconsistent and ineffective.

WHAT ARE THE PARTS OF A TOURISM INFORMATION SYSTEM?

We have covered the fact that a tourism information system is made up of different related and interdependent information channels. But what are these channels?

Examples of these channels include:

- State promotional messages,
- Regional tourist associations,
- Travel information centres,
- Individual business promotion,
- Employee knowledge,
- Brochures, signs,
- The community's visual image (appearance):
- Storefronts, billboards, etc.
- Its hospitality
- Community awareness and pride,
- Other travellers,
- Repeat visitors.

While this list is not exhaustive, it gives you some idea of what can be used as channels. The only limitation is your imagination in how you present your message.

WHY MANAGE YOUR TOURIST INFORMATION SYSTEM?

There are three major reasons why it is necessary to manage information systems. The first reason is that travellers need organized information so that it becomes easier to acquire information and make decisions. They do not want to, nor have time to, sort through information that is confusing and disorganized. The easier it is to get information, the more comfortable travellers feel and the more enjoyable the trip will be for them. Travellers who are satisfied with their trip will be more likely to return and to tell others about the good time they had. By managing your information system, you can make it easy for travellers to get the information they want.

The second reason to manage tourism information systems is to present your theme and identify it to travellers in a clear, concise, and consistent manner. By managing your information system, you have some control over what information travellers receive and through what channels. This way you can make sure that all the delivered information relates to your theme, and you are better able to develop continuity and coherence throughout your system.

The third reason why it is important to manage tourism information systems is that they play an important role in community development. This is especially important in tourism because travellers see the community as a whole, rather than as individual parts. People base their image of a community on the information received from the community's information system. A community's image is important because tourists often become future investors and residents in communities that they find attractive. You want to be able to manage your information system so that the image you want is projected.

HOW CAN YOU MANAGE YOUR TOURISM INFORMATION SYSTEM

There are a variety of tools that you can use to manage your tourism information system. Here we want to deal with four that experts believe are the most effective. These tools are most effective when used together, but they can be used individually.

1. Establish a committee or organization to manage your tourism information system. It should control what information is used and how it is distributed throughout the system. It should also be responsible for evaluating the system's effectiveness.
2. Establish a set of standards, or guidelines, for deciding what, how, and through what channels information will be presented. This will help ensure that information used will accurately reflect your community's identity and theme and that it reaches the right target market.
3. Develop community cooperation in the system. Explain the benefits of being involved in the system to local business person and to community residents, and develop community awareness and pride.
4. Consider Zoning-A community's appearance plays a significant role in its tourism information system. A tourist's image of a community is significantly influenced by its appearance. Zoning can be used to make sure that a community's appearance will have a positive influence on it image. Zoning provides the following advantages. It gives you control over "street level environment," meaning such things as side walks, shopping malls and centres, town squares, and the avenues of access and travel to and through each. Zoning gives the control needed to maintain adequate amounts of space for people to move freely in, around, and through these areas.

Zoning can also be used to manage the outward appearance of you "street level environment." All structures constructed, such as storefronts, signs, etc., can be required to reflect your community's identity and theme.. Zoning also allows you to save older, historical buildings while allowing the development of surrounding property. There are two types of zoning: prestated design features, and transfer of rights.

Prestated design features can be used as incentive zoning or as mandated design features.

With incentive zoning, developers are granted building privileges for including a prestated design feature(s) in the building design. Mandated design features require developers to include a certain prestated design feature in the building. Transfer of rights is used to transfer the rights to development of a particular piece of property from one developer to another.

When using zoning, the zoning commission, or board, must be easily accessible and flexible. Then, when changes in zoning regulations are needed, they can be made.

WHAT WILL A TOURIST INFORMATION SYSTEM DO FOR YOU?

A well organized tourism information system will benefit local businesses, the community, and local residents as well as travellers. It helps area residents and travellers locate recreation activities, sites, and service outlets.

It helps build community pride and establish long term ties with satisfied visitors. It will also avoid confusion and other problems that can result from poorly oriented, directed, and managed travellers, such as traffic problems.

This bulletin was written to help you understand what a tourism information system is, why it needs to be managed, and to give you some ideas on how to manage it. But managing one is not easy, and it does not happen over night. It takes a lot of long range planning, and foresight, as well as some expertise and being able to stick-to-it to overcome any obstacles encountered.

SUSTAINABLE TOURISM: A LOCAL AUTHORITY PERSPECTIVE

1. A primary challenge of local governance, both today and in decades ahead, is to steerincreasingly external, global forces on local development so that development achieves the sharedvision of the local population. In cities, towns and villages throughout the world, the primary responsibility for this steering process rests with the institution of local government and its diverselocal authorities.
2. As providers of social services, builders of economic infrastructure, regulators of economicactivity, and managers of the natural environment, local authorities have many direct instruments attheir disposal to influence development. Yet in addition to their direct roles in the development process, perhaps the most important role that local authorities can play in a global economy is thatof facilitator among the diverse interests seeking to influence the direction of local development. Only with such a facilitator can a community of diverse interests define a shared vision and actconsistent with this vision.
3. The role of local authorities as facilitators in the development process is reinforced through municipal international cooperation (MIC). With globalisation, the governance challenges facinglocal authorities in different parts of the world have increased in their similarities, transcending thenational political and economic systems upon which different communities rely. These shared challenges of governance have instigated thousands of local authorities to establish

municipalinter national cooperation projects and to join international local government organisations (LGOs)to advocate for local self-governance and control over the development process.

4. Even prior to the UN Conference on Environment and Development, but particularly sincethe adoption of Agenda 21, many local authorities and their LGOs have focused on the uniquechallenges of governance for sustainable development. At the local level, sustainable developmentis achieved by steering local development activities to simultaneously achieve three objectives:
   - Increased local social welfare;
   - Greater, and more equitably distributed, local economic wealth; and
   - Enhanced integrity of local ecosystems.
5. Thousands of local authorities, in partnership with their communities and supported by MIC activities, have instigated Local Agenda 21 processes to create a shared vision for local development that is consistent with the sustainable development concept. In response to thesevisions, local authorities have been adapting their practices and activities to steer local developmentalong the sustainable development path. Local Agenda 21 processes, in conjunction with decentralisation policies originating at the national level, are transforming local governance and reorienting the process of local development in communities throughout the world.
6. Tourism is one of the many external forces influencing the direction and options for localdevelopment. The question of whether tourism can be sustainable—that is, whether it can contribute to local sustainable development—is rightfully addressed in the context of the Local Agenda process.
7. A truly legitimate and practical discussion on sustainable tourism must take place in and with the communities that are being influenced by tourist industry development. It must create accountability of the tourism industry to locally-defined development visions. This paper provides an general call for the tourism industry, through both its local and transnational agents, to join and support the Local Agenda 21 processes in communities where tourism is a fundamental development force.
8. The true proof of "sustainable tourism" will be the sustainable development of local communities that serve as tourist destinations. It is time for the sustainable tourism debate to focuson this challenge. Local authorities worldwide welcome the leadership of the UN Commission on Sustainable Development, and the interest of the tourism industry, to reduce tourism's negative impacts and to increase

the positive contribution of tourism business and consumption activity to local sustainable development.

DEVELOPING AN EFFECTIVE TOURISM MARKETING PROGRAMME

Tourism has started to receive increased attention as an important sector of New Mexico's economy, and has provided a much needed boost to New Mexico's economy. Travellers generated $1.94 billion in revenue for New Mexico in 1987. There were 45,700 jobs generated through tourism within the state and the state collected $93.3 million in tax revenues from tourism expenditures. Capitalizing on this expanding tourism interest in New Mexico will require each community or region to have a detailed plan for the development, marketing and evaluation of its tourist market.

This pamphlet will help develop marketing and evaluation plans for tourism by New Mexico communities and regions. However, with minor modifications, the process can be used for any organization or business. A well-developed marketing plan is necessary to have an effective marketing programme, regardless of the type or size of the business or organization.

Step-by-step instructions describe how to inventory attractions, assess current marketing efforts, find existing market research, determine target markets, determine tourist motivators, develop promotional goals, determine campaign themes, find an advertising media, develop public relations and gather the correct data for an evaluation. It is important to read all the material presented here, then complete the work sheets as thoroughly as possible. Use the information summarized in the work sheets to direct future marketing and evaluation efforts.

The effectiveness of a marketing plan is determined by the evaluation process, which helps make future strategies more effective.

INVENTORY OF ATTRACTIONS AND ACCOMMODATIONS

The first step in developing effective marketing plans is to inventory the attractions a community has to offer tourists. A community must know what it has to offer or sell before plans can be laid for marketing the product. These can include natural, manmade, historical, cultural or ethnic, festivals, special events and recreational attractions. Using Work sheet as a guide, inventory all attractions to complete the first step of developing a market plan.

ASSESSING CURRENT MARKETING EFFORTS

Listing current advertising efforts for all attractions is necessary to assess the present promotional campaign's successfulness, and to develop new campaigns. With the assistance of Work sheet, write down all current advertising and public relation activities, and the objectives to be accomplished with each.

MARKET RESEARCH

Market research is an important part of developing a market plan. Several important pieces of information are needed to develop a market plan. These include:

1. An inventory of tourist attractions in the area, region, or destination
2. Market trends
3. Tourist motivations
4. Tourist profiles, including expenditures

It helps to review other successful marketing plans, remembering that a marketing plan should meet the individual needs of the area, region or destination for which it was developed. Learning from previous mistakes is a key to developing better programmes.

There are two types of research data that can provide this information. The first is primary research gathered through phone calls, surveys, or other interviewing techniques. Secondary data has been compiled by outside organizations (*e.g.*, U.S. Census, New Mexico Tourism and Travel Division). Be careful when using secondary data; confirm the reliability of the source.

Target Market

Trying to appeal to everyone is a common mistake made in marketing. Not everyone looks for the same thing in a destination, and every destination cannot be all things to all people. Target marketing, focusing on a particular segment or segments of the market, allows for a more effective marketing plan. Market research will define the market segments, which will find those tourists most interested in what a community has to offer. Data on past visitors can indicate the type of tourist or the geographic region on which to focus. A target market can be a geographic region, a type of tourist, a combination of the two or any grouping that makes sense.

One target market could be those people living in Lubbock, Texas (geographic region), while another could be those people in Lubbock with an income above $50,000 a year (geographic region and demographic characteristic). Work sheet can help determine target markets. Begin collecting any data that is missing.

Determine Tourist Motivators

Tourist motivators should be studied once a target market has been defined. Discovering where and why tourists travel is important when focusing advertising. Enticing the tourist to chose a historical destination because of its mystique, or choosing a full-service resort where every need can be catered to requires different motivational factors. Work sheet includes target market questions that can help determine a target market and related motivations.

DEVELOPING PROMOTIONAL GOALS

Establishing goals provides the basis to determine what a community wants its marketing and promotion programme to accomplish. Goals should be well thought out and be measurable, and can also serve as controls. Writing down goals provides directional guidelines. It can be difficult to get feedback on promotional goals, but with specific goals set, an evaluation and feedback plan can be implemented. This will gather the necessary data for the evaluation process, which can determine the successfulness of a community's plans and programme. Note: Providing feedback on goals and accomplishments is the purpose of an evaluation.

Several examples of promotional goals are as follows: To create and measure the awareness of a particular tourism attraction in a specific market.

Example: Awareness in Et Paso, Texas of the Deming Duck Races

What are the Deming Duck Races? Where are they held? To communicate a specific tourism appeal in promotion to a specific market, then determine how many people can recall it.

Example: Promoting a Ruidoso golf course as a specific appeal to a Roswell market Conduct a random survey in the Roswell market to determine the effectiveness of the golf course advertising.

To communicate a basic campaign theme to a specific market, then determine how many people can restate the premise without aided recall.

Example: More to Explore, New Mexico USA Is this campaign theme easily recalled by readers of the New Mexico Vacation Guide? Was it recalled without any hints?

To communicate a particular image or try to create a particular attitude about a tourism site, then determine if the message registered in the potential prospect's mind creates the correct image.

Example: Hang Your Hat in Clayton What image does this create for people living in Amarillo, Texas? To measure the effectiveness of advertising materials by tracking inquiry coupon responses.

Example: Old West Country advertisement placed in New Mexico Vacation Guide How many inquiries were received? How many of the people inquiring actually visited Old West Country? Use Work sheet to help develop promotional goals.

6

Tourism Marketing Strategy

STRATEGIES IN MARKETING

Marketing strategy is a powerful process that gives an organization a competitive advantage in the marketplace. While just defining a marketing strategy will not automatically create a competitive advantage, it will allow the organization to concentrate its resources on the greatest opportunities to increase sales and achieve a sustainable competitive advantage. The word strategy comes from the Greek word strategies meaning general. Strategy is what generals use to win battles. Thus properly understood, marketing strategy is a high-level exercise involving the "generals" of the organization in determining how to build on the firm's strengths while taking advantage of competitors' weaknesses. Marketing strategy is most effective when it is a vital component of corporate strategy, defining how the organization will engage customers, prospects and the competition in the market arena for consistent success.

A marketing strategy also serves as the foundation of a marketing plan. A marketing plan contains a set of specific actions required to successfully implement a specific marketing strategy. For example: "Use a low cost product to attract consumers. Once our organization, via our low cost product, has established a relationship with consumers, our organization will sell additional, higher-margin products and services that enhance the consumer's interaction with the low-cost product or service."

A strategy is different from a tactic. While it is possible to write a tactical marketing plan without a sound, well-considered strategy, it is not recommended. Without a sound marketing strategy, a marketing plan has no foundation.

Marketing strategies serve as the fundamental underpinning of marketing plans designed to reach marketing objectives. It is important that these objectives have measurable results. A good marketing strategy should integrate an organization's marketing goals, policies, and action sequences into a cohesive whole.

The objective of a marketing strategy is to provide a foundation from which a tactical plan is developed.

This allows the organization to carry out its mission effectively and efficiently. Marketing strategies are partially derived from broader corporate strategies, corporate missions, and corporate goals. They should flow from the firm's mission statement. They are also influenced by a range of microenvironmental factors. Marketing strategies are dynamic and interactive. They are partially planned and partially unplanned.

Commercial Planning

In the modern world of business, it is useless to be a creative original thinker unless you can also sell what you create. Management cannot be expected to recognize a good idea unless it is presented to them by a good salesman. The success of a new product depends not only on the idea behind the product, but also on the marketing of the new product before, during and after the product launch. Commercializing a product is commonly known as Commercial Planning. No concrete methods are currently available for New Product Launching. However, to launch a new product. This describes a set of activities and products, that are essential for launching a new product. New Product Launching is part of the New Product Development method.

Strategic Management

An organization's strategy must be appropriate for its resources, environmental circumstances, and core objectives. The process involves matching the company's internal resources and capabilities to the external business environment the organization faces.

Strategy formulation involves:

- Doing a situation analysis: Both internal and external; both micro-environmental and macro-environmental.
- Concurrent with this assessment, objectives are set. This involves crafting vision statements, mission statements, overall corporate objectives, strategic business unit objectives, and tactical objectives.
- These objectives should, in the light of the situation analysis, suggest a strategic plan. The plan provides the details of how to achieve these objectives.

This three-step strategy formulation process is sometimes referred to as determining where you are now, determining where you want to go, and then determining how to get there. These three questions are the essence of strategic planning. SWOT Analysis: I/O Economics for the external factors and RBV for the internal factors.

Strategy implementation involves:

- Allocation of sufficient resources

- Establishing a chain of command or some alternative structure
- Assigning responsibility of specific tasks or processes to specific individuals or groups
- It also involves managing the process. This includes monitoring results, comparing to benchmarks and best practices, evaluating the efficacy and efficiency of the process, controlling for variances, and making adjustments to the process as necessary.
- When implementing specific programmes, this involves acquiring the requisite resources, developing the process, training, process testing, documentation, and integration with legacy processes.

Strategy formulation and implementation is an on-going, never-ending, integrated process requiring continuous reassessment and reformation. Strategic management is dynamic. It involves a complex pattern of actions and reactions.

It is partially planned and partially unplanned. Strategy is both planned and emergent, dynamic, and interactive. Some people feel that there are critical points at which a strategy must take a new direction in order to be in step with a changing business environment. These critical points of change are called strategic inflection points.

Strategic management operates on several time scales. Short term strategies involve planning and managing for the present. Long term strategies involve preparing for and preempting the future. Marketing strategist Derek Abell has suggested that understanding this dual nature of strategic management is the least understood part of the process. He claims that balancing the temporal aspects of strategic planning requires the use of dual strategies simultaneously. Strategic Management is actually a solid foundation or a framework within which all the functioning managerial operations are bundled together. This is the highest level corporate activity that sets the terms and goals for a company that it should follow for prosperity.

Strategic management techniques can be viewed as bottom-up, top-down, or collaborative processes. In the bottom-up approach, employees submit proposals to their managers who, in turn, funnel the best ideas further up the organization. This is often accomplished by a capital budgeting process. Proposals are assessed using financial criteria such as return on investment or cost-benefit analysis.

The proposals that are approved form the substance of a new strategy, all of which is done without a grand strategic design or a strategic architect. The top-down approach is the most common by far. In it, the CEO, possibly with the assistance of a strategic planning team, decides on the overall direction the company should take. Some organizations are starting to experiment with collaborative strategic planning techniques that recognize the emergent nature of strategic decisions.

In most corporations there are several levels of strategy. Strategic management is the highest in the sense that it is the broadest, applying to all parts of the firm. It gives direction to corporate values, corporate culture, corporate goals, and corporate missions. Under this broad corporate strategy there are often functional or business unit strategies. Functional strategies include marketing strategies, new product development strategies, human resource strategies, financial strategies, legal strategies, and information technology management strategies.

The emphasis is on short and medium term plans and is limited to the domain of each department's functional responsibility. Each functional department attempts to do its part in meeting overall corporate objectives, and hence to some extent their strategies are derived from broader corporate strategies. Many companies feel that a functional organizational structure is not an efficient way to organize activities so they have re-engineered according to processes or strategic business units. A strategic business unit is a semi-autonomous unit within an organization. It is usually responsible for its own budgeting, new product decisions, hiring decisions, and price setting. An SBU is treated as an internal profit centre by corporate headquarters. Each SBU is responsible for developing its business strategies, strategies that must be in tune with broader corporate strategies.

The "lowest" level of strategy is operational strategy. It is very narrow in focus and deals with day-to-day operational activities such as scheduling criteria. It must operate within a budget but is not at liberty to adjust or create that budget. Operational level strategy was encouraged by Peter Drucker in his theory of management by objectives. Operational level strategies are informed by business level strategies which, in turn, are informed by corporate level strategies. Business strategy, which refers to the aggregated operational strategies of single business firm or that of an SBU in a diversified corporation refers to the way in which a firm competes in its chosen arenas.

Corporate strategy, then, refers to the overarching strategy of the diversified firm. Such corporate strategy answers the questions of "in which businesses should we compete?" and "how does being in one business add to the competitive advantage of another portfolio firm, as well as the competitive advantage of the corporation as a whole?" Since the turn of the millennium, there has been a tendency in some firms to revert to a simpler strategic structure. This is being driven by information technology.

It is felt that knowledge management systems should be used to share information and create common goals. Strategic divisions are thought to hamper this process. Most recently, this notion of strategy has been captured under the rubric of dynamic strategy, popularized by the strategic management textbook authored by Carpenter and Sanders. This work builds on that of Brown and Eisenhart as well as Christensen and portrays firm strategy, both business and corporate, as necessarily embracing ongoing strategic change, and the seamless integration of strategy formulation and implementation. Such change and implementation are usually built into the strategy through the staging and pacing facets. Management by Objectives is a process of agreeing upon objectives within an organization so that management and employees buy in to the objectives and understand what they are. Management By Objectives term was first popularized by Peter Drucker in 1954 in his book 'The Practice of Management'. It is all too easy for managers to fail to outline, and agree with their employees, what it is that everyone is trying to achieve. MBO substitutes for good intentions a process that requires rather precise written description of objectives and timelines for their monitoring and achievement. The process requires that the manager and the employee agree to what the employee will attempt to achieve in the period ahead, and that the employee accept and buy into the objectives.

For example, whatever else a manager and employee may discuss and agree in their regular discussions, let us suppose that they feel that it will be sensible to introduce a key performance indicator to show the development of sales revenue in a part of the firm. Then the manager and the employee need to discuss what is being planned, what the time-schedule is and what the indicator might or might not be. Thereafter the two of them should liaise to ensure that the objective is being attended to and will be delivered on time.

Organizations have scarce resources and so it is incumbent on the managers to consider the level of resourcing but also to consider whether the objectives that are jointly agreed within the firm are the right ones and represent the best allocation of effort. Also, reliable Management information systems are needed to establish relevant objectives and monitor their "reach ratio" in an objective way. MBO is often achieved using set targets. MBO introduced the SMART criteria: Objectives for MBO must be SMART. However, it has been reported in recent years that this style of management receives criticism in that it triggers employees' unethical behaviour of distorting the system or financial figures to achieve the targets set by their short-term, narrow bottom-line, and completely self-centered thinking.

THE ACCIDENTAL TOURIST

"For Newfoundland and Labrador, there's no such thing as an accidental tourist. It takes deliberate planning and determined effort to visit here, compelled by curiosity and the promise of what's unique and different in our people, culture, lifestyle, and dramatic scenery."

Barriers & Opportunities

Travel distance, access, and cost continue to be significant barriers for visitors, and a competitive disadvantage for the tourism industry in Newfoundland and Labrador.

A short peak season, capacity constraints during peak season, and increasing problems and delays at border crossings and in airports make increasing tourism visitors and revenue even more difficult. Competing with well-known tourism destinations that are well-funded and heavily advertised makes the job even tougher. Despite these barriers, there are opportunities open to Newfoundland and Labrador Tourism.

Baby bloomers are entering the empty nest stage of the family lifestyle. They have money, time, and keen interest to explore destinations that are off the beaten track, unusual and unspoiled places where few have gone before. Places like Newfoundland and Labrador. Ontario, our largest non-resident market, still remains largely underdeveloped for Newfoundland and Labrador tourism. Our greatest opportunity may lay in the launch of the new Tourism brand positioning and personality for Newfoundland and Labrador – and the creative strategy which we use to express it. Our coastline, rich history, unique culture, people, and natural environment remain our key strengths.

Marketing Objectives

The marketing objectives for Newfoundland and Labrador Tourism are to increase non-resident visitation and expenditures from our core markets, thereby increasing the tourism industry's annual contribution to the economy. The strategies and campaigns created to achieve these marketing objectives will also be guided by the desire of government and the Tourism Board to extend the tourism season beyond the core summer season in order to increase the economic benefit and the long-term viability of the industry.

Marketing Strategy

Newfoundland and Labrador Tourism will take a growth-strategy approach to marketing Newfoundland and Labrador as a tourism destination. Advertising will reach and persuade visitors to come to Newfoundland and Labrador, rather than to other destinations in their evoked set.

Public and media relations will reinforce the key messages, delivering a consistent and relevant brand image of the province, while sales and online initiatives will "close the loop."

The tourism product – in the form of attractions, experiences, and infrastructure – has a larger role to play in increasing length of stay, amount of money spent per trip, and overall tourism revenues.

To be successful in attracting customers from competitors, it's essential that we focus and concentrate our resources on the best opportunity – and create programmes and campaigns that are fully integrated.

Target Markets

Newfoundland and Labrador Tourism will focus and concentrate its resources against the target audiences and markets which offer the best opportunity and the highest return on investment. The target market is the non-resident touring and explorer market with concentration in Toronto, Ottawa, Calgary, Halifax and Montreal. Additional geographic markets include the Mid-Atlantic Region of the United States, California and the UK. Activity-based markets include Meetings, Convention and Incentive Travel market, the Hunting and Fishing market, the Hiking market and partnerships in Outdoor Adventure and Cruise markets.

Touring & Explorer Market

The touring and explorer group is a broad leisure market seeking sightseeing and soft-adventure experiences – from nature viewing to cultural experiences to hiking, birding, and whale-watching. Demographically, research reveals them to be singles and couples in the pre- and post-full nest stage of the family life cycle. Not surprisingly, they tend to be in two age groups: 25 to 34 and (skewed) 45+ years of age.

They also tend to be well-educated and have a higher than average proportion who are university-educated and have higher than average household incomes. Psychographically, they see themselves as increasingly sophisticated and experienced travellers, seeking more unusual places and experiences 'off the beaten track'. They are looking for an antidote to the stress and plastic composition of urban life and modern times. They're interested in discovering and experiencing the unspoiled natural environment. They are curious people, more interested in unexpected and intriguing experiences than repeat trips to conventional 'tourist' destinations: "been there, done that."

Marketing efforts in the United States will shift from the New England region to the Mid-Atlantic region for Newfoundland and Labrador. These travellers are seeking adventure and cultural experiences in new destinations. To maximize our efforts, Newfoundland and Labrador works cooperatively with the Atlantic Canada Tourism Partnership (ACTP).

ACTP is a nine-member, pan-Atlantic partnership comprising of the Atlantic Canada Opportunities Agency, the four Atlantic Canada Tourism Industry Associations, and the four provincial departments responsible for tourism. The international market is developmental for Newfoundland and Labrador, with low penetration but with long-term potential and high-spend per visitor. Newfoundland and Labrador Tourism will continue to pursue this market in partnership with its Atlantic Canada Partners (ACTP), with primary focus being on the United States and the United Kingdom.

Marketing activities include travel trade partnerships, familiarization tours, trade shows, media relations, and joint marketing with the Canadian Tourism Commission (CTC). The CTC and its industry partners have launched a new global advertising campaign in the UK, Germany, and France. ACTP is a partner in this UK programme to build more consumer awareness of the region.

MEETINGS, CONVENTIONS & INCENTIVE TRAVEL MARKET

Newfoundland and Labrador Tourism provides consultation, materials support, and mailing assistance to international, national, and regional conference organizers hosting conventions and meetings in Newfoundland and Labrador.

Incentive travel is a global management tool that uses an exceptional travel experience to motivate and/or recognize staff for increased levels of performance in support of organizational goals. Newfoundland and Labrador Tourism provides consultation, marketing, and product development support to industry suppliers in this lucrative market. Trade shows and marketplaces are available through partnership opportunities in North American markets.

Outdoor Adventure Market

Outdoor and nature activities such as hiking, birding and kayaking are core to our tourism experiences. These experiences appeal to outdoor enthusiasts and have a broad appeal to our touring and explorer market. Newfoundland and Labrador Tourism partners with the Newfoundland and Labrador Adventure Tourism Association at consumer and trade shows.

Hunting & Fishing Market

Newfoundland and Labrador offers hunters and sport fish enthusiasts some of the most amazing and rewarding outdoor recreation experiences in the world.

Newfoundland and Labrador Tourism partners with the Newfoundland and Labrador Outfitters Association (NLOA) to develop a fully-integrated marketing programme for the hunting and fishing market.

NEWFOUNDLAND AND LABRADOR BRAND

Brand Positioning

Most tourism brands are positioned on tangible products and features. Not surprisingly, most advertising presents an inventory of 'products' – places to go, sights to see, and things to do. But people don't buy 'products', they buy benefits. The real benefit lies several layers below the tangible tourism 'product' – in the emotion of the brand, and the feelings it evokes.

Newfoundland and Labrador will stand for 'creativity'. 'Creativity' is true to the brand of Newfoundland and Labrador. Creativity – natural, spontaneous, and uncomplicated – defines who we are, what we do, and the place around us. We express it in everything we do and say. It will differentiate the Newfoundland and Labrador brand and become our strongest unique selling point. 'Creativity', as the brand positioning, will be expressed and supported by three pillars:

People: The very real character of our people, their attitude, and way of life. Real, genuine people – warm, friendly, welcoming, uncomplicated, witty, humorous, and fun-loving. All the more powerfully felt because of the historical undercurrent of an unrelenting and unforgiving environment, mastered only through a fierce independence, steeped in self-reliance, quiet pride, and creative ingenuity.

Culture: Our history, heritage, music, art, language, architecture, folklore, traditions, values, and the vitality of colour and texture in everything we touch. It links our past with our present and expresses our spiritual and creative and intellectual qualities.

Natural Environment: This place of fierce beauty that lives by the sea. A rugged land with 29,000 kms of coastline, rich icons of whales and wildlife and icebergs, and a sensuous magic light that pours over the landscape and into the art and culture, and hearts of our people.

Brand Personality

A tourism brand personality is the feeling or image that people have about a place. Newfoundland and Labrador's brand personality will personify the creativity of our people and our culture and guide all marketing programmes. The Newfoundland and Labrador Tourism brand personality is the natural and spontaneous expression of who we are:

- Natural and uncomplicated.
- Warm and friendly.
- Genuine and authentic.
- Quietly and proudly independent.
- Spontaneous, rather than practiced or self-conscious.
- Witty and funny, with a natural spontaneity.
- Creative – not only in art and culture, but in our natural ingenuity and inventiveness.
- Comfortable in our own skin.

TOURING & EXPLORER MARKETING ACTIVITIES

Canada Market (Newspaper Campaign)

Online Campaign:A series of online advertising including leader boards, big-box, skyscraper, and banners on a variety of business/news-related websites such as The Globe and Mail, travel-specific websites including Air Canada, Expedia, Travelocity & Yahoo and interest/activity websites dedicated to activities such as birding, hiking, whales, and nature viewing.

Ontario Market (Television Campaign)

Ambient Campaign: Newfoundland and Labrador Tourism is finalizing its ambient marketing activities for the upcoming campaign. Ambient marketing is also called guerilla marketing or place-based marketing; it is marketing or advertising that occurs wherever customers happen to be, it is memorable because it is usually unexpected and unconventional.

Newspaper Campaign: A combination of full-page ads and 4-colour preprinted inserts in Ottawa Citizen.

Radio Campaign: Sponsorship of weather and air quality reports on selected radio stations in Toronto.

United States Market: Marketing efforts in the United States will shift from the New England region to the Mid-Atlantic region for Newfoundland and Labrador. These travellers are seeking adventure and cultural experiences in new destinations. To maximize our efforts, Newfoundland and Labrador works cooperatively with the Atlantic Canada Tourism Partnership (ACTP). ACTP is a nine-member, pan-Atlantic partnership comprising of the Atlantic Canada Opportunities Agency, the four Atlantic Canada Tourism Industry Associations, and the four provincial departments responsible for tourism. In 2009, Newfoundland and Labrador will continue to focus its efforts in the United States with an emphasis on the hiking and walking activity markets.

Magazine Campaign: Newfoundland and Labrador Tourism advertisements in Audubon, Harpers, National Geographic Traveller, and Smithsonian.

Online Campaign: A series of online advertising including leader boards, big-box, skyscrapers, and banners on websites such as Audubon, Smithsonian, Yahoo, Google, National Geo and activity websites such as Backpacking Light.

Overview: The international market is developmental for Newfoundland and Labrador, with low penetration but with long-term potential and high-spend per visitor. Newfoundland and Labrador Tourism will continue to pursue this market in partnership with its Atlantic Canada Tourism Partnership (ACTP), with primary focus being on the United Kingdom. Marketing activities include travel trade partnerships, familiarization tours, trade shows, media relations, and joint marketing agreements with Overseas Tour Operators/Wholesale and with the Canadian Tourism Commission (CTC).

INTERNATIONAL TRAVEL MEDIA PROGRAMME

The Travel Media Programme plays an integral role in maximizing consumer and trade awareness of Newfoundland and Labrador through unpaid media coverage in key overseas markets. Travel media includes freelance journalists, travel editors, broadcasters, producers, and travel trade media. Newfoundland and Labrador Tourism, along with our International counterparts, estimates editorial value from travel stories is four times that of paid advertising. In 2008-09, Newfoundland and Labrador received in excess of $45 million in media coverage and was featured in numerous international newspapers and magazines.

Help us keep media informed of what's new in Newfoundland and Labrador. We welcome your information on new travel products, events, personalities, folklore, and regional descriptions for unique travel story opportunities. The information you give us is used to pitch unique story ideas to media and to initiate and plan media tours to Newfoundland and Labrador for qualified journalists. You are also encouraged to submit articles on new tourism products and attractions for the CTC and various media outlets.

Co-host travel media at your business as they tour Newfoundland and Labrador to experience our tourism products first-hand. You may participate by sharing costs or providing in-kind contributions for these tours.

Media events, promotions, and sales calls in our key international markets are crucial elements in our travel media programme. Many of these activities are undertaken in partnership with the CTC and the Atlantic Canada Tourism Partnership (ACTP).

IN-PROVINCE RESIDENT MARKETING ACTIVITIES

Newfoundland and Labrador Tourism will continue a season extension programme for the in-province market. The programme covers all four seasons and provides opportunities for tourism operators to promote seasonal packages and create partnerships with other operators in their region.

The objectives for the programme are:

- To increase resident in-province travel and expenditures by motivating residents to travel at home.
- To increase resident knowledge of activities and attractions that occurs during fall, spring, and winter seasons as well as the summer period.
- To increase frequency of travel by motivating residents to take additional and more frequent short trips during the shoulder seasons as well as their annual summer vacation. Increase focus on the shoulder seasons.

MARKETING STRATEGY: TARGETING AND POSITIONING

No area of the marketing plan surpasses the selection of target markets in importance. If inappropriate markets are selected, marketing resources will be wasted. High-level expenditures on advertising or sales will not compensate for misdirected marketing effort. Target markets should be selected from a previously developed list of available segments. These include segments currently served by the organization and newly recognized markets. A target market is simply the segment at which the organization aims its marketing message.

Implicitly, the non-profitable customers should be given less attention. A target market generally has four characteristics. It should comprise groups of people or businesses that are well defined, identifiable and accessible; members should have common characteristics; they should have a networking system so that they can readily refer the organization to one another; and they should have common needs and similar reasons to purchase the product or service. The target market for Wine for Dudes (Generation X) fulfils these characteristics.

The family market is a popular target market for many tourism organizations. Family travel is growing as more parents are choosing to share travel experiences with their children. Club Med is a good example. Once known for its ability to cater to young singles, it now has more than 60 family-friendly holiday villages worldwide. Adventure tours for families are also on the increase.

A family-oriented, 13-day tour of South Africa offered by Explore is one example. Other tour operators are choosing to target the baby boomers. This sector, born between 1947 and 1966, generates the highest travel volume in North America, and is a very attractive market for the tourism and hospitality industry. Two other target markets growing in attractiveness for the tourism industry are the gay market and the senior market.

The gay tourism market offers enormous growth for the tourism industry. The British Tourist Authority's (BTA) campaign to attract gay and lesbian travellers from the United States is evidenced by the launch of the 2002 edition of its gay travel guide, as well as by new strategies for building a market niche that it says has already produced 'gratifying' results. The decision to begin targeting gay and lesbian travellers from the United States was made in 1997. The BTA has subsequently expanded the campaign, with the introduction of a larger travel guide and a dedicated gay and lesbian web site. Positioning

Once the market has been segmented and a target market identified, the next step in the marketing plan is positioning. Positioning is a communications strategy that is a natural follow-through from market segmentation and target marketing. Market positioning is ultimately how the consumer perceives the product or service in a given market, and is used to achieve a sustainable advantage over competitors. The Snapshot below on Four Seasons Hotels and Resorts is an excellent example of distinctive positioning leading to global competitive success. Best Western recently changed its positioning strategy in China in the hope of going beyond its traditional image as a purveyor of budget hotels. In 2006, the Phoenix-based chain scrapped plans to build a network of 100 three-star hotels in China by 2007. Instead, it plans to triple the number of its four- and five-star hotels in the country to 60 by 2009 (Fong, 2006).

Three steps are necessary to develop an effective position in the target market segment: product differentiation; prioritizing and selecting the competitive advantage; and communicating and delivering the position.

- *Step One: Product Differentiation:* Product differentiation, a phrase coined by Michael Porter, describes a technique that enables organizations to gain competitive advantage by offering a product that has features not offered by its competitors. Product differentiation can give companies a competitive edge and competitive advantages, which offer greater value to the consumer by providing benefits that justify a higher price. These advantages can be established through product attributes, features, services, level of quality, style and image, and price range. The key elements will shape how the consumer perceives the product. Physical attribute differentiation is achieved by enhancing or creating an image in the consumer's mind through tangible evidence. For example, Quality Inn offers a very simple physical appearance, communicating a clean, safe, cheap place to sleep. Fairmont Hotels and Resorts, on the other hand, combines an elaborate exterior with a luxurious interior to inspire feelings of comfort, relaxation, and prestige.

Service differentiation is an increasingly important way of gaining competitive advantage. The process by which customers evaluate a purchase, thereby determining satisfaction and likelihood of repurchase, is important to all marketers, but especially to services marketers because, unlike their manufacturing counterparts, they have fewer objective measures of quality by which to judge their production (Zeithaml *et al.*, 1988).

Several studies have examined the association between service quality and more specific behavioural intentions, and there is a positive and significant relationship between customers' perceptions of service quality and their willingness to recommend the company or destination (Zeithaml *et al.*, 1996). Likewise, research on service quality and retaining customers suggests that willingness to purchase again declines considerably once services are rated below good (Gale, 1992).

- *Step Two: Prioritizing and Selecting the Competitive Advantage:* Positioning is much like a ranking system, and an organization must decide where it wants to be in the hierarchy. Some companies have an image of high quality, service, and price; others, of being low budget. Neither image is better or worse. However, once the position is established, it is very difficult to change it in the consumer's mind. Therefore, companies must be very cautious in selecting the most effective combination of competitive advantages to promote.

It is important to promote not only one benefit to the target market, but to develop a unique selling proposition (USP), a feature of a product that is so unique that it distinguishes the product from all other products. The goal of a USP is for a company to establish itself as the number one provider of a specific attribute in the mind of the target market.

The attribute chosen should be desired and highly valued by target consumers. If the marketing mix elements build the brand and help it to connect with the customer year after year, the total personality of the brand, rather than the trivial product differences, will decide its ultimate position in the market. Although it is difficult in the tourism industry to find an effective USP in such a competitive and free market, it is essential to offer something new, as Freedom Paradise in Mexico has done. Package holidays tend to offer similar deals, with only minor differences. Therefore, it is important for a company to create a new good, service, or benefit that can be offered to consumers by that company alone. An example of a company offering a unique transportation service to tourists is TucTuc Ltd in the UK.

The company imports motorized rickshaws from Delhi to Brighton, England. Owner Dominic Ponniah says,'I guess they're so popular because they have a certain romance and because, running on natural gas, they're environmentally sound.'

- *Step Three: Communicating and Delivering the Position:* The final goal of an organization in the positioning process is to build and maintain a consistent positioning strategy. The overall aim of tourism providers is to attract attention from potential customers and to delight them with product offerings that cannot be beaten by competitors. Programmes and slogans that support the organizations position must be continuously developed and promoted in order to establish and maintain the organizations desired position in the consumer's mind. Quality, frequency, and exposure in the media will determine how successful the positioning strategy will be.

Tourism and hospitality providers try to differentiate their products by using branding, a method of establishing a distinctive identity for a product based on competitive differentiation from other products. Branded products are those whose name conjures up certain images - preferably positive ones - in consumers' minds. These images may relate to fashion, value, prestige, quality, or reliability.

Image is an important element of customer perception. If a hotel chain has an image of quality, staying at the hotel will provide benefits to business customers who want to project a successful image to their clients or colleagues.

Some brands are recognized for their reliability.

It is comforting for many travellers, for example, to know that a Best Western property will meet certain standards, and that selecting one will be a reliable choice, even if the traveller is unfamiliar with the specific property or region. Hotels, in particular, brand specific properties within their group to identify different categories of product.

TACTICS AND ACTION PLANS

Although no single strategy will be suitable for all organizations, marketing planning provides the opportunity to understand the operating environment and to choose options that will meet the organization's goals and objectives. Planning involves selecting and developing a series of strategies that effectively bring about the required results.

Among the types of strategies that can be considered are:

1. Making good investment decisions. Selecting the best, most effective use of financial resources is crucial. This will include reviewing the product's life cycle and doing a portfolio analysis;
2. Diversifying. While it is important to ensure that resources are allocated to those markets showing the best potential yields, the possibility of disruptions to markets must also be taken into account. Diversification can provide an important cushion;
3. Planning for the long term. Tourism marketing campaigns can have long lead times. The cumulative effect of promotions may take a while to produce measurable results. Building effectiveness over time is just as important as generating instant results;
4. Seizing new opportunities. Being aware of consumer trends, fads, fashions, and attitudinal shifts will also help an organization to identify opportunities. Being flexible enough to respond to market developments will give an organization a strong competitive edge;
5. Developing strategic partnerships. It is important to identify customers, suppliers, and competitors with whom it is possible to develop an enhanced working relationship. Strategic alliances offer the opportunity to increase profits for all participants.

APPLYING THE MARKETING MIX

Marketing strategies are designed as the vehicle to achieve marketing objectives. In turn, marketing tactics are tools to support strategies. Action programmes comprise a mix of marketing activities that are undertaken to influence and motivate buyers to choose targeted volumes of particular products.

The third column lists the chapters in this book where these topics are covered in detail. A marketing mix programme or marketing campaign expresses exactly what activities will take place in support of each identified product/market subgroup on a week-by-week basis. Roots Air implemented a major advertising campaign to win new customers, with a jazzy web site, large banners inside and outside major airports, and moody, black-and-white print ads in major daily newspapers. However, the airline did not forge a clear marketing message – one of the reasons it eventually failed.

RESOURCE REQUIREMENTS

The marketing plan needs to address the resources required to support the marketing strategies and meet the objectives. Such resources include personnel, equipment and space, budgets, intra-organizational support, research, consultation and training. A common error in writing a marketing plan is developing strategies that may well be highly workable, but for which there is insufficient support. Generally, the most costly and difficult resource needed to ensure the success of marketing/sales strategies in tourism and hospitality businesses is personnel. Management commonly views the addition of personnel as unnecessary, impractical or unwise, given budgetary restrictions.

Of prime importance in analysing resource requirements is the budget. Setting a budget that provides the marketing department with sufficient resources to deliver its plan is essential. However, in most organizations, various departments compete for funds, and it is not always easy to convince management that the marketing budget should have a priority claim on limited funds.

Although this is less of an issue in commercially oriented organizations, it can be a major problem in arts and entertainment organizations and non-profit groups. The idea of spending money on marketing (which is frequently not viewed as a core activity) at the expense of collections, maintenance, acquisitions, or expanding performance programmes is often a very contentious issue.

MARKETING CONTROL

The penultimate step in the planning process is to ensure that objectives will be achieved in the required time, using the funds and resources requested. In order to measure effectiveness, evaluation programmes have to be put in place, and regular monitoring needs to occur. There is little value in preparing a one-year marketing plan and including an evaluation methodology that commences towards the end of the operating year. This will not allow enough time to identify potential problems or initiate remedial action.

Because objectives have been set in quantifiable terms, regular reviews of sales forecasts and quotas, assessments of expenditure against budget, and data collection and analysis will provide guidance on how well objectives are being met. If a problem arises, contingency plans can be activated.

Effective contingency plans are considered long before emergencies or problems arise. Reacting under pressure is rarely as effective as preplanning. If, as part of the original process, alternatives are considered, it is more likely that they will be successful.

The most important reason for insisting on precision in setting objectives is to make it possible to measure results. Such results for a tourism business might be flow of bookings against planned capacity, enquiry and sales response related to any advertising, customer awareness of advertising messages measured by research surveys, sales response to any price discounts and sales promotions, sales response to any merchandising efforts by travel agents, consumer use of web sites and flow of bookings achieved, and customer satisfaction measurements. Most marketing plans are written to cover a one-year action plan in detail, with references made to the longer term – traditionally three years and five years. While the corporate goals may be longer term (often as long as ten or 20 years), the actual objectives are usually defined in terms of a much shorter time frame.

Some organizations base their marketing plans on their funding cycles. Some art organizations or government departments on three-year funding cycles prepare business and marketing plans that cover the full funding period.

Even these, however, stress the importance of regular reviews, and re-evaluate their action plan sections on a 12-month basis.

COMMUNICATING THE PLAN

Involving as many staff members as possible in the process of setting objectives and drawing up plans that communicate well is an important aspect of motivating staff at all levels and securing enthusiastic participation in the implementation process.

This involvement is a subject of increasing attention in many tourism and hospitality organizations (Middleton and Clarke, 2001). It is especially important for service businesses, in which so many staff members have direct contact with customers on the premises. It is a good idea to time the stages in marketing planning so that managers and as many staff as possible in all departments can take some part in initiating or commenting on draft objectives and plans.

Motivation can be damaged if objectives are continuously changed or if there is no opportunity to debate their practicality in operation. While marketing planning is conducted primarily to achieve more efficient business decisions, its secondary benefit is to provide a means of internal participation and communication, vital in creating and sustaining a high level of organizational morale.

Marketing plans must be sold to many people. Internally, these include members of the marketing and sales department, vendors and advertising agencies, and top management. Marketing plans are also important in communicating with stakeholders outside the company.

Approaching banks or other investors – for example, in tourism projects funded by government sources – invariably requires a business plan in which marketing is a primary component. Where money is granted, evidence of results will be required through a formal evaluation process.

In terms of presenting the report, many readers, both inside and outside the organization, will be impatient and will want the conclusions immediately. The executive summary is therefore a key section of the report. Indeed, it can be assumed that some staff – and perhaps senior executives and board members – will read only the executive summary. In general, an executive summary should be between two and six pages. It should avoid the use of jargon, and it should highlight the key objectives and action aspects of the plan and budget, leaving the analysis of current situations and detailed market analyses for the main document.

MARKETING STRATEGY TOOLS AND MODELS

A common tool used within marketing was developed by Igor Ansoff in 1957. His model gives organisation five strategic business options.

1. *Market Penetration:* This involves increasing sales of an existing product and penetrating the market further by either promoting the product heavily or reducing prices to increase sales.
2. *Product Development:* The organisation develops new products to aim within their existing market, in the hope that they will gain more custom and market share. For Example Sony launching the Playstation 2 to replace their existing model.
3. *Market Development:* The organisation here adopts a strategy of selling existing products to new markets. This can be done either by a better understanding of segmentation, *i.e* who else can possibly purchase the product or selling the product to new markets overseas.
4. *Diversification:* Moving away from what you are selling to providing something new *e.g.* Moving over from selling foods to selling cars.
5. *Consolidation:* Where the organisation adopts a strategy of withdrawing from particular markets, scaling back on operations and concentrating on its existing products in existing markets.

PRODUCT LIFE CYCLE

The product life cycle concept suggests that a product passes through four stages of evolution. Introduction, growth, maturity and decline. As a product evolves and passes through theses four stages profit is affected, and different strategies have to be employed to ensure that the product is a success within its market. As a new product much time will be spent by the organisation to create awareness of it presence amongst its target market. Profits are negative or low because of this reason.

Growth: If consumer clearly feels that this product will benefit them in some ways and they accept it, the organisation will see a period of rapid sales growth. Maturity: Rapid sales growth cannot last forever. Sales slow down as the product sales reach peak as it has been accepted by most buyers.

Decline: Sales and profits start to decline, the organisation may try to change their pricing strategy to stimulate growth, however the product will either have to be re-modified, or replaced within the market.

Value Chain Analysis

Michael Porter in 1985 introduced in his book ' The competitive advantage' the concept of the Value Chain. He suggested that activities within the organisation add value to the service and products that the organisation produces, and all these activities should be run at optimum level if the organisation is to gain any real competitive advantage. If they are run efficiently the value obtained should exceed the costs of running them *i.e.* customers should return to the organisation and transact freely and willingly. Michael Porter suggested that the organisation is split into 'primary activities' and 'support activities'.

Primary Activities

- *Inbound logistics*: Refers to goods being obtained from the organisations suppliers ready to be used for producing the end product.
- *Operations*: The raw materials and goods obtained are manufactured into the final product. Value is added to the product at this stage as it moves through the production line.
- *Outbound logistics*: Once the products have been manufactured they are ready to be distributed to distribution centres, wholesalers, retailers or customers.
- *Marketing and Sales*: Marketing must make sure that the product is targeted towards the correct customer group. The marketing mix is used to establish an effective strategy, any competitive advantage is clearly communicated to the target group by the use of the promotional mix.
- *Services:* After the product/service has been sold what support services does the organisation have to offer. This may come in the form of after sales training, guarantees and warranties.

With the above activities, any or a combination of them, maybe essential for the firm to develop the competitive advantage which Porter talks about in his book.

Support Activities

The support activities assist the primary activities in helping the organisation achieve its competitive advantage.

They include:

- *Procurement:* This department must source raw materials for the organisation and obtain the best price for doing so. For the price they must obtain the best possible quality
- *Technology development:* The use of technology to obtain a competitive advantage within the organisation. This is very important in today's technological driven environment. Technology can be used in production to reduce cost thus add value, or in research and development to develop new products, or via the use of the internet so customers have access to online facilities.

- *Human resource management*: The organisation will have to recruit, train and develop the correct people for the organisation if they are to succeed in their objectives. Staff will have to be motivated and paid the 'market rate' if they are to stay with the organisation and add value to it over their duration of employment. Within the service sector *e.g.* airlines it is the 'staff' who may offer the competitive advantage that is needed within the field.
- *Firm infrastructure:* Every organisations needs to ensure that their finances, legal structure and management structure works efficiently and helps drive the organisation forward.

As you can see the value chain encompasses the whole organisation and looks at how primary and support activities can work together effectively and efficiently to help gain the organisation a superior competitive advantage.

SWOT Analysis

A tool used by organisations to help the firm establish its Strengths, Weaknesses, Opportunities and Threats. A SWOT analysis is used as a framework to help the firm develop its overall corporate, marketing, or product strategies. Note: Strengths and Weaknesses are internal factors which are controllable by the organisation. Opportunities and threats are external factors which are uncontrollable by the organisation.

Strength examples could include:

- A strong brand name.
- Market share.
- Good reputation.
- Expertise and skill.
- Weaknesses could include:
- Low or no market share.
- No brand loyalty.
- Lack of experience.
- Opportunities could include:
- A growing market.
- Increased consumer spending.
- Selling internationally.
- Changes in society beneficial to your company.

Threats could include:

- Competitors
- Government policy *e.g.* taxation, laws
- Changes in society not beneficial to your company

A SWOT analysis is an excellent tool to use if the organisation wants to take a step back and assess the situation they are in. Issues raised from the analysis are then used to assist the organisation in developing their marketing mix strategy. A SWOT analysis must form the part of any prudent marketing strategy.

TOURISM MARKETING ENVIRONMENT

MICROENVIRONMENT

The marketing environment is made up of a microenvironment and a macroenvironment. The microenvironment consists of forces close to the organization that can affect its ability to serve its customers: the organization itself, marketing channel firms, customer markets, and a broad range of stakeholders or publics. For a tourism marketer, these factors will affect the degree of success in attracting target markets, so it is important to understand their importance.

Marketing managers need to work closely with other departments in the company, as all of these departments will have some impact on the success of marketing plans. Every tourism organization will differ as to how many departments it has and what they are called. However, finance is normally responsible for finding and using the funds required to carry out marketing plans, accounting has to measure revenues and costs in order to evaluate marketing objectives, and human resources will be crucial in supporting a service marketing culture. Suppliers also have an important role to play in supporting marketing objectives. Suppliers are firms and individuals that provide the resources needed by the company to produce its goods and services. Marketing management must pay close attention to trends and developments affecting suppliers, and to changes in supply availability and supply costs. At a micro level, hotels and exhibition centres contract with restaurant companies to supply food and beverage services. In turn, these restaurants will have their own favoured suppliers of produce. On a macro basis, tourist destinations will need suppliers in the form of airlines, hotels, restaurants, ground operations, meeting facilities, and entertainment.

Macroenvironment

The macroenvironment comprises the larger societal forces that affect the entire microenvi-ronment, and this will shape opportunities and pose threats.

Although an organization cannot control many of these external factors, they should never be allowed to come as a total surprise. A planned response to potential environmental issues allows for a balanced, thoughtful reaction – a process often referred to as 'environmental scanning'.

Competitive Forces: Being aware of who the competition is, knowing what their strengths and weaknesses are, and anticipating what they may do are important aspects of understanding the macroenviron-ment. The marketing concept states that to be successful, a company must satisfy the needs and wants of consumers better than its competitors. Furthermore, competitive advantage is now widely accepted as being of central importance to the success of organizations, regions, and countries. As we enter the third millennium, the world of tourism is becoming increasingly competitive. Although competition occurs between hotels, airlines, tour operators, travel agents, and other tourism services, this inter-enterprise competition is dependent upon and derived from the choices tourists make between alternative destinations. Competition therefore centres on the destination. Countries, states, regions and cities now take their role as tourist destinations very seriously, committing considerable effort and funds toward enhancing their touristic image and attractiveness. As a consequence, destination competitiveness has become a significant part of tourism literature, and evaluation of the competitiveness of tourism destinations is increasingly being recognized as an important tool in the strategic positioning and marketing analysis of destinations.

As a result of globalization, a growing number of countries are aware of the importance of tourism to their economies, as was mentioned at the beginning of this chapter. These countries have therefore increasingly targeted international tourism markets, augmenting their investment in marketing to attract international visitors and increase foreign earnings. For example, competition is intensifying to grab a larger share of the expected growth in outbound travel from China. The World Tourism Organization expects that by the year 2020, China will become one of the world's major outbound tourism markets, generating globally 100 million tourists, or 6.2 per cent of the world total. Competitive product, price, and quality, as well as access to and delivery of tourism goods and services will be the major success factors in attracting new Chinese outbound tourists and encouraging repeat travellers in the next decade and beyond.

Demographic Forces: Demographics are statistics that describe the observable characteristics of individuals, including our physical traits, such as gender, race, age, and height; our economic traits, such as income, savings, and net worth; our occupation-related traits, including education; our location-related traits; and our family-related traits, such as marital status and number and age of children. According to David Foot, author of *Boom, Bust & Echo* (2000), demographics explain about two-thirds of everything. For example, the dramatic increase in popularity of golf over the last 25 years is explained by golf's popularity among aging baby boomers who are entering a stage of life that enables them to spend more time on the golf course.

In fact, the single most notable demographic trend in many countries is the aging population. The over-50 segment, sometimes referred to as the maturing or greying market, constitutes nearly 30 per cent of many western countries, and this market has a keen interest in travel and leisure services. Other demographic trends affecting the marketing of tourism worldwide include the relatively slow population growth, the continued increase in education and service sector employment, increasing ethnic diversity, the demise of the traditional family, and the geographic mobility of the population. In addition to understanding general demographic trends, marketers must recognize demographic groupings that may turn out to be market segments because of their enormous size, similar socioeconomic characteristics, or shared values.

Economic Forces: Economic forces in the environment are those that affect consumer purchasing power and spending patterns. Total purchasing power depends on current income, prices, savings and credit, so marketers must be aware of major economic trends in income and of changing consumer spending patterns. For example, newly rich Russians, Indians and Chinese and a wider rise in disposable income are expected to boost the luxury goods market over the next decade. As a consequence, the luxury travel market will grow considerably. The market is already a lucrative one. In 2005, Virtuoso, a network of over 6,000 travel consultants that specialize in the luxury travel segment, booked more than US$4.2 billion in travel for their clients.

Price changes and exchange rates can also have a significant impact on tourism. How price increases in Cephalonia, as a result of the island's increased popularity following the *Captain Corelli* movie, led to dissatisfaction amongst both locals and prospective tourists. In 2006, Moscow replaced Tokyo as the world's most expensive city, and this will undoubtedly impact on visitors to the city. New York city remains the most expensive city in North America with currency appreciation being the main cause, although price increases in fuel and certain consumer goods have also contributed.

Environmental and Natural Forces: The last four decades have witnessed a dramatic increase in environmental consciousness worldwide. Media attention given to the greenhouse effect, acid rain, oil spills, ocean pollution, tropical deforestation and other topics has raised public awareness, which has had an impact on the tourism industry. International leisure travellers are increasingly motivated by the quality of destination landscapes, in terms of environmental health and the diversity and integrity of natural and cultural resources. Studies of German and US travel markets indicate that environmental considerations are now a significant element of travellers' destination-choosing process, down to – in the case of the Germans – the environmental programmes operated by individual hotels.

The growing concern amongst consumers for the protection of the environment has clearly attracted the attention of companies seeking to profit from environmentally sound marketing practices. Surveys have shown that consumers are more likely to choose one brand over another if they believe the brand will help the environment, and environmental quality is a prevailing issue in making travel-related decisions. This has led to the 'greening' of attractions, hotels, and even resorts, and to an increase in the number of environmentally friendly tourism products. An increasing emphasis is also being placed upon evaluating the likely environmental impacts of any tourism development, with environmental audits, environmental impact analysis, and carrying capacity issues being taken more seriously. A recent report from the UK (2005) suggested that there are a growing number of concerned individuals in Britain who have begun to turn away from international travel because of its environmental price.

Finally, uncontrollable natural forces can have a negative impact on the tourism industry. For example, the South Asian tsunami of 2004, due to the number of victims among foreign visitors and among workers of the tourism sector, constitutes the greatest catastrophe ever recorded in the history of tourism. Before the tsunami, tourism was at an all-time high in many of the affected countries. A two-year cease-fire between the Sri Lankan government and the Tamil Tigers had helped produce an 11 per cent increase in the number of tourists. Thailand was continuing its strong growth with a 20 per cent rise from the previous year. Even Bali, which was unaffected by the tsunami, had seen an almost complete recuperation of tourism revenues, to the level they were at prior to the Al-Qaeda bombings in October 2002. The tsunami devastated tourism in many of these countries. Due to its magnitude and repercussions the disaster took on a global scale, reflecting the worldwide reach tourism has today.

Technological Forces: The most dramatic force shaping the future of tourism and hospitality is technology. The accelerated rate of technological advancement has forced tourism organizations to adapt their products accordingly, particularly in terms of how they develop, price, distribute, and promote their products. Technology facilitates the continual development of new systems and features that improve the tourism product. It has allowed for extra security in hotels and resorts, thanks to security systems and safety designs. It has also created new entertainment options for travellers, such as in-room movies and video games. Increasingly, hotels and even airplanes are offering internet services to cater to the technological needs of today's consumer.

The internet fits the theoretical marketing principle in the travel industry because it allows suppliers to set up direct links of communication with their customers. Travellers are turning in increasing numbers to the internet to help them plan and book their travel. Technology is also beginning to have an impact on consumer research, as tourism organizations realize the potential of database management and the value of relationship marketing. Databases of customer profiles and customer behaviour are the basis for effective direct marketing. In tourism, the collection and analysis of data streams that now flow continuously through distribution channels and booking systems provide the modern information base for strategic and operational decisions of large organizations. The rate of technological change as databases connect and interact indicates that the speed and quality of information flows will be further enhanced in the coming decade.

Political Forces: Marketing decisions are strongly affected by developments in the political environment. This environment is made up of government agencies and pressure groups that influence and limit the activities of various organizations and individuals in society.

Government policies can have far-reaching implications for the tourism industry. For example, the nation of Myanmar (formerly called Burma) receives very few tourists because of the turbulent political situation in the country. The Case Study at the end of this chapter explores these issues in more depth. In Fiji, tourism is often influenced by political forces. A military coup in December 2006 – the country's fourth in 20 years – had a negative impact on tourism arrivals.

Terrorism can also have a devastating impact on tourism around the world. Since 11 September 2001 there have been more than 3,000 major terrorist attacks worldwide, most of which have impacted on the tourism industry. The media attention given to these attacks is usually enough to persuade many international travellers to reconsider their vacation plans. The terrorists themselves target tourism destinations in order to force governments to rethink and abandon specific policies, or to deny governments the commercial and economic benefits of tourism. The response by governments and the private sector to the impact of terrorism on tourism is given more attention.

Political actions can also have a positive impact on tourism. In some parts of the world, the relaxing of political barriers is making areas more accessible to tourists. An example is Mongolia, where Soviet influence smothered Mongolia's cultural traditions and closed off outside access until recently. But now, adventurous Westerners are exploring central Asia's vast wilderness of grasslands, deserts, and alpine terrain.

Cultural and Social Forces: Marketing's consumer focus relies on an understanding of who the markets are, what motivates them, and how to appeal to them. Understanding the cultural environment is thus crucial for marketing decision-making. This cultural environment includes institutions and other forces that affect society's basic values, perceptions, preferences, and behaviours.

Cultural values influence consumer behaviour, and marketers tend to concentrate on dominant cultural values or core values. A grouping technique that is used to track trends in cultural values is psychographics, which determines how people spend their time and resources (activities), what they consider important (interests and values), and what they think of themselves and the world around them (opinions). Core values are slow and difficult to change, but secondary values are less permanent and can sometimes be influenced by marketers.

INTEGRATED MARKETING COMMUNICATIONS (IMC) IN TOURISM

Perhaps one of the most important advances in marketing in recent decades has been the rise of integrated marketing communications (IMC) – the unification of all marketing communications tools, as well as corporate and brand messages, so they send a consistent, persuasive message to target audiences. This approach recognizes that advertising can no longer be crafted and executed in isolation from other promotional mix elements. As tourism markets and the media have grown more complex and fragmented, consumers find themselves in an ever more confusing marketing environment. Tourism marketers must address this situation by conveying a consistent, unified message in all their promotional activities. IMC programmes co-ordinate all communication messages and sources of an organization. An IMC campaign includes traditional marketing communication tools, such as advertising or sales promotion, but recognizes that other areas of the marketing mix are also used in communications. Planning and managing these elements so they work together helps to build a consistent brand or company image.

Two cases in this chapter highlight how both VisitBritain and Carnival Cruises used a number of promotional techniques to achieve their promotional objectives. Carnival, for example, in an effort to promote the concept of giving cruise vacations as holiday gifts, used television and print ads, banner ads, point-of-purchase promotional items, postcards, flyers and e-cards. The end-of-chapter Case Study is another example of a company integrating different promotional tools as part of its marketing strategy. Saatchi and Saatchi were given the task in 2004 of eradicating sex and drink from Club 18–30's promotional material in order to change its image. The famous ad agency came up with an 'underground' campaign based on teaser advertising techniques, which banished the company logo from all marketing material and from the resorts themselves. Cryptic advertisements with no mention of Club 18–30 directed viewers to a website, and the new up-market, trendy image was disseminated via posters, magazines, and radio as well as the viral email advertising. The Global Spotlight below highlights how Visit Britain used an integrated marketing strategy to leverage the fact that the Harry Potter movies were made in Britain.

PUSH AND PULL PROMOTIONAL STRATEGIES

One final factor to consider in the promotional strategy is the position of the organization in the distribution channel. For example, does a retailer (*i.e.*, the travel agent or the venue) carry out its own promotion for the travel product? Or does the producer (*i.e.*, the tour operator or destination organization) have to promote the product in order to bring the public into the travel agency to buy it? This is known as the choice between push and pull promotional strategies. A push strategy uses the sales force and trade promotion to push the product forward; the producer promotes the product to wholesalers, the wholesalers promote to retailers, and the retailers to consumers. In contrast, a pull strategy calls for spending a large amount on advertising and consumer promotion to build up consumer demand; if successful, consumers will ask their retailers for the product, the retailers will ask the wholesalers, and the wholesalers will ask the producers.

The choice of strategy depends on the degree of influence each member of the distribution channel has on the consumer's decision process, and on the relative power of the producer's and the retailer's brand names. In most cases, a combination of the two strategies are used, with each player in the channel marketing itself to the others and providing support for joint promotions. In the Snapshot on Carnival Cruise below, a pull strategy was used to entice consumers to purchase cruise vouchers as gifts using advertising and promotion, whereas a push strategy was used to promote the idea using virtual sales kits for travel agents, which were available on the cruise line's travel agent internet portal.

TOURISM ADVERTISING

Advertising has emerged as a key marketing tool in the tourism and hospitality industries. These industries require potential customers to base buying decisions upon mental images of product offerings, since they are not able to sample alternatives physically. As a result, advertising is a critical variable in the tourism marketing mix, and it covers a wide range of activities and agencies. Its role reflects that of promotion in general, which is to influence the attitudes and behaviour of audiences in three main ways: confirming and reinforcing, creating new patterns of behaviours, or changing attitudes and behaviour. Thus tourism and hospitality companies use images to portray their products in brochures, posters and media advertising. Destinations do the same, attempting to construct an image of a destination that will force it into the potential tourist's list of options, leading ultimately to a purchase. Whatever the tourism or hospitality product, its identity is the public face of how it is marketed, and the importance of advertising in tourism marketing should therefore not be underestimated.

Defining Advertising

Advertising can be defined as paid non-personal presentation and promotion of ideas, goods, or services by an identified sponsor, using mass media to persuade or influence an audience. This standard definition of advertising has six elements. First, advertising is a paid form of communication, although some forms of advertising, such as public service announcements, use donated space and time. Second, not only is the space paid for, but the sponsor is identified. Third, most advertising tries to persuade or influence the consumer to do something, although in some cases the point of the message is simply to make consumers aware of the product or company.

Fourth, the message is conveyed through many different kinds of mass media, and fifth, advertising reaches an audience of potential consumers. Finally, because advertising is a form of mass communication, it is also non-personal.

Developing an Advertising Programme

The process of developing an advertising programme includes six important stages. *Setting the Objectives:* In planning and managing advertising, a key factor is the setting of objectives. An advertising objective can be defined as a specific communication task designed to reach a specific target audience during a specific period of time. In general terms, advertising has four major tasks: informing, persuading, reminding, and selling. However, advertising in tourism and hospitality can have many uses. These might include creating awareness; informing about new products; expanding the market to new buyers; announcing a modification to a service; announcing a price change; making a special offer; selling directly; educating consumers; reminding consumers; challenging competition; reversing negative sales trends; pleasing intermediaries; recruiting staff; attracting investors; announcing trading results; influencing a destination image; creating a corporate image; soliciting customer information; improving employee morale; and contributing to co-operative/partnership advertising ventures.

In the Opening Vignette, the objective of the 'What Happens in Vegas Stays in Vegas' advertising campaign was to assist in re-branding Las Vegas as 'Sin City' after a failed attempt to reposition it as a family destination. The advertising objective was to change the perception of the company and create a new up-market, trendy image. However, the Snapshot on Brazil later in this chapter describes how the Brazilian tourism industry used prevention ads to discourage unwanted behaviours - rather the opposite of the normal behavioural responses sought through advertising.

Setting the Budget: Ideally, the advertising budget should be calculated on the basis of the objectives set in the first stage of the process. The media plan must reach sufficient numbers in the target market to produce the size of response that will achieve the sales target. Several methods can be used to set the advertising budget. The objective and task method involves developing the promotion budget by (1) defining specific objectives, (2) determining the tasks that must be performed to achieve these objectives, and (3) estimating the costs of performing these tasks. Using this method requires considerable experience of response rates and media costs, as well as confidence in the accuracy of predictions. Cautious managers prefer to base the advertising budget on what they know, from previous experience, they can afford to spend. This is often referred to as the affordable method. The percentage of sales method involves setting the promotion budget at a certain percentage of current or forecasted sales or as a percentage of sales price. In tourism and hospitality, the percentage of gross sales generally set aside for marketing is somewhere between 4 and 12 per cent, advertising being allocated about a quarter of this amount. Cheddar Caves & Gorge in the UK, for example, spend about 10 per cent of gross turnover on marketing and publicity. The actual percentage will vary according to the products position on the product life cycle. For example, new products will require more advertising to launch them into the market. The budget size for communications can have a tremendous range. For example the Las Vegas Convention and Visitors Authority spent US$60 million on their 'What Happens in Vegas Stays in Vegas' advertising campaign, whereas at the other end of the scale, Club 18-30 had only £1.5 million to spend on their promotional campaign.

Another way of setting the budget is the competitive parity method, which sets the promotion budget at the level needed to achieve parity or 'equal share of voice' with competitors. It may seem unwise to spend significantly less than competitors if you are aiming for a similar share of the same market. In the hotel business the advertising expenditure for the average hotel is 1 per cent of sales, but for limited-service hotels, advertising expenditure is higher, representing 2 per cent of sales.

Advertising Agency Decisions: Since advertising is usually considered the most important tool in the marketing communications mix, companies must decide carefully whether they are going to do the work themselves or hire an outside agency. Only very small businesses, such as guesthouses or local visitor attractions, are likely to undertake their own advertising without professional help. At the very least, advertising agencies can help with the purchase of advertising space at discounted rates. Most advertising agencies enjoy working on tourism and hospitality accounts as they involve intrinsically interesting products, and may welcome the account as a stimulating break from their usual subject matter.

The best advertising agencies create value for their clients, as seen in the Club 18–30 example. An agency can clearly interpret what the customer wants and then communicate information about the client's product so meaningfully, so uniquely, and so consistently that customers reward that product with their loyalty. An agency can add perceived value to the product by giving it a personality, by communicating in a manner that shapes basic understanding of the product, by creating an image or memorable picture of the product, and by setting the product apart from its competitors.

There are two main types of advertising agency: the full-service agency and the specialized agency. In advertising, a full-service agency is one that provides the four major staff functions: account management, creative services, media planning and buying, and account planning (which is also known as research). A full-service advertising agency will also have its own accounting department, a traffic department to handle internal tracking on completion of projects, a department for broadcast and print production, and a human resources department. However, tourism and hospitality organizations often use the services of a specialized agency. This type of agency will specialize in certain functions (*e.g.*, writing copy, producing art, media buying), audiences (*e.g.*, minority, youth), or industries (*e.g.*, health care, computers, leisure), or in certain marketing communication areas, such as direct marketing, sales promotion, public relations, events and sports marketing, and packaging and point-of-sale.

Message Strategy: The message strategy is the fourth stage in the process of developing an advertising programme. Studies have shown that creative advertising messages can be more important than the number of dollars spent on the message. Creative strategy plays an increasingly important role in advertising success. Developing a creative strategy requires three message steps: generation, evaluation and selection, and execution.

Providers of tourism and hospitality products face an inherent barrier to effective communication with their customers: the intangibility of the product. A hotel or airline flight is experienced only at or after the time of purchase. This characteristic of services in general poses genuine challenges for message generation. Advertisers need to make tangible an intangible product, using emotion and experience. An example of a very creative and successful print ad produced on a low budget is the Dog & Sock ad for Calgary Zoo. It was developed through the zoo's advertising agency (Parallel Strategies which is now Trigger Communications). Strategically the zoo wanted something that would convey a very simple message but have a strong, funny, visual appeal to both young and old and work in all mediums. The budget was low at only $35,000 for the entire campaign, including creative design, fees, production, photography and media buys. However, the campaign was so successful the zoo continued it for another three years and now has 17 'No Substitute for the Zoo' ad executions. The campaign has won several awards including the Trans-Canada Agency Network Award for Best in Show (2003), Extra Award of Merit (Certificate of Excellence) in 2004, Ad Rodeo Anvil 2004, International Association of Amusement Parks & Attractions (IAAPA) Brass Ring for Best Outdoor and Best of Show for the same in 2004.

Although advertisers may create many possible messages, only a few will be used in the campaign, and the second step in developing a creative strategy – evaluation and selection – will determine the final message to be used. According to Kotler *et al.*, (2003) the advertiser must evaluate possible ads on the basis of three characteristics. First, messages should be meaningful and should point out benefits that make the product more desirable or interesting to consumers. Second, messages should be distinctive. They should tell the consumer how the product is better than competing brands. Finally, messages must be believable. This goal is difficult to achieve, as many consumers doubt the truth of advertising.

In the third step of developing a creative strategy execution, the creative staff must find a style, tone, words and format for executing the message. Any message can be presented in a variety of styles. The following are commonly used in tourism and hospitality:

1. Slice of life. This style shows people using the product in a normal setting.
2. Fantasy. This style creates a wonder-world around the product or its use. The human psyche is receptive to fantasy, so companies like Disney have capitalized on this type of advertising, which is particularly effective in an industry that appeals to one's desire to escape.
3. Mood or image. This style builds a mood or image around the product or service, such as beauty, love or serenity. Destination marketers often attempt to create an emotional relationship between the destination and potential visitors. In this type of advertising, branding activities concentrate on communicating the essence or the spirit of a destination via a few key attributes and associations.
4. Lifestyle. This style shows how a product fits with a lifestyle. For example, British Airways, advertising its business class, featured a businessman sitting in an upholstered chair in the living room, having a drink and enjoying the paper. The other side of the ad featured the same person in the same relaxed position with a drink and a paper in one of the airline's business-class seats.
5. Musical. This style shows one or more people or cartoon characters singing a song about a product. Almost 30 years ago, Coca-Cola wanted to 'teach the world to sing in perfect harmony', and the pattern was set for an important ingredient in successful advertising. Airlines have used music to good effect. Delta Airlines used music effectively in its 'We Love to Fly' campaign, as did British Airways in its 'World Images' campaign. The association various destinations have with music is often used in advertising campaigns. For instance, the haunting strains of Irish music are the background sounds in an ad for Ireland.
6. Te sti m onia l e v i d en ce. In this style, celebrities we admire, created characters (McDonald's Ronald McDonald, for example), experts we respect, or people 'just like us' whose advice we might seek out, speak on behalf of the product to build credibility. An example is a print ad that appeared extensively in travel magazines in 2006 for Samsonite luggage, in which Richard Branson, Chairman of Virgin, endorses the products. In 2005 Elton John appeared on 20 AirTran jets in a move to promote the Florida-based airline's launch of satellite radio at each passenger seat. In return John was given a $50,000 cheque for the Elton John AIDS Foundation.

7. Technical expertise. In this style of advertisement, the company shows its expertise. Hotels, for example, may use this style in advertising to meeting and convention planners, to show that they have the technical ability to support them. Airlines also sometimes make use of expertise to reassure the consumer about the technical qualities of their pilots and mechanics.

Media Strategy: The media plan section in an advertising plan includes media objectives (reach and frequency), media strategies (targeting, continuity and timing), media selection (the specific vehicles), geographic strategies, schedules and the media budget. The range of advertising media available to today's advertiser is increasingly bewildering and is becoming ever more fragmented. While these changes offer the prospect of greater targeting, they also make the job of the media planner more difficult. In the Carnival Cruise campaign, the media plan included T V, radio, newspapers, trade magazines and other promotional vehicles to stimulate people to purchase cruise holiday gift vouchers. All these media outlets are referred to as the media mix – created by media planners by selecting the best combination of traditional media vehicles (print, broadcast, etc.), non-traditional media (internet, cell phones, unexpected places like the floors of stores), and marketing communication tools such as public relations, direct marketing and sales promotion to reach the targeted stakeholder audiences. Given cost constraints, media planners usually select the media that will expose the product to the largest target audience for the lowest possible cost. The process of measuring this ratio is called efficiency – or cost per thousand (CPM). To calculate the CPM, two figures are needed: the costs of the unit (*e.g.*, time on TV or space in a magazine) and the estimated target audience. The cost of the unit is divided by the target audience's gross impressions to determine the advertising dollars needed to expose the product to 1,000 members of the target.

CPM : For example, if the show *Pilot Guides* has 92,000 target viewers, and the cost of a 30-second announcement during the show is $850, the CPM will be $9.42 (CPM = $850/92 000 × 1000 = $9.24).

There are many components to the media mix, and how an organization blends them depends on a number of factors, particularly the nature of the product or service and the target audience. For example, tour operators and major destinations rely heavily on television advertising, but niche players such as special interest operators tend to focus their advertising in specialist publications. Decisions also have to be made about reach and frequency. Marketers for Cheddar Caves & Gorge have decided that printing 1.5 million leaflets and distributing them within a 50-mile radius of the attraction is the best way of spending the bulk of their promotional budget. While tourism and hospitality advertising makes use of all of the main media, the key vehicles are print and electronic media advertisements and brochures. In fact, the most popular medium used by tourism advertisers is undoubtedly the travel brochure. For many organizations, the design, production and distribution of their annual tourism brochure is the single most important and most expensive item in the marketing budget. However, the position of the brochure as a major travel medium is being threatened by new technology, such as CD-ROMs, videos and the internet.

One of the fastest growing sectors of media is ambient advertising. This approach includes place-based advertising and uses new, unexpected ways of getting messages across. Examples of ambient advertising include ads on the back of grocery receipts, on gas pumps, in elevators, on ATM screens, on shop floors, on washroom walls, on toilet paper, on pizza boxes, on welcome mats and on tickets. Such tactics might involve live advertising. Golden Palace Casino has been advertising on the back of professional boxers for many years using large tattoos. Sony Ericsson Mobile Communications Ltd. hired actors to create buzz about a new mobile phone that was also a digital camera. The actors pretended to be tourists who wanted their picture taken, thus persuading consumers to try the product. The use of hyper-tag technology by Whistler and its partner in the UK, Neilson, referred to later in this chapter, is an example of ambient advertising. Another is the 'talking urinal' developed by Wizmark that uses a sensor to detect someone approaching, which then activates an attention-grabbing display of lights flashing in a pre-programmed pattern. This draws the eye to the graphics incorporated within the waterproof 9 cm viewing screen at the base of the urinal. After a period of animation, the display automatically resets itself in anticipation of the next viewer.

In 1999, Virgin Atlantic made innovative use of ambient media in the tourism sector when it painted the traditionally green and white Hong Kong harbour's Star Ferry bright red with its own logo. A further use of ambient advertising is the use of airfields as a context in which to view ads cut into crop fields. An example of such an attempt to capture the interest of the business traveller occurred at Munich airport, where arriving passengers saw a giant ad for Swissair growing in the fields below. A 250-metre-long aircraft, grown in green barley against a background of brown straw, depicted the red and white Swissair logo, the colours created by using pigments.

Campaign Evaluation: Managers of advertising programmes should regularly evaluate the communication and sales objectives of advertising. The campaign evaluation stage is often the most difficult in the advertising cycle, largely because while it is relatively easy to establish certain advertising measures (such as consumers' awareness of a brand before and after the campaign), it is much harder to establish shifts in consumer attitudes or brand perception. Despite such uncertainties, the evaluation stage is significant not only because it establishes what a campaign has achieved but also because it will provide guidance as to how future campaigns could be improved and developed. There are many evaluative research techniques available to marketers to measure advertising effectiveness. Memory tests are often used, and are based on the assumption that a communication leaves a mental residue with the person who has been exposed to it. Memory tests fall into two major groups: recall tests and recognition tests. In a traditional recall test, a commercial is run on a television network and the next evening interviewers ask viewers if they remember seeing it. This type of test, in which the specific brand is mentioned, is called aided recall. Alternatively, the interviewers may ask consumers what particular ads they remembered from the previous day; this is known as unaided recall. If the commercial fails to establish a tight connection between the brand name and the selling message, the commercial will not receive a high recall score. Another method of measuring memory, called a recognition test, involves showing the advertisement to people and asking them whether they remember having seen it before.

The persuasion test is another evaluative research technique used to measure effectiveness after execution of a campaign. In this technique, consumers are first asked how likely they are to buy a particular brand. Next, they are exposed to an advertisement for the brand.

After exposure, researchers again ask them what they intend to purchase. The researcher analyses the results to determine whether intention to buy has increased as a result of exposure to the advertisement. Persuasion tests are expensive and have problems associated with audience composition, the environment and brand familiarity. However, persuasion is a key objective for many advertisers, so even a rough estimate of an advertisement's persuasive power is useful.

International Advertising and the Global versus Local Debate: In 2006, global expenditure on advertising worldwide was about US$450 billion and is expected to rise to $511 billion by 2009. Of all the elements of the marketing mix, decisions involving advertising are those most often affected by cultural differences among country markets. Consumers respond in terms of their culture, value systems, attitudes, beliefs and perceptions. Because advertising's function is to interpret or translate the qualities of products and services in terms of consumer needs, wants, desires, and aspirations, the emotional appeals, symbols, persuasive approaches, and other characteristics of an advertisement must coincide with cultural norms if the ad is to be effective. The end-of-chapter Case Study looks at the success of Australia's 'Where the Bloody Hell Are You?' campaign. The television ads resonated with consumers in Japan, UK, USA, Germany, China, New Zealand and South Korea, even with subtitles. The phrase 'bloody hell' was expressed in English by an Australian but caught the attention of all those cultures, while the local translation in subtitles, in colloquial language, conveyed the same sentiment and meaning.

Reconciling an international advertising campaign with the cultural uniqueness of markets is the challenge confronting the global marketer. A classic

Harvard Business Review article by Theodore Levitt ignited a debate over how to conduct global marketing. He argued that companies should operate as if there were only one global market. He believed that differences among nations and cultures were not only diminishing but should be ignored, because people throughout the world are motivated by the same desires and wants. Other scholars like Philip Kotler disagreed, pointing to companies like Coca-Cola, PepsiCo and McDonalds, and arguing that they did not offer the same product everywhere. The outcome of this debate has been three schools of thought on advertising in another country:

1. Standardization. This school of thought contends, like Levitt, that differences between countries are a matter of degree, so advertisers should focus on the similarities of consumers around the world.
2. Localization. The localization or adaptation school of thought argues that advertisers must consider differences between countries, including local culture, stage of economic and industrial development, stage of life cycle, media availability and legal restrictions.
3. Combination. The belief here is that a combination of standardization and localization may produce the most effective advertising. Some elements of brand identity or strategy, for example, may be standardized, but advertising executions may need to be adapted to the local culture.

The reality of global advertising suggests that a combination approach will work best, and most companies tend to use this or even lean towards localization. Starbucks, for example, offers more tea in the Far East, stronger coffees in Europe and gourmet coffees in the US. The company has standardized its product name, logo, and packaging to maintain brand consistency even though there is variation in its product line.

HOSPITALITY MARKETING STRATEGY TOOLS AND MODELS

Ansoffs Matrix

A common tool used within marketing was developed by Igor Ansoff in 1957. His model gives organisation five strategic business options.

1. Market Penetration: This involves increasing sales of an existing product and penetrating the market further by either promoting the product heavily or reducing prices to increase sales.
2. Product Development: The organisation develops new products to aim within their existing market, in the hope that they will gain more custom and market share. For Example Sony launching the Playstation 2 to replace their existing model.
3. Market Development: The organisation here adopts a strategy of selling existing products to new markets. This can be done either by a better understanding of segmentation, i.e who else can possibly

purchase the product or selling the product to new markets overseas.

4. Diversification: Moving away from what you are selling (your core activities) to providing something new eg Moving over from selling foods to selling cars.
5. Consolidation: Where the organisation adopts a strategy of withdrawing from particular markets, scaling back on operations and concentrating on its existing products in existing markets.

Product Life Cycle

The product life cycle concept suggests that a product passes through four stages of evolution. Introduction, growth, maturity and decline. As a product evolves and passes through theses four stages profit is affected, and different strategies have to be employed to ensure that the product is a success within its market. As a new product much time will be spent by the organisation to create awareness of it presence amongst its target market. Profits are negative or low because of this reason.

Growth: If consumer clearly feels that this product will benefit them in some ways and they accept it, the organisation will see a period of rapid sales growth.

Maturity: Rapid sales growth cannot last forever. Sales slow down as the product sales reach peak as it has been accepted by most buyers.

Decline: Sales and profits start to decline, the organisation may try to change their pricing strategy to stimulate growth, however the product will either have to be re-modified, or replaced within the market.

Value Chain Analysis

Michael Porter in 1985 introduced in his book ' The competitive advantage' the concept of the Value Chain. He suggested that activities within the organisation add value to the service and products that the organisation produces, and all these activities should be run at optimum level if the organisation is to gain any real competitive advantage. If they are run efficiently the value obtained should exceed the costs of running them i.e. customers should return to the organisation and transact freely and willingly. Michael Porter suggested that the organisation is split into 'primary activities' and 'support activities'.

Primary Activities

Inbound logistics : Refers to goods being obtained from the organisations suppliers ready to be used for producing the end product.

Operations : The raw materials and goods obtained are manufactured into the final product. Value is added to the product at this stage as it moves through the production line.

Outbound logistics : Once the products have been manufactured they are ready to be distributed to distribution centres, wholesalers, retailers or customers. Marketing and Sales: Marketing must make sure that the product is targeted towards the correct customer group. The marketing mix is used to establish an effective strategy, any competitive advantage is clearly communicated to the target group by the use of the promotional mix.

Services: After the product/service has been sold what support services does the organisation have to offer. This may come in the form of after sales training, guarantees and warranties. With the above activities, any or a combination of them, maybe essential for the firm to develop the competitive advantage which Porter talks about in his book.

Support Activities

The support activities assist the primary activities in helping the organisation achieve its competitive advantage. They include:

Procurement: This department must source raw materials for the organisation and obtain the best price for doing so. For the price they must obtain the best possible quality Technology development: The use of technology to obtain a competitive advantage within the organisation. This is very important in today's technological driven environment. Technology can be used in production to reduce cost thus add value, or in research and development to develop new products, or via the use of the internet so customers have access to online facilities. Human resource management: The organisation will have to recruit, train and develop the correct people for the organisation if they are to succeed in their objectives. Staff will have to be motivated and paid the 'market rate' if they are to stay with the organisation and add value to it over their duration of employment. Within the service sector eg airlines it is the 'staff' who may offer the competitive advantage that is needed within the field.

Firm infrastructure: Every organisations needs to ensure that their finances, legal structure and management structure works efficiently and helps drive the organisation forward.

As you can see the value chain encompasses the whole organisation and looks at how primary and support activities can work together effectively and efficiently to help gain the organisation a superior competitive advantage.

SWOT Analysis

A tool used by organisations to help the firm establish its Strengths, Weaknesses, Opportunities and Threats (SWOT). A SWOT analysis is used as a framework to help the firm develop its overall corporate, marketing, or product strategies. Note:Strengths and Weaknesses are internal factors which are controllable by the organisation. Opportunities & threats are external factors which are uncontrollable by the organisation.

Strength examples could include:

- A strong brand name.
- Market share.
- Good reputation.
- Expertise and skill.
- Weaknesses could include:
- Low or no market share.
- No brand loyalty.
- Lack of experience.
- Opportunities could include:
- A growing market.
- Increased consumer spending.
- Selling internationally.
- Changes in society beneficial to your company.

Threats could include:

- Competitors
- Government policy eg taxation, laws
- Changes in society not beneficial to your company

A SWOT analysis is an excellent tool to use if the organisation wants to take a step back and assess the situation they are in. Issues raised from the analysis are then used to assist the organisation in developing their marketing mix strategy. A SWOT analysis must form the part of any prudent marketing strategy.

Generic Strategies

For an organisation to obtain a sustainable competitive advantage Michael Porter suggested that they should follow either one of three generic strategies.

Strategy one: Cost Leadership

This strategy involves the organisation aiming to be the lowest cost producer within their industry. The orgainisation aims to drive cost down through all the elements of the production of the product from sourcing, to labour costs. The cost leader usually aims at a broad market, so sufficient sales can cover costs. Low cost producers include Easyjet airline, Ryan air, Asda and Walmart. Some organisation may aim to drive costs down but will not pass on these cost savings to their customers aiming for increased profits clearly because their brand can command a premium rate.

Strategy 2: Differentiation

To be different, is what organisations strive for. Having a competitive advantage which allows the company and its products ranges to stand out is crucial for their success. With a differentiation strategy the organisation aims to focus its effort on particular segments and charge for the added differentiated value. If we look at Brompton folding cycles their compact design differentiates them from other folding bike companies. New concepts which allow for differentiation can be patented, however patents have a certain life span and organisation always face the danger that their idea that gives the competitive advantage will be copied in one form or another.

Strategy 3: Niche strategies

Here the organisation focuses its effort on one particular segment and becomes well known for providing products/services within the segment. They form a competitive advantage for this niche market and either succeed by being a low cost producer or differentiator within that particular segment. Examples include Roll Royce and Bentley.

Are you 'Stuck in the Middle'

The danger some organisation face is that they try to do all three and become what is known as stuck in the middle. The have no clear business strategy, be all to all consumers, which adds to their running costs causing a fall in sales and market share. 'Stuck in the middle' companies are usually subject to a takeover or merger.

Industry Analysis Model

Porters fives forces model is an excellent model to use to analyse a particular environment of an industry. So for example, if we were entering the PC industry, we would use porters model to help us find out about:

1) Competitive Rivalry
2) Power of suppliers
3) Power of buyers
4) Threats of substitutes
5) Threat of new entrants.

The above five main factors are key factors that influence industry performance, hence it is common sense and practical to find out about these factors before you enter the industry.

Competitive Rivalry

A starting point to analysing the industry is to look at competitive rivalry. If entry to an industry is easy then competitive rivalry will likely to be high. If it is easy for customers to move to substitute products for example from coke to water then again rivalry will be high. Generally competitive rivalry will be high if:

- There is little differentiation between the products sold between customers.
- Competitors are approximately the same size of each other.
- If the competitors all have similar strategies.

- It is costly to leave the industry hence they fight to just stay in (exit barriers)

Power of Suppliers

Suppliers are also essential for the success of an organisation. Raw materials are needed to complete the finish product of the organisation. Suppliers do have power. This power comes from:

- If they are the only supplier or one of few suppliers who supply that particular raw material.
- If it costly for the organisation to move from one supplier to another (known also as switching cost)
- If there is no other substitute for their product.

Power of Buyers

Buyers or customers can exert influence and control over an industry in certain circumstances. This happens when:

- There is little differentiation over the product and substitutes can be found easily.
- Customers are sensitive to price.
- Switching to another product is not costly.

Threat of Substitutes

Are there alternative products that customers can purchase over your product that offer the same benefit for the same or less price? The threat of substitute is high when:

- Price of that substitute product falls.
- It is easy for consumers to switch from one substitute product to another.
- Buyers are willing to substitute.

Threat of New Entrant

The threat of a new organisation entering the industry is high when it is easy for an organisation to enter the industry i.e. entry barriers are low.

An organisation will look at how loyal customers are to existing products, how quickly they can achieve economy of scales, would they have access to suppliers, would government legislation prevent them or encourage them to enter the industry. So to summaries porters five forces model is essential to carry to help you understand your industry in depth before you enter it.

Diffusion of Innovation

This extension of the product life cycle was developed by Everett M. Rogers in 1962 and simply looks who adopts products at the different stages of the life cycle.

Rogers identified five types of purchasers as the product moves through its life cycle stage. He suggested:

1. Innovator who make up 2.5% of all purchases of the product, purchase the product at the beginning of the life cycle. They are not afraid of trying new products that suit their lifestyle and will also pay a premium for that benefit.
2. Early Adopters make up 13.5% of purchases, they are usually opinion leaders and naturally adopt products after the innovators. This group of purchasers are crucial because adoption by them means the product becomes acceptable, spurring on later purchasers.
3. Early Majority make up 34% of purchases and have been spurred on by the early adopters. They wait to see if the product will be adopted by society and will purchase only when this has happened. They early majority usually have some status in society.
4. Late Majority make up another 34% of sales and usually purchase the product at the late stages of majority within the life cycle.
5. Laggards make up 16% of total sales and usually purchase the product near the end of its life. They are the 'wait and see' group. They wait to see if the product will get cheaper. Usually when they purchase the product a new version is already on the market. Some may call Laggards, bargain hunters!

Boston Consultancy Group (BCG Matrix)

This product portfolio matrix classifies product lines into four categories. The BCG models suggests that organisations should have a healthy balance of products within their range. The Boston Consultancy Group classified these products as following:

Question Mark/Problem Child

These are products with low market share but operate in high market growth rates. The company puts a lot of resources in this product in the hope that it will eventually increase market share and generate cash returns in the future.

Star

Stars have high market shares that operate in growing markets. The product at this stage should be generating positive returns for the company.

Cash Cow

Cash Cow are products at the mature stage of the lifecycle, they generate high amounts of cash for the company, but growth rate is slowing. There are chances that the product may slip into decline, appropriate marketing mix strategies should be employed to try to prevent this from happening.

7

Business Travel and Tourism

INTRODUCTION

Given the complexity of business travel and tourism, any attempt to seek to measure its volume is almost certainly doomed to failure. Data is collected on different bases in different countries and it can be a considerable time between the collection of data and its publication. Furthermore, much data is collected for commercial purposes and is never published.

There is also considerably more data available on conferences and meetings than on incentive travel or exhibitions, for example. This chapter, therefore, has a bias towards conferences and meetings, although it does endeavour to consider all types of business travel and tourism. However, before we begin to look at the demand for business travel and tourism, in statistical terms, we need to say a few words about the nature of demand, in this field, in general.

First, we need to recognize that demand in business travel and tourism has two dimensions, namely, the customer and the consumer.

While this is clearly a gross simplification of the situation it is still valid and helps explain one of the key perceived characteristics of the business travel and tourism market, namely the idea that business travel is less price elastic than leisure travel because, often, the business traveller him or herself is not paying the bill. However, this generalization does not apply to the self-employed, who constitute a significant proportion of the business travel and tourism market. At the same time the customer and consumer can often be one and the same person or body. For example, the scientific committee of an international association conference will be both customer and consumer. They decide on the conference venue, pay to attend the event, and then attend and consume a range of travel and tourism services in so doing.

Motivators

The motivators for business travel will be different for the customers and consumers and perhaps in relation to different types of business travel. Let us look at some hypothetical examples to illustrate this point.

The managing director of a UK-based food company books a stand for the company at a trade fair in France. He wants to raise the profile of the company and increase sales in France, as cheaply as possible. He selects Mr 'A' to represent the company at this event because he speaks good French. Mr 'A' also has a taste for French food and wine and sees this as an ideal opportunity to indulge in both at the company's expense! He also sees it as an ideal opportunity to make contact with French companies to help him get a job in France. He spends lots of money but devotes little time to selling his own company's products.

Playtime Inc., a young computer games company decides to take staff on an incentive travel trip to help with team-building and to encourage staff to work harder in the future. The company does not explain this to the staff, who therefore think the trip is a reward for past efforts which, to be honest, have not been that great. The staff see this trip as a 'freebie', a perk, some fun at the company's expense. Not surprisingly, the trip is not a great success.

The head of the Philosophy School at Newton University gives permission for Dr Socrates to attend the International Symposium on German philosophers and their work, in Acapulco. This conference is part of Dr Socrates' staff development and is designed to help her keep up to date with developments in her field. It is also intended to give her an opportunity to network and raise the profile of the university's new MA in the Philosophical Aspects of Mobile Phone Use. Dr Socrates has other ideas, however, and prefers to spend most of the conference discussing the philosophy of coastal tourism, on the beach, with an attractive male philosopher from the University of Nether Hampton! All three scenarios illustrate the potential for a gap in the motivators of customers and consumers in the different areas of business travel and tourism.

BUSINESS TRAVEL

Business travel is the practice of people traveling for purposes related to their work. It is on the rise especially with foreign business markets opening up. 432 million business trips were completed by United States residents in 2009, this accounted for approximately $215 billion dollars towards the economy. Many airlines began to concentrate on providing premium service on long haul flights especially for the first and business class business traveler with the development of more sophisticated business traveler needs over the last 15 years.

American Airlines was the first airline to offer a frequent flier programme to customers. The AAdvantage programme began in May 1981 and included Hertz car rental and Hyatt hotel. The first hotel to start an independent hotel programme was Holiday Inn; they began in January 1983. National Car Rental was the first car rental company to introduce a programme back in March 1987. Airlines have also been working on tools that benefit the business travellers such as: Improved and competitive mileage programmes, quick check in and online check in, lounges with broadband connection, etc. Hotels are not far behind. They are also on the competition for the business travellers by offering flexible points programmes, broadband connection in all rooms and fast check in and check out services.

While internet booking engines have become the first destination for around 60% of leisure travelers, business travelers, especially with the need for itineraries that may include more than one destination, have still found that a knowledgeable travel agent may be their best resource for better ticket pricing, less hassle and better air and land travel planning. For larger business travel accounts these travel agents take on a travel management role, and are referred to as Travel Management Companies (TMCs), providing services such as consultancy, traveller tracking, data and negotiation assistance and policy advice. Recent trends in this market have extended to the implementation of Self Booking Tools (SBTs) which allow automated booking of trips within company policy, an increase in the inclusion of Duty of care practices in the booking and monitoring process and more consideration for the environmental impact of business travel.

THE STRUCTURE OF DEMAND

Business travel and tourism demand has a number of dimensions. Clearly, in its simplest sense it is the number of people travelling for business purposes in a particular region, country or worldwide.

THE FACTORS WHICH INFLUENCE BUSINESS TRAVEL AND TOURISM DEMAND

Business travel and tourism demand is influenced by a broad range of factors found in both the generating region and the destination.

The forces that will influence demand between a specific generating region and a particular destination. It also gives an indication of the factors that will influence demand overall in any particular generating region.

However, this is a highly generalized picture and specific factors will influence the demand for particular forms of business tourism such as incentive travel and training courses. Let us now look at how the market can be subdivided and segmented.

The growing segments in the market appear to be:

- Business travellers from newly industrialized countries such as South Korea or Taiwan
- Business travellers from Eastern Europe where political change has led to growth of business tourism
- Female business travellers
- People taking incentive travel packages

- Frequent travellers
- Long-haul business travellers.

The situation is constantly changing and the ways of segmenting the business travel market are likely to change, too, over time.

There are three other issues we would like to consider at this stage:

- The nature of demand for different types of business travel and tourism
- The levels of business travel and tourism and different industries
- The question of seasonality of demand.

THE NATURE OF DEMAND AND DIFFERENT TYPES OF BUSINESS TRAVEL AND TOURISM

The nature of demand obviously differs between types of business tourism. While much of the data in this chapter relates to the meetings market, other types of business travel and tourism have very different market characteristics. This can be seen if we look, for example, at the exhibition market in Europe.

THE EXHIBITION MARKET

In spring 2000 *Travel and Tourism Analyst* published a report on the European Exhibition and Trade Fair Market, based on data obtained from its markets by the European Major Exhibition Centres Association. These are the main findings of this survey:

1 It was suggested that Europe hosts more than 3000 major exhibitions and trade fairs every year.
2 In 1996 it was estimated that 50 million people visited exhibitions and trade fairs in Europe.
3 Expenditure by exhibitors and visitors to trade fairs was thought to be worth between £6 billion and £15 billion to the European economy.
4 The average size of a major exhibition in 1996 was 14 900 square metres compared with 18 000 square metres in 1990.
5 Most exhibitions lasted from three to nine days, with an average duration of from three days in London to nearly six in Hanover, in 1998.
6 More than 5 million visitors attended exhibitions and trade fairs in Paris in 1998.
7 Individual exhibition centres hosted events with an economic impact of nearly £1 billion.

Levels of business tourism demand and different industries

The level of demand for business travel varies dramatically between different industries. The market for the services of conference and incentive travel agencies in the UK.

Seasonality

It is often said that one of the advantages of business travel and tourism is that it is less seasonal than leisure tourism. While the season is longer and less pronounced than leisure tourism, business travel still does have an element of seasonality.

In general it is an activity which takes place outside the summer holiday months, in the Northern Hemisphere at least, and is predominantly a Monday to Friday activity. It is now time for us to move on to look at the geographical pattern of demand for business travel and tourism.

THE GEOGRAPHY OF DEMAND

By definition, business travel and tourism involves the movement of people so its pattern of demand will clearly have a strong geographical dimension. This is manifested in two ways:

1 A distinction, as with leisure travel, between domestic, inbound and outbound travel. The balance of these three types of demand will vary significantly between destinations.

2 Geographical differences, in terms of countries or regions of the world, from which a destination attracts the majority of its business travellers.

The global picture

It has been estimated that the value of the global business travel market in 1995 was approximately US$398 billion of which 47 per cent came from Europe and 30 per cent from the USA. The International Convention and Congress Association estimated that, in 1999, 56 per cent of international meetings took place in Europe, 15 per cent in Asia, 11 per cent in North America, 10 per cent in Australasia/Pacific, 6 per cent in Central/South America and 2 per cent in Africa (Spiller and Ladkin, 2000). Within the world, there are, however, great variations in levels of demand for business travel and tourism. We will now look at these at three different levels:

- Regions of the world, focusing on Europe and Asia
- Different countries of the world
- Different cities of the world.

Regions of the world

Here we will concentrate on the issue of demand in what are probably the two leading business tourism areas of the world, namely, Europe and Asia.

BUSINESS TRAVEL MANAGEMENT

Many corporations had introduced a down-scaling of mobility; even a de facto stop of all travel was observed in some cases. As the "VDR Business

Travel Report Germany 2009" states, some 86,000 German companies reported that the recession had by then impacted their travel management. Of those enterprises that have implemented restrictive business travel measures as a reaction to economic developments, two out of three had reduced travel volume. One in three companies was reacting by cutting down on events.

On the other hand, in two out of three small to medium-sized enterprises (SMEs) the financial crisis has had few consequences for business travel until then, VDR – The Business Travel Association of Germany found out. The bigger the company, the more pronounced the impact and the more extensive the packages of measures. In the public sector only 11% of organizations were affected, which can be attributed in part to their activities and travel patterns (more domestic travel, fewer overnight stays).

The situation was and is at the time of writing this chapter far more dramatic, however, in companies with intensive business travel, for example VDR members. According to a survey, over 80% had felt the impact of the crisis by mid-February. This share was 60% in the months before. Over 90% of travel managers asked predicted a decline of business travel spending for the running year. About 70% thought the meltdown will be 10% or more. 44% expected a slump of 20% or more. 72% said that travel authorization had been toughened. 46% reported revised travel policies. Over 60% predicted normalization no sooner than in a year. More than 20% thought, this will take longer – or the old level will not be reached at all again.

Over 70% of German cities registered a decrease in incoming domestic business travel in the early summer of 2009, according to Deutscher Tourism usverband e.V. (DTV). For incoming international business travel, 60% of German cities reported a drop. The financial crisis began to take hold in Germany in the fourth quarter of 2008. But already in the third quarter 19% of the affected businesses had begun to introduce control measures. This previously unknown finding supports the thesis that business travel is an early indicator for the state of the overall economy.

The economic crisis and subsequent job cuts mean declining travel volume for all suppliers. Airlines and airports are likely to be the biggest losers in the crisis, at least in the short term – 37% of German businesses anticipated decreasing demand for air travel in the current year. The forecast doesn't look much better for hotels (33%) and rental cars (29%). The railways likewise have to count on some losses (26%), but 11% of organizations at least have plans for more rail travel in 2009 – in keeping with the demands of corporate social responsibility. Travel in the public sector was not affected to the same extent; one in three of the organizations surveyed believed that travel volume will remain the same.

The first signs of an economic upswing are felt, business travel is hoped to pick up again. But it is probable, VDR warns, that a boost in demand cannot, and will not, help all areas of business travel to resume their former significance in proportion and in synchrony with the economic upturn. One can expect instead to see partial distortions of the market, leading some to lose their market and negotiating positions (both on the supplier and customer side), as well as structural adjustments. The business travel association comes up with these examples and scenarios:

- Companies whose airline ticket demand has dropped drastically can expect fewer turnover bonuses, or none at all. Frequent flyers' statuses will be downgraded and they will need some time to get back their privileges (lounge use, preferred check-in and boarding, etc.).
- Businesses that neglect to book regular room contingents for major events (such as fairs), might possibly be placed on waiting lists and forced to make new plans, as capacities will in some cases have been blocked in the meantime by other customers.
- The government car-wrecking scheme ("cash for clunkers") has had drastic effects on the residual value of used cars, upsetting the calculations of car hire and leasing businesses. Some market players are already insolvent, and others are completely revising their business concepts. Car model policies and conditions are being redefined, with mobility managers' CSR approaches increasingly playing a role.
- Service-oriented suppliers, such as travel management companies or travel agencies, will utilize the phase of short-time work even more than in the past to become leaner. Personnel will in future be deployed more productively. This goes along with a general trend toward minimizing the range and depth of basic products offered. In order to compensate for these pared-down services, customer relation management will take on increasing importance.
- Airlines risk their claim to time slots at airports ("Grandfather Rights") if they do not use these slots at least 80% – which is what is happening now. For the summer 2009 schedules, the European Parliament had passed a directive that temporarily suspends the principle of "expiry if not used". The future of these "hereditary rights" is open, however. The slump might have the effect of opening up historical chances to competitors, leading to shifts in air traffic choices, especially at secondary airports.
- An increasingly critical view will be taken of long business trips to remote destinations. The demand for regional services and products, for example for meetings and events, will rise sharply.
- In times of travel restrictions, people will take more frequently advantage of the versatile possibilities offered by modern

telecommunications. Their high quality, further waves of innovations, the low price of hardware and network use, the affinity of the younger generation for technology and a habituation effect will lead to a fraction of business trips being replaced for good by virtual alternatives ("intelligent travel avoidance"). This is even more the case as CSR becomes obligatory and tangible dangers increase (there is no risk of terrorist attacks or medical infection at a web conference) and might even be reinforced by the increasingly relevant argument of the "duty of care".

Intelligent travel avoidance is increasingly part of the standard repertoire of mobility management. Two out of three businesses already now make use of video, web and/or teleconferences as an alternative to business trips. Virtual meetings also top the priority list when it comes to demonstrating corporate social responsibility in business travel. There's no question that telecommunications have become a major rival to travel. And with the trend pointing toward the mobile office, things are likely to stay that way.

So what can companies do in those areas where they have control over? Considerable synergy reserves still lay dormant, VDR claims. This is because those in charge tend to rely on organizational traditions rather than looking for strategic opportunities. Travel expense accounting tops the list of common travel management tasks with 42%. Other important mobility-relevant cost factors are taken into consideration much more rarely, for example event management (28%), fleet management (16%), travel insurance (13%) or mobile communications (11%). VDR's view is, what belongs together should grow together.

As is so often the case, small to medium-sized enterprises have the most homework to do when it comes to recognizing significant savings potential. Although travel expense accounting is typically part of the domain of those in charge of business travel, as stated above, this routine operational task is still carried out "by hand" in a surprising number of companies. A dramatic 85% of businesses with 10 to 250 employees choose to do without the (inexpensive) software available for this assignment.

The area of business travel has taken on substantially greater significance for businesses lately. Some 48,000 persons are involved today in Germany in organizational tasks having to do in a broader sense with business travel. The topic of travel management has penetrated through to the management level in two thirds of Germany's businesses. Today management is examining more closely than it did five years ago the purpose and necessity of business trips and the expenses involved. Particularly in the crisis year 2009, corporate boards are taking advantage of the savings potential offered by travel management.

But in two-thirds of companies today, business travel, although ostensibly a top management priority, is still not part of any discernible strategic plan.

And the concept of a "Travel Management Competence Centre" has not been able to gain any appreciable ground in the past five years. This is unfortunate, because crises are the best time to call in the specialists.

Two out of three businesses in Germany work with a travel agency. However, the use of such services has gone down overall during the last five years. Online offerings have gained market share in this sector, with standard services increasingly found and booked on the Internet. As travel volume rises, so does the potential for saving costs. While half of small to medium-sized enterprises do without the services of a travel management company, 84% of businesses with over 1,500 employees do take advantage of such services.

Consider also this, VDR says: Business partners that have come to be held dear can be an expensive luxury. Travel experts are astounded at how the "corner travel agency" is still the partner of choice for German businesses. Without casting doubt on the expertise of independents, businesses are surely more likely to find state-of the- art access to cost-saving technologies and value-added networks at the larger travel management companies. A (first-time?) request for proposals from various travel management companies could lead to an undreamt-of boost in efficiency. Do difficult times blindfold corporations in respect of their resolutions made during better days? Do they now ignore Corporate Social Responsibility (CSR) – which refers to the principles and concepts that form the basis for companies to voluntarily integrate social aspects and environmental concerns in their activities and in their relationships with others? Three quarters of German organizations do not incorporate CSR approaches into their business travel, VDR found out. But, in absolute figures, around 45,000 companies actively take into consideration CSR in their business trips, and almost half of companies with over 1,500 employees do so (46%). In 58% of companies which pursue CSR, these concerns also have an influence on travel management tasks.

Suppliers of transport services are particularly likely to feel the competitive impact of CSR. The choice of mode of transportation is directly influenced in two-thirds of companies, but this goes even deeper: When companies are preparing to choose the right partner or services in the transport field, the principles of sustainability are important to about one in four of them.

In larger companies business trips are avoided more frequently and replaced by virtual meetings than in medium-sized businesses. One in five organizations with over 500 employees takes part in a programme for climate compensation. Among the beneficiaries of this trend are suppliers of products and services for virtual meetings. Two out of three companies with more than 500 employees cited virtual meetings as an alternative, whereby their frequency in the private sector is significantly higher (66%) than in the public sector (38%). In 42% of the businesses that pursue CSR approaches, they also have an effect on bids for tender and a concrete influence on decisions in the business travel area. This is even more the case in companies with 500-1500 employees (53%). There is still a lot to be done in the traffic sector to reduce CO2 emissions, Anja Hänel, Project Manager Transport Club Germany (VCD), said at ITB Berlin Business Travel Days 2009. This is difficult because it is necessary to change the behavior of people and this cannot be done by end-of-pipe technologies as used in the industry sector, she added. But the goal is clear: A reduction of another 26 million metric tons is necessary to avoid the worst damages. What catches the eye when looking at the modal split is the fact that the means of transport used the most in relation with business travel is the car. Studies reveal that travelling by plane, even though it is very often criticized, is not the main problem.

What are the most important points when it comes to environmentally friendly travelling? One reason for environmentally friendly travelling is "to be fit for the future". This implies that you need to be prepared for the changes to come, which may for example include car taxes in relation to CO2 emissions or low emission zones. Furthermore, air traffic will become part of the emissions trade in 2012, so there are a lot of things you need to factor in as these will make your business travelling and your fleet a lot more expensive, VCD urges.

"Positive effects" is another motive for environmentally friendly travelling, and CSR strategies play a vital role for all kinds of companies in this context. Siemens is a perfect example for the positive effects the reorganization of the company fleet can have in the press, Ms. Hänel said. Even SMEs are currently making some effort in the field of CSR. CSR does of course not only comprise the environment and environmentally friendly travelling. But rather, mobility is a way to increase your credibility as it is connected to changing your behavior and cannot simply be bought but has to be lived. "Green washing" has a rather negative effect here, she warned.

Travel management has a lot of potential concerning improvement, efficiency and cost cutting. There are many possibilities for you to reduce your travelling costs when you know about your requirements and the necessary means of transport. This is also a significant plus when negotiating with travel agencies, Ms. Hänel advised.

Current studies about environmental awareness in Germany show that many people do care about the environment and almost 50% feel threatened by the climate change. Your employees are also a part of these 50%, she reminded the Berlin audience. The decision to accept a certain job is related to many different criteria. Among these is the fact that you do not only like your job but that your are also convinced of the quality of your company, that you can tell your friends about it and the sense that you are actively involved in protecting the environment.

The following points need to be considered, according to VCD, when companies wish to develop and follow an overall strategy:

- Are there any unnecessary travels? A common alternative to travelling is the video conference. However, video conferences are often technically complex and not suitable for every company. By now there are also lowlevel possibilities to enter this field especially in the area of web conferences and last but not least there is still the good old telephone. By having a look at the guidelines, employees can find out which trips they should and can substitute by virtual conferences. Every trip they can substitute does definitely save costs and CO2 emissions and in most cases gives some additional life quality to employees.
- Combine your trips. This is basically very easy, but the devil is in the details. What about the organization of travel management? Is it possible to know today that several employees will take part in the same meeting? In order to combine trips companies will have to integrate all their divisions and departments into travel management. By this all the different destinations of the employees are known which creates some room for interaction.
- Choosing the right means of transport. When it comes to business travel it is of course important to be flexible. It is vital for travel management to show the advantages of alternatives. The company "Infras" for example paid attention to the fact that its new business site was well connected to public transport and trains. They also coordinate time and place of an event with the timetables of public means of transport. An easy place to start the improvement of travel management is fleet management. This means buying fuel efficient cars and showing employees how to save fuel. Also car sharing should be considered. For short distances it makes sense to use bicycles.
- When it comes to means of transport companies should also take railway services into account as they are often better than their reputation, especially considering costs and delay.

Giving advice to a large audience at ITB Berlin Business Travel Days 2009, Lutz I. Stammnitz, President Procurement, Mobility and Logistics of Siemens AG, stated that the travel manager has never been so important than today. He nowadays should be a variation of the cost manager, the responsible person for mobility, logistic, work place environment, marketing communication and event management, he added. Siemens has its own spend manager who compares supply and demand to achieve the best price for the company.

One of the first things he changed concerning business travel management at Siemens was the way visa are acquisitioned. That topic is underestimated, Jochen Mesenberg from CIBT Visum Centrale, agreed. Difficulties are becoming bigger. In a lot of cases, tourist visa instead of business visa are issued, what may lead to serious problems with the authorities. Visa acquisition is a stepchild of business travel management, as time is very important and visas are often organized too late, Christoph Wolf, Director Law of International Trade, Trade Facilitation of Association of German Chambers of Industry and Commerce, assents. Furthermore it has to be stressed that a visa is just the request for entry and not an entry permit. A final advice at ITB Berlin Business Travel Days 2009 came from Michael Schneider of AirPlus. A good contract considers the interests of both parties, he said. What does a travel manager need to know about the negotiating range of his key account manager to achieve economic, effective and sustainable compromises?

The first aim of the salesman is influence on the buyer in the form of concession of the other. This influence can also be used by the buyer, while the buyer has different aims such as quality assurance, cost cutting, efficiency, problem solving and security of supply. It can be said that airlines are in any kind of crisis all the time and use this for negotiations, Mr. Schneider revealed. During the negotiations a lot of psychology can be found on both sides. The complexity between the objective targets, the preparation and the implementation has to be solved during the negotiation. A preparation like the multidimensional SWOT analysis doesn't take too long to prepare and conveys a feeling about the tenor of the buyer.

THE EUROPEAN BUSINESS TRAVEL MARKET

O'Brien, in 1998, published an interesting paper on the situation in the European business travel market in 1997 and 1998, using a variety of sources. The main conclusions of his work were as follows:

1 Europe, in 1998 accounted for an estimated 47 per cent of all business trips (international and domestic) throughout the world.
2 The split of revenues from business travel in Europe in 1998 were estimated to be: Western Europe $180.2 billion; Eastern Europe $5.8 billion.
3 The top four business travel markets in Europe in terms of expenditure in 1998 were, in descending order of importance: France; Italy; Germany and the UK. France had a 17 per cent share of all European expenditure on business travel in 1998.
4 Business travel expenditure as a percentage of all travel expenditure varied from 13 per cent in Germany to 37 per cent in Turkey.
5 The highest proportion of outbound business travel in 1998 came from the UK market.
6 The market share in national outbound markets of the five leading agencies in business travel in European countries ranged from 15 per cent in Italy to 80 per cent in Norway.
7 European business travellers accounted for approximately 17 per cent of international business trips but contributed more than 80 per cent of the total revenues for major European airlines.

8 European business travellers accounted for 43 per cent of the bed nights in hotels worldwide.
9 Fewer than 15 per cent of European business travellers were under 35 years of age.
10 Less than 15 per cent of European business travellers worked for organizations with more than 550 employees.
11 Approximately 62 per cent of European business travellers made their reservations via a travel agent.
12 Only 24 per cent of those questioned had ever accessed the Internet for travel information.
13 Twenty per cent of UK companies were unable to estimate how much they spent on travel.
14 There was a growing interest amongst European business travellers in new forms of longer-stay accommodation such as serviced apartments.
15 It was generally agreed that business travel costs have risen significantly in recent years, particularly in terms of business class air fares.

Major force in global business travel demand and that there are significant differences between the business travel market in different European countries.

THE CONFERENCE, MEETINGS AND INCENTIVES MARKET IN ASIA

Until the late 1990s the booming 'tiger economies' of Asia were recording impressive increases in business travel – inbound, outbound and domestic – year on year.

Research reported in 1997 by Muqbil estimated that 10 000–20 000 meetings, incentive events, conferences and exhibitions (MICE) were taking place in Asia each year, involving as many as 14 million participants. Of these people it was thought around 80 per cent were attending exhibitions and trade shows. This flourishing MICE market was being fuelled by annual economic growth rates of up to 8 per cent per annum on average.

The leading destinations in the mid-1990s for hosting MICE events were, in order of importance:

1 Singapore.
2 Japan.
3 Thailand.
4 Hong Kong.
5 China.

The region was particularly successful at attracting both international events and incentive travel events.

Because of this growth, investment in new facilities and infrastructure took place all over the region. For example, in the late 1990s Hong Kong opened its new airport and unveiled its new conference and exhibition centre which offers over 25 000 square metres of exhibition space.

Confidence was high in the mid-1990s. The number of exhibitions held in Bangkok was expected to rise by 17 per cent between 1996 and 1999, for instance, and the Putra World Trade Centre in Malaysia targeted a 30 per cent increase in business between 1996 and 1997. Muqbil, in *Travel and Tourism Analyst* in 1997, boldly predicted that: 'The confluence of economic progress, booming trade centres... as well as increased tourism are going to lead to sustained growth in the region's MICE industry'.

Then everything changed and the picture became more negative between 1997 and 1999, due to several factors, including:

- a severe economic crisis in most of the countries of South East Asia
- a serious reduction in the value of the currencies of many Asian countries such as Thailand and Malaysia
- political instability in Indonesia
- the 'smog' which affected large areas of the region in 1998
- the uncertainty surrounding the implications of the return of Hong Kong to China in 1997.

While one or two countries such as Singapore weathered the storm quite well, the economic crisis dealt a serious blow to most countries in the region. We can illustrate this point by looking at Indonesia.

While it is impossible in the statistics to separate leisure travel from business travel, it seems reasonable to assume that the fall in business travel to Indonesia from different markets fell at least as much as the general figures, between 1997 and 1998. Demand for travel relating to business between the countries in the region, as well as with the rest of the world, fell. Airlines and hotels reduced their prices as the problems mounted. However, paradoxically, the weak currencies made Asia an attractive destination for incentive travel groups from other regions of the world.

Now that the economies of Asia are recovering we may well see them re-establish their strong position in the global business travel market.

THE ORIGINS OF BUSINESS TRAVEL AND TOURISM

Business travel and tourism originated with trade between communities. Once agriculture developed beyond the subsistence level in areas of Africa, Asia and Europe, thousands of years before Christ was born, communities began to trade agricultural products. This led to the growth of markets, and producers travelled sometimes hundreds of kilometres to take their produce to market.

Then urban settlements began to grow and develop. These were home to artisans producing a range of products including clothes, tools and decorative arts.

These were traded with the surrounding countryside for foodstuffs. However, they were also marketed further afield, particularly if they were of high quality or were made of materials not available in other countries. Archaeological evidence shows us that this trading often took goods thousands of kilometres from where they were made. The earliest business travellers were, therefore, artisans and small-scale traders.

THE GREAT EMPIRES OF EGYPT, PERSIA, GREECE AND ROME

The rise of great empires including those of Egypt, Persia, Greece and Rome, among others, further stimulated this growth of trade-based business travel.

For example, in the Roman Empire, well-established trade routes developed across the empire, transporting goods in all directions. The museums of Europe, the Middle East and North Africa are full of evidence of this fact. A local museum of the Roman period in the UK, for example, could well contain pottery made in Italy, olive stones from Spain, wine jars from Greece and precious stones from Asia and the Middle East.

However, once these empires fell, there was often a period of economic and political instability, and as ever such instability was seen as undesirable and tended to temporarily reduce the volume of business travel and tourism.

THE MEDIEVAL TRADE FAIRS

By the medieval period business travel for trade was well established and its infrastructure included a number of massive trade fairs in strategically located towns and cities. These were vital days in the calendar for medieval merchants. The fairs might last for several weeks during which time great use was made of local accommodation, eating and entertainment facilities. One of the most famous of these fairs was the Beaucaire trade fair on the Rhoˆne river in Southern France, which attracted tens of thousands of visitors.

THE SILK ROUTE

In the Middle Ages, perhaps the greatest business travel route of all time, the Silk Route, reached its peak. Although named after one commodity, this route was a conduit for the transportation of a wide variety of goods from Asia to Europe and vice versa. And while the term Silk Route implies a single route, the fact is that there were a number of routes, starting and ending in different places.

The Silk Route was very important in two main ways:

1 It stimulated the growth of a sophisticated set of support systems for business travellers including accommodation and restaurants – the 'Caravanserai' – transport services such as camel traders and guides.

2 The route was also the way in which scientific inventions and ideas, as well as goods, moved from Asia to Europe and vice versa. It is

this route which brought phenomena as diverse as gunpowder, new religions, knowledge of astronomy and advances in medicine to Europe and the Middle East, from Asia.

The Silk Route also created a network of major stopping points on the route which have tended to remain major trading cities ever since. For example, the role of Istanbul, a great trading centre, linking Asia and Europe, was established partly due to the Silk Route.

OTHER EARLY FORMS OF SPECIALIST BUSINESS TRAVEL

Throughout history, there have been three highly specialist but important forms of specialist business travel, notably:

1. Priests of all religions, who have often had to travel with their employment, making pilgrimages to shrines.
2. Soldiers, particularly mercenaries, travelling to take part in battles or moving into newly occupied territory. Even more often they simply moved because they were ordered to move to a different garrison.
3. Workers migrating temporarily in connection with their trade. In many rural communities in France, for example, there was until recently a tradition of crafts people moving to cities to practise their trade for a few months every year when there was little demand for their services at home on the farms at certain times of the year.

Interestingly, while very ancient in origin, all three forms of business travel survive in many parts of the world.

THE INDUSTRIAL AGE AND BUSINESS TRAVEL

Business travel and tourism in Europe grew dramatically between 1750 and 1900, for three main reasons:

1. The Industrial Revolution, which began in the UK, steadily spread to many other European countries. This movement increased the scale of production of industrial goods which then had to be marketed and transported. This stimulated a growth in business travel and tourism, particularly with the rise of the on-the-road salesperson, the commercial traveller.
2. Many European countries developed empires in Africa, the Middle East and Asia, and these colonies created a demand for business travel. Industrialists needed the raw materials from these countries while their populations also provided a market for the finished goods. Furthermore, administering the colonies created a demand for business travel for the 'army' of colonial administrators from the home country to the colony, and within the colony.
3. This period saw the improvement of roads in general in Europe which made business travel easier. However, more importantly, the railway

was born. Rail travel was faster than road transport and allowed business travellers to make business trips to more distant cities without it costing too much in terms of time or money.

Because of these factors, in Europe at least, the late nineteenth century in particular was a major period of growth for international business travel and tourism.

THE EARLY TWENTIETH CENTURY

As the twentieth century dawned, the next major development in business travel and tourism was taking place in the USA. Meetings have gone on since time immemorial, but the concept of the conference or convention was developed, at this time, in the USA. Trade and scientific associations, together with the political parties, began to organize large-scale gatherings in the late nineteenth century. This activity gathered pace in the early decades of the twentieth century. Cities soon realized that hosting such events brought great economic benefits and convention bureaux began to appear to market cities as convention destinations.

As Rogers (1998) notes, the first was established in Detroit in 1896, followed soon after by Cleveland (1904), Atlantic City (1908), Denver and St Louis (1909) and Louisville and Los Angeles (1910). The phenomenon of the convention bureau is now well established around the world.

The development of the private car in the first half of the twentieth century further stimulated the growth of domestic business travel, primarily in Europe and North America.

THE EXPLOSION OF BUSINESS TRAVEL AND TOURISM SINCE 1950

While there is little hard data, it is clear that business travel and tourism has grown dramatically worldwide, since around 1950. There are two types of reason for this growth:

- Factors leading to a growth in demand
- Positive changes on the supply side which have facilitated the growth of business travel and tourism.

We can also distinguish between the reasons for the growth of business travel and tourism as a whole, and the reasons why particular sectors of business tourism have grown. Let us now look at these issues in a little more detail.

THE GROWTH OF BUSINESS TRAVEL AND TOURISM AS A WHOLE

Business travel and tourism overall, has grown worldwide because of a number of factors relating to both the demand and supply sides.

DEMAND-RELATED FACTORS

The demand-side factors which stimulated the growth of business travel and tourism worldwide in the second half of the twentieth century.

SUPPLY-RELATED FACTORS

Supply-side factors

The increase in business travel and tourism has only been possible because of developments on the supply side.

A TYPOLOGY OF BUSINESS TRAVEL AND TOURISM

For example, an individual general business trip could involve:

- A salesperson trying to sell his or her company's food product to a new customer
- A computer consultant visiting a client to sort out the client's problem
- The senior manager of a major multinational corporation visiting a branch factory
- A business person visiting a government department to apply for an export licence.

It is clear, therefore, that business travel and tourism is a diverse, complex field. However, this book will focus on the main areas of meetings, conferences, conventions, exhibitions, training courses, product launches and incentive travel. We will therefore, now, define these terms, to ensure that we all understand what we are talking about.

MEETINGS, CONFERENCES AND CONVENTIONS

According to Davidson, a meeting is: an organised event which brings people together to discuss a topic of shared interest.

[It may] be commercial or non-commercial... may be attended by 6, or many hundreds... it may last from a few hours to a week... [What makes] a meeting qualify as part of business tourism is that it engages some of the services of the tourism industry, and (is usually) held away from the premises of the organisation running it.

The terms used to describe meetings tend to vary depending on the size of the event and where it is held. A small gathering is a meeting but a large meeting is usually called a conference in the UK, a convention in the USA and a congress in much of mainland Europe.

EXHIBITIONS

Davidson defines exhibitions as: presentations of products or services to an invited audience with the object of inducing a sale or informing the visitor... Exhibitions are considered part of the business tourism industry because they stimulate travel (for both exhibitors and visitors). [They also] create a high level of demand for travel services, catering, and accommodation.

Exhibitions may also be called trade fairs or expositions in different parts of the world.

TRAINING COURSES

These are events where participants gather together at a specific time and place to receive information or to be helped to develop their skills. These can be 'internal' training courses where all the participants are employed by a single organization, or 'open' events where the training organization offers a programme which is available to all those who feel it might benefit them.

PRODUCT LAUNCHES

These are the high-profile special events which many organizations now use to attract publicity for new products and services they are launching. They usually have a range of audiences including the media, retailers and consumers. They often take place over a short time period – as little as a few minutes – but often involve a very large budget.

INCENTIVE TRAVEL

The key professional body, the Society of Incentive Travel Executives (SITE) defines this form of business tourism as follows:

Incentive Travel is a global management tool that uses an exceptional travel experience to motivate and/or recognize participants for increased levels of performance in support of the organizational goals. (SITE, 1998)

The italic words are those identified by SITE as being elements of the definition. Interestingly, incentive travel uses leisure tourism as a reward for good performance at work. It therefore bridges the divide between leisure tourism and business tourism.

8

Tourism Product

A tourism product can be defined as the sum of the physical and psychological satisfaction it provides to tourists during their travelling en route to the destination. The tourist product focuses on facilities and services designed to meet the needs of the tourist. It can be seen as a composite product, as the sum total of a country's tourist attractions, transport, and accommodation and of entertainment which result in customer satisfaction. Each of the components of a tourist product is supplied by individual providers of services like hotel companies, airlines, travel agencies, etc. The tourist product can be analysed in terms of its attraction, accessibility and accommodation.

ATTRACTIONS

Of the three basic components of a tourist product, attractions are very important. Unless there is an attraction, the tourist will not be motivated to go to a particular place. Attractions are those elements in a product which determine the choice made by particular tourist to visit one particular destination rather than another.

The attractions could be cultural, like sites and areas of archaeological interest, historical buildings and monuments, flora and fauna, beach resorts, mountains, national parks or events like trade fairs, exhibitions, arts and music festivals, games, etc. Tourist demands are also very much susceptible to changes in fashion. Fashion is an important factor in the demand for various tourist attractions and amenities. The tourist who visits a particular place for its natural beauty may decide to visit some other attractions due to a change in fashion. Peter has drawn up an inventory of the various attractions which are of significance in tourism. However, the attractions of tourism are, to a very large extent, geographical in character.

Location and accessibility (whether a place has a coastal or inland position and the ease with which a given place can be reached) are important. Physical space may be thought of as a component for those who seek the wilderness and solitude. Scenery or landscape is a compound of landforms; water and the vegetation and has an aesthetic and recreative value. Climate conditions, especially in relation to the amount of sunshine, temperature and precipitation (snow as well as rain), are of special significance.

Animal life may be an important attraction, firstly in relation to, bird watching or viewing game in their natural habitat and secondly, for sports purposes, eg. fishing and hunting. Man's impact on the natural landscape in the form of his settlements, historical monuments and archaeological remains is also a major attraction. Finally, a variety of cultural features-ways of life, folklore, artistic expressions, etc. provide valuable attractions to many.

ACCESSIBILITY

It is a means by which a tourist can reach the area where attractions are located. Tourist attractions of whatever type would be of little importance if their locations are inaccessible by the normal means of transport.

A Tourist in order to get to his destination needs some mode of transport. This mode may be a motor car, a coach, an aeroplane, a ship or a train which enables him to reach his predetermined destination.

If tourist destinations are located at places where no transport can reach or where there are inadequate transport facilities, they become of little value.

The tourist attractions, which are located near the tourist-generating markets and are linked by a network of efficient means of transport, receive the maximum number of tourists. The distance factor also plays an important role in determining a tourist's choice of a destination. Longer distances cost much more in the way of expenses on travel as compared to short distances.

An example can be that of India. About two and a half million tourist arrivals for a country of the size of India may look rather unimpressive. However if one looks at certain factors like the country's distance from the affluent tourist markets of the world such as the United States, Europe, Canada, Japan and Australia, one may conclude that the long distance is one of the factors responsible for low arrivals.

It costs a visitor from these countries, quite a substantial amount, to visit India for a holiday. It has been stated earlier that Europe and North America continue to be the main generating and receiving areas for international tourism, accounting for as much as 70% and 20% respectively, of international tourist arrivals. Easy accessibility, thus is a key factor for the growth and development of tourist movements.

ACCOMMODATION

The accommodation and other facilities complement the attractions. Accommodation plays a central role and is very basic to tourist destinations. World Tourism Organization in its definition of a tourist has stated that he must spend at least one night in the destination visited, to qualify as a tourist.

This presupposes availability of some kind of accommodation. The demand for accommodation away from one's home is met by a variety of facilities. The range and type of accommodation is quite varied and has undergone considerable change since the last half century.

There has been a decline in the use of boarding houses and small private hotels. Larger hotels are increasing their share of holiday trade, especially in big metropolitan areas and popular spots. In more traditional holiday and sea-side resorts in Europe and elsewhere, big hotels are keeping their share of holiday resorts. In recent years, some changes have been reflected in the type of accommodation.

There has been an increasing demand for more non-traditional and informal types of accommodation. The latest trends in accommodation are holiday villages. In recent years there has been an increase in the popularity of such accommodation.

Accommodation may in itself be an important tourist attraction. In fact, a large number of tourists visit a particular destination or town simply because there is a first class luxury hotel or resort which provides excellent services and facilities. Some countries like Switzerland, Holland, France, Austria, and Belgium have gained a reputation for providing excellent accommodation with good cuisine.

Many hotel establishments elsewhere in various countries, especially the resort hotels, have gained a reputation for their excellent cuisine, services and facilities. The French government for instance, paved the way for tourist development of Corsica by launching a big hotel development programme.

NATURAL TOURISM PRODUCTS

These include natural resources such as areas, climate and its setting, landscape and natural environment. Natural resources are frequently the key elements in a destination's attraction.

Let us look at some examples:

- Countryside
- Climate- temperature, rains, snowfall, days of sunshine
- Natural Beauty- landforms, hills, rocks, gorges, terrain
- Water- lakes, ponds, rivers, waterfalls, springs
- Flora and Fauna
- Wildlife
- Beaches
- Islands
- Spas
- Scenic Attractions

The climate of a tourist destination is often an important attraction. Good weather plays an important role in making a holiday. Millions of tourists from countries with extreme climates visit beaches in search of fine weather and sunshine. The sunshine and clear sea breeze at the beaches have attracted many people for a very long time. In fact, development of spas and resorts along the sea coasts in many countries were a result of the travellers. urge to enjoy good weather and sunshine. In Europe, countries like France, Italy, Spain and Greece have developed beautiful beach resorts.

North Europeans visit the Mediterranean coast searching for older resorts like Monte Carlo, Nice and Cannes on the Riviera and new resorts in Spain and Italy. Beautiful beaches of India, Sri Lanka, and Thailand, Indonesia and Australia and some other new destinations are more examples of how good weather can attract tourists. All these areas capitalise on good weather. Destinations with attractive winter climates, winter warmth and sunshine are also important centres of tourist attraction.

Many areas have become important winter holiday resorts attracting a large number of tourists. Around these winter resorts, winter sport facilities have been installed to cater to the increasing needs of tourists. People from warm climates travel especially to see snowfall and enjoy the cold climate. In countries with tropical climates, many upland cool areas have been developed as 'hill stations'. Hence climate is of great significance as a tourism product. The scenery and natural beauty of places has always attracted tourists. Tourists enjoy nature in all its various forms. There are land forms like mountains, canyons, coral reefs, cliffs, etc. One of the great all time favourite tourist destination is the Grand Canyon, Arizona. Mountain ranges like the Himalayas, Kilimanjaro, and Swiss Alps, etc.

There are water forms like rivers, lakes waterfalls, geysers, glaciers, etc. The Niagara Falls shared by Canada and the United States is an example of how scenic waterfalls attract tourists. Lake Tahoe in California and the, deserts of Egypt are other examples of great tourist products. Other great natural wonders that attract tourists are the Giants Causeway of Northern Ireland, the Geysers of Iceland, the glaciers of the Alps, the forests of Africa etc. Vegetation like forests, grasslands, moors deserts, etc. has all been developed as tourist products. Flora and Fauna attract many a tourist. Tourists like to know the various types of plants and trees that they see and which trees are seen in which seasons.

There are many plants which are specific to certain regions and many times students and travellers visit those areas especially to see those varieties of plants. Thick forest covers, attract tourists who enjoy trekking and hunting activities. Fauna attracts tourists who like to watch birds, wild mammals, reptiles and other exotic and rare animals. Countries in South East Asia have crocodile gardens, bird sanctuaries, and other tourist products that display the fauna of their region. Spas are gaining popularity as modern tourism products all over the world. While most parts of the world have their own therapies and treatments that are effective in restoring the wellness and beauty of people.

New kinds of health tours that are gaining popularity are spa tours. Spas offer the unique advantages of taking the best from the West and the East, combining them with the indigenous system and offering best of the two worlds. For example Swedish massages work well with the Javanese Mandy, lulur, aromatherapy, reflexology and traditional ayurvedic procedures. Now various spa products are being combined with yoga, meditation, and pranayama, giving a holistic experience to tourists. Spa treatments are now combined with other medical treatments to treat blood pressure, insomnia, depression, paralysis and some other diseases. People are now travelling to spas and clinics for curative baths and medical treatment.

In some countries like Italy, Austria and Germany, great importance is given to spa treatments. In Russia along the Black Sea coast and in the foothills of the Caucasus Mountains, there are many world famous sanatoria where millions of Russians and international tourists throng every year. Beach tourism is very popular among the tourists today. Tourists of all age groups, backgrounds, cultures and countries enjoy this tourism product. Besides attraction and saleability, beach holidaying has lead to overall development of tourism in many parts of the world.

The basic importance of beaches is that they provide aesthetic and environmental value of the beach such as beautiful natural scenery with golden sands, lush green vegetation and bright blue sky. The water should be clear, free of currents and underwater rocks. Beach tourism activities include water and land resource use. The water usage involves swimming, surfing, sailing, wind surfing, water scootering, Para- sailing, motorboat rides, etc. The land use has multifacets like sunbathing, recreational areas for tourists (parks, playgrounds, clubs, theatre, amusement parks, casinos, cultural museums, etc.), accommodation facilities (hotels, cottages, villas, camping sites, etc.), car and bus parking areas, entertainment and shopping complexes, access roads and transportation network.

Due to its multidimensional requirements the beach product needs special care. A beach resort needs to be developed as an integrated complex to function as a self-contained community. Environmental management should also ensure the availability of necessary infrastructure in the immediate hinterland to the coastal region in support of the development on the coast to maintain its ecosystem. Islands abound with natural beauty, with the rare flora and fauna and tribes. This makes islands an ideal place for adventure, nature and culture lovers to visit. This tourist product has great scope as these islands are being developed as tourist paradises. For example, Hawaii, Maldives, Mauritius, Tahiti, Andaman and Nicobar Islands, etc. has developed with tourism activity over the past few decades.

The topography is generally undulating and they offer natural scenic beauty with exotic flora and fauna. Most of these islands have places of worship like churches, temples, etc. As an added attraction some of these islands have developed as tax havens thereby encouraging commercial development of these economies. They offer social and cultural attractions as tourists can experience the local lifestyle, local food, fairs and festivals, etc. Scenic attractions, like good weather, are very important factors in the development of tourism.

Breath-taking mountain scenery and the coastal stretches exert a strong fascination on the tourist the magnificent mountain ranges provide an atmosphere of peace and tranquillity. Tourists visiting the northern slopes of the Alps in Switzerland and Austria and the southern slopes in Italy and also the Himalayan slopes of India and Nepal for the first time, cannot but be charmed by their physical magnificence.

PRODUCT IN TOURISM

The needs of the tourist relate to comfort and pleasure in travel, stay, food arrangements and visiting spots of interest and attraction.

Hence, the tourist expectations are:

- Able to experience the new places–their life-styles, food, culture, heritage, etc. as per one's own choice.
- Be able to visit places of interest, spend adequate time at such places.
- Facility of transportation available.
- Facing no risk to one's person or belongings, etc.
- Getting suitable food to one's tastes and health.
- Not to be hurried or hustled against the preferred place.
- To be looked after and cared for.

The three basic components of a tourist product are:

- Attractions,
- Facilities, and
- Accessibility.

Attractions constitute an important feature of the product. Attractions are those elements in the tourist product, which determine the choice of the particular tourist product, to visit one particular destination rather than another. These are things to see and enjoy like cultural sites, historical buildings, beaches, mountains, national parks, or events like trade fairs, exhibitions, music festivals, etc.

Facilities are those elements in the tourist product, which are a necessary aid to the tourist centre. The facilities complement the attractions. These include accommodation, food, communications, guides and so on. Accessibility is a means by which a tourist can reach the areas where attractions are located. Tourists' attractions are of little importance if their locations are inaccessible by the normal means of transport. It also relates to the formalities in reaching the places like visas, customs, bookings etc.

In Tourism, the products are varied. A travel agent may arrange for itineraries and airline bookings and may also help in getting passport, visas, foreign exchange clearances, embarkation facilities at airport and so on. Similarly attractions are added to a destination. For example, 18 rooms of Buckingham Palace have been opened to visitors, which are a major tourist attraction to visitors.

Apart from the Throne Room, Drawing Room and the Picture Gallery, the Souvenir shop selling white china mugs with Buckingham Palace written on it or Crystal Balls with details from the State Dining Room is also a part of the attraction. A product in tourism is the place of destination and what one may experience while proceedings to and staying at that destination.

For example,

- Sentose islands of Singapore, is packaged as a place where there are no shops, no skyscrapers, no offices- a place of quiet and tranquility, to relax and be with nature, so different from Singapore. Travelling by cable car to the island is also a part of the package.
- Places in Rajasthan like Jaisalmer are being offered as tourism products to experience the life-style of Maharajas, living in real palaces with kingly comforts, travelling on ' Palace on Wheels', the luxuriously fitted railway train, going hunting on elephant back and so on. The product is not merely the city of Jaisalmer and what it may offer as historical and cultural importance. The product is the total experience of travel and other attractions, all related to the royalty of Jaisalmer.

The tourism product may be developed with emphasis on art, architecture, culture, religion, history, sports, leisure, temples, life-styles, etc.

- Himalayas are a product not only for sports and adventure tourism, but also for nature lovers and spirituality.
- Varanasi is a product based on religion, the Ganges capturing the essence of Oldest Hindu heritage.
- The accommodation provided, is as much a part of the safari in the African forests as the prospect of seeing wild-life. Many prefer and pay more to live in the open country 'with nature' instead of in five-star comfort.

CHARACTERISTICS OF TOURISM PRODUCT MANAGEMENT

By now, you must have understood what a tourism product is. Now let us look at some of its characteristics:-

INTANGIBLE

Unlike a tangible product, say, a motor car or refrigerator, no transfer of ownership of goods is involved in tourism. The product here cannot be seen or inspected before its purchase. Instead, certain facilities, installations, items of equipment are made available for a specified time and for a specified use. For example, a seat in an aeroplane is provided only for a specified time.

PSYCHOLOGICAL

A large component of tourism product is the satisfaction the consumer derives from its use. A tourist acquires experiences while interacting with the new environment and his experiences help to attract and motivate potential customers.

HIGHLY PERISHABLE

A travel agent or tour operator who sells a tourism product cannot store it. Production can only take place if the customer is actually present. And once consumption begins, it cannot be stopped, interrupted or modified. If the product remains unused, the chances are lost *i.e.* if tourists do not visit a particular place, the opportunity at that time is lost. It is due to this reason that heavy discount is offered by hotels and transport generating organisations during off season.

COMPOSITE PRODUCT

The tourist product cannot be provided by a single enterprise unlike a manufactured product. The tourist product covers the complete experience of a visit to a particular place. And many providers contribute to this experience. For instance, airline supplies seats, a hotel provides rooms and restaurants, travel agents make bookings for stay and sightseeing, etc.

UNSTABLE DEMAND

Tourism demand is influenced by seasonal, economic political and others such factors. There are certain times of the year which see a greater demand than others. At these times there is a greater strain on services like hotel bookings, employment, the transport system, etc.

FIXED SUPPLY IN THE SHORT RUN

The tourism product unlike a manufactured product cannot be brought to the consumer; the consumer must go to the product. This requires an in-depth study of users' behaviour, taste preferences, likes and dislikes so that expectations and realities coincide for the maximum satisfaction of the consumer. The supply of a tourism product is fixed in the short run and can only be increased in the long run following increased demand patterns.

ABSENCE OF OWNERSHIP

When you buy a car, the ownership of the car is transferred to you, but when you hire a taxi you buy the right to be transported to a predetermined destination at a predetermined price (fare). You neither own the automobile nor the driver of the vehicle. Similarly, hotel rooms, airline tickets, etc. can be used but not owned. These services can be bought for consumption but ownership remains with the provider of the service. So, a dance can be enjoyed by viewing it, but the dancer cannot be owned.

HETEROGENEOUS

Tourism is not a homogeneous product since it tends to vary in standard and quality over time, unlike a T.V set or any other manufactured product. A package tour or even a flight on an aircraft can't be consistent at all times. The reason is that this product is a service and services are people based. Due to this, there is variability in this product. All individuals vary and even the same individual may not perform the same every time. For instance, all air hostesses cannot provide the same quality of service and even the same air hostess may not perform uniformly in the morning and evening. Thus, services cannot be standardised.

RISKY

The risk involved in the use of a tourism product is heightened since it has to be purchased before its consumption. An element of chance is always present in its consumption. Like, a show might not be as entertaining as it promises to be or a beach holiday might be disappointing due to heavy rain.

MARKETABLE

Tourism product is marketed at two levels. At the first level, national and regional organisations engage in persuading potential tourists to visit the country or a certain region. These official tourist organisations first create knowledge of its country in tourist -generating markets and persuade visitors in these markets to visit the country. At the second level, the various individual firms providing tourist services, market their own components of the total tourist product to persuade potential tourists to visit that region for which they are responsible.

APPROACHES TO NEW PRODUCT DEVELOPMENT IN HOSPITALITY AND TOURISM

A company must develop new products to survive. New products can be obtained through acquisition or through new product development (NPD). There is a reasonably established approach to NPD, but Scheuing and Johnson (1989) have proposed a model for new service development (NSD), based on a review of other models and research into 66 US-based service firms. The model has 15 steps and four main stages. The first stage (steps 1–3) of NSD focuses on how new ideas are generated and developed. The development process must begin with a precise formulation of objectives and strategy. A well-designed strategy drives and directs the entire innovation effort and imbues it with effectiveness and efficiency. The second step is for companies to ensure that they have organized or structured their plan in such a way as to enable innovation to take place. In large companies, this may involve setting up a research and development (R & D) department. The third step consists of idea generation and screening. New ideas can be drawn from external sources, or be generated internally through consultation and brainstorming. Often the most powerful idea source is customer feedback.

The idea generation and development stage of NSD is followed by the second stage – the 'go/no-go' stage – comprising four steps (steps 4–7) that enable the company to decide whether or not it will proceed with the new development. Concept development requires that the surviving ideas be expanded into fully fledged concepts, especially if there is a significant service element. Concept testing is a research technique designed to evaluate whether a prospective user understands the idea of the proposed good or service, reacts favourably to it, and feels it provides benefits that answer unmet needs. The sixth step, business analysis, should represent a comprehensive investigation into the business implications of each concept.

The project authorization step occurs when top management commits corporate resources to the implementation of a new idea. In an industry such as tourism, which consists of many small organizations, it is likely that 90 per cent of companies have just one person or department to authorize all innovative projects.

Once the go-ahead has been given, the third stage of NSD – test design – is reached, in which detailed design and implementation of the innovation is carried out (steps 8–11). At this point, the new concept is converted into an operational entity. This requires design and testing. For a service, this activity should involve both the input of prospective users and the active co-operation of the operations personnel who will ultimately be delivering the service. It may also be necessary to design new production processes or develop new equipment.

This stage also includes marketing design and testing. To complete the test design phase, all employees should be familiarized with the nature and operational details of the new service. For instance, research into flight catering has showed that 91 per cent of airlines engage in personnel training, whereas only 68 per cent of food manufacturers do so.

The final stage of NSD is the evaluation of the new innovation, comprising four steps. *Service testing* should be used to determine potential customer acceptance of the new service, while a pilot run ensures its smooth functioning. The Marriott Corporation designed a new chain of hotels for business travellers – Courtyard by Marriott – but tested the concept under real-world conditions before subsequently developing the large chain that filled a gap in the market.

The next step, *test marketing*, examines the saleability of the new service, and a field test should be carried out with a limited sample of customers. With the delivery system and marketing in place and with the service thoroughly tested, the company should next initiate the full-scale *launch*, introducing the service product to the entire market area.

Different sectors tend to evaluate their new services/products in slightly different ways. For instance, fast-food operators use market surveys, whereas food service contractors rely more on after-sales customer feedback. The final step, *post-launch review*, should be aimed at determining whether the strategic objectives were achieved or whether further adjustments are needed.

Sheuing and Johnson suggest that firms should not rigidly follow this model but instead consider it as a framework from which to select those activities they deem necessary for a specific development. In fact, research studies have shown that tourism organizations do not follow a systematic NSD process.

It has been suggested that the systematic and formal approach to innovation is likely to be adopted only when one of the following is true: new products with major process impact are developed; a number of interrelated innovations are being developed simultaneously; product life cycles are long; competitors are unlikely to enter the market with a similar product or service; the new product is protected by license or patent; or the innovation is original or 'new to the world'.The tourism and hospitality market clearly has few of these characteristics.

Innovation is likely to follow a shorter, simplified development process when minor modifications are made to existing products or services; there is no license protection; the 'new' product is largely a copy of a competitor's product; innovation is not part of a major change programme; and competitors are actively innovating.

An organization creates internal conditions that either foster or hinder innovation. Often, these are strongly influenced by the external environment. Conditions that may encourage a systematic but rigid approach to innovation are a bureaucratic culture, mature marketplace, the involvement of external consultants, and formal research and development departments.

Conditions that encourage a dynamic and flexible approach to innovation are the following: growing supply chain integration; an organizational culture founded on innovation; industry association sponsorship; creative and entrepreneurial leadership; and deregulated markets.

These conditions are likely to be more typical of organizations in tourism and hospitality, as there are many small, highly entrepreneurial firms, such as weekendtrips.com, operating in a largely deregulated marketplace.

However, large companies can also encourage innovation. Virgin, has always been innovative, largely because of the entrepreneurial leadership of Richard Branson. His entrepreneurship has always led him to take on challenges, risks and new projects, which he calls 'brand stretching'.

PHYSICAL EVIDENCE AND THE SERVICESCAPE IN HOSPITALITY

An important part of the augmented product is the physical environment. Because many tourism and hospitality services are intangible, customers often rely on tangible cues, or physical evidence, to evaluate the service before its purchase and to assess their satisfaction with the service during and after consumption. The physical evidence is the environment in which the service is delivered and in which the firm and customer interact, and any tangible components that facilitate performance or communication of the service. The physical facility is often referred to as the servicescape, and is very important for tourism and hospitality products such as hotels, restaurants and theme parks, which are dominated by experience attributes. Disney, for example, effectively uses the servicescape to excite its customers. The brightly coloured displays, the music, the rides, and the costumed characters all reinforce the feelings of fun and excitement that Disney seeks to generate in its customers. The Global Spotlight on Sweden's Icehotel shows how important the servicescape is for accommodations. In this case, the hotel is made entirely of ice and snow, and provides a unique experience for tourists.

They include all aspects of the organization's servicescape that affect customers, including both exterior attributes (such as parking and landscape) and interior attributes (such as design, layout, equipment and décor). Signage is also part of the physical evidence; in 2007, Beijing attempted to stamp out embarrassingly bad English on bilingual signs in the run-up to the 2008 Olympics. The municipal government issued translation guidelines for signs in hotels, shopping malls, public transport and tourist attractions. At the time, the Park of Ethnic Minorities was identified as 'Racist Park', while the emergency exits at Beijing's international airport read, 'No entry on peacetime'. Consumer researchers know that the design of the servicescape can influence customer choices, expectations, satisfaction and other behaviours. Retailers know that customers are influenced by smell, décor, music and layout. Arby's, a fast-food chain in North America, uses the servicescape to position its restaurants as a step above other quick-service outlets. With carpeted floors, cushioned seating and a décor 'superior' to other fast-food chains, the company asserts that the interior ambience of Arby's outlets contributes to attracting diners. Design of work environments can also affect employees' productivity, motivation and satisfaction. The challenge in many tourism and hospitality settings is to design the physical space in a way that supports the needs and preferences of customers and employees simultaneously.

Employees and customers in service firms respond to their physical surroundings in three ways – cognitively, emotionally, and physiologically – and these responses influence their behaviours in that environment. First, the perceived servicescape may elicit *cognitive* responses, including people's beliefs about a place and their beliefs about the people and products found there. For example, a consumer study found that a travel agent's office décor affected customer understanding of the travel agent's behaviour. In addition to influencing cognitions, the perceived servicescape may elicit *emotional* responses that in turn influence behaviours. The colours, décor, music, and other elements of the atmosphere can have an unexplained and sometimes subconscious affect on the moods of people in the place. According to Russell *et al.* (1981), servicescapes that are both pleasant and arousing are 'exciting', while those that are pleasant and non-arousing, or sleepy, are 'relaxing'. Unpleasant servicescapes that are arousing are 'distressing', while unpleasant, sleepy ser-vicescapes are 'gloomy'. Finally, the servicescape may affect people in purely *physiological* ways. Noise that is too loud may cause physical discomfort, the temperature of a room may cause people to shiver or perspire, the air quality may make it difficult to breathe, and the glare of lighting may decrease ability to see and may cause physical pain. All of these physical responses will influence whether people remain in and enjoy a particular environment. In 2004, a Vancouver-based company, Enhanced Air Technologies, developed Commercaire pheromone, a synthetic compound that mimics the maternal sense of comfort piped to children when they are crying or unhappy. Filtered into a store, the odourless substance is meant to relax customers so they stay longer and buy more. The firm claims retailers can expect revenue growth of between 9 per cent and 20 per cent when using the product. While Enhanced Air's sales-stimulating pheromone may be a first, there is a long history of retailers using fake sawdust or fresh bread smells to foster favourable emotions in patrons.

The discussion of consumer trends pointed out that today's consumer desires experiences, and more and more businesses are responding by explicitly designing experiences with themed servicescapes. At themed restaurants such as the Hard Rock Café, Planet Hollywood or the Rainforest Café, the food is just a prop for what's known as 'eatertainment'. Retailers are also creating themes that tie merchandising presentations together in a staged experience. A popular tourist attraction in Las Vegas is the Forum, a mall that displays its distinctive theme – an ancient Roman marketplace – in every detail. The Simon DeBartolo Group, which developed the mall, disperses this motif through a panoply of architectural effects. These include marble floors, stark white pillars, 'outdoor' cafes, living trees, flowing fountains – and even a painted blue sky with fluffy white clouds that yield regularly to simulated storm, complete with lighting and thunder. Every mall entrance and every storefront is an elaborate Roman replica. Hourly, inside the main entrance, statues of Julius Caesar and other Roman luminaries come to life and speak. 'Hail, Caesar!' is a frequent cry, and Roman centurions periodically march through on their way to the adjacent Caesar's Palace casino.

Despite the increased emphasis on the servicescape in designing experiences, companies that fail to provide consistently engaging experiences, overprice their experiences relative to the value perceived, or overbuild their capacity to stage them will see pressure on demand, pricing, or both. The Rainforest Café and Planet Hollywood have both encountered trouble because they have failed to refresh their experiences. Guests find nothing different from one visit to the next. Disney, on the other hand, avoids staleness by frequently adding new attractions and even whole parks, such as the Animal Kingdom in 1998 and California Adventure in 2001.

The latter US$1.4 billion project, which also included construction of a first-class hotel, was designed to accommodate 30,000 people a day, to add to the 70,000 visitors that come to Disneyland across the street. Covering 55 acres, California Adventure is a high-energy park, celebrating the dreams of the many Americans who came to California and reflecting the highlights and the pop culture of the state today. It features attractions a little wilder and a lot more grown up than the original Disneyland. These attractions are situated in three themed areas: Paradise Pier, Golden State and Hollywood Pictures Backlot.

The Snapshot below about the new Churchill Museum in London shows how designers of a museum have used technology to enhance the servicescape, creating an interactive educational experience for visitors.

PRODUCT PLANNING

Product Mix

The most basic decisions a tourism organization has to make are what business it is in and what product mix is appropriate to it. The product mix is the portfolio of products that an organization offers to one market or several.

According to Seaton and Bennett (1996), five basic market/product options exist:

1. Several markets with multi-product mixes for each (*e.g.*, mass tour operators that offer a wide range of multi-destination packages to a variety of market segments);
2. Several markets with a single product for each (*e.g.*, airlines with a product for business and economy class travellers);
3. Several markets with a single product for all (*e.g.*, a national tourist organization promoting a country);
4. Single market with a multi-product mix (*e.g.*, a specialist tour operator with a range of cultural tours aimed at a wealthy, educated market); and
5. Single market with a single product (*e.g.*, a heli-skiing operator targeting the very rich).

The decision as to which product mix option to adopt depends upon many factors, including the strength and value of consumer demand in the different markets, the level of competition in each market, and the distinctive competence of the organization to service the markets adequately. The starting point in product analysis and planning is thus an analysis of the consumer and competitive offerings in relation to the goals and product capacity of the tourism organization. The most successful products emerge when the marketing planning steps. Portfolio and SWOT analysis are discussed there; another useful method of analysing the tourism product is by considering its features and benefits. Features consist of the objective attributes of a tourism product; benefits are the rewards the product gives the consumer. Hong Kong International Airport was recently named the world's best airport in a survey of over 50,000 frequent travellers. Part of the reason is the features of the airport and the benefits they offer passengers. As well as shops that sell everything from rare white tea to cell phones, there are free plasma televisions to watch, a children's play area, wireless broadband, internet cafés, a prayer room, a pharmacy, nap rooms, a beauty salon, shower facilities, a medical centre (complete with on-site vaccinations and x-ray machines) and displays from Hong Kong museums.

Product Life Cycle

One of the most basic product analysis tools is the product life cycle (PLC) analysis, the Opening Vignette described the journey of Concorde through this life cycle. Plotting products or services to identify what stage they are at in their PLC is a valuable way of reviewing a product's past and current position and making predictions about its future. As part of a portfolio analysis, an organization should access each good and service in terms of its position in the product life cycle. *Product development* begins when the company finds and develops a new product idea. The Snapshot later in this chapter about the Sydney BridgeClimb describes how its founder conceived the idea nine years before it was put into action.

The *introduction* phase is a period of slow sales and low profits because of the investment required for product introduction. The new Churchill Museum in London could be considered to be in this phase. The *growth* phase is characterized by increasing market acceptance and substantial improvement in profits. This is the case for the Sydney BridgeClimb, as it now takes tourists on the climb 12 hours a day, 363 days a year. The *maturity* phase is a period of slow sales marked by high profits, as the product is well entrenched in the marketplace and has an acceptable market share. An example would be Sweden's Icehotel. However, when sales begin to drop because competitors are moving into the marketplace, the product enters the *decline* stage. Profits and market share decline, and major costs may be involved in redeveloping, refurbishing, or maintaining the product. This is the case for many small ski resorts around the world.

Using the PLC concept to develop marketing strategy can be difficult. Strategy is both a cause and a result of the PLC. At the introduction stage, promotion spending is likely to be high in order to inform consumers about the new product and encourage them to buy it. A company will focus on selling to buyers who are ready to buy, usually higher-income groups. Prices tend to be on the high side because of low output, production problems, high promotion costs and other expenses. At the growth stage, the early adopters will continue to buy, and later buyers will start following their lead, encouraged by favourable word of mouth. Competitors will enter the market, attracted by the opportunity for profit, and they will introduce more product features that will expand the market. In the growth stage, the organization faces a tradeoff between high market share and high current profit. By investing heavily in product improvement, promotion and distribution, it can capture a dominant position. But it sacrifices maximum current profit in the hope of making this up in the next stage.

When sales start to slow down, the product will enter the maturity stage; this lasts longer than the previous two stages and poses stronger challenges to marketing management. Most products or services are in this stage, and it is a phase that is characterized by heavy competition. The only way to increase sales is to lure customers away from competition, and so price wars and heavy advertising are common. At this stage, an aggressive product manager will seek to increase consumption by modifying markets and/or products. The product manager may also try to improve sales by changing one or more of the marketing mix elements.

In the decline stage, some firms will withdraw from the market. Those that remain may reduce the number of their product offerings or the number of market segments they are targeting. They may also reduce the promotion budget, and prices. For each declining product, management must decide whether to maintain, harvest, or drop it.

However, the PLC is not as simple as it sounds in theory, and according to Mercer (1992), 'its supposed universal applicability is largely a myth'. The study of the PLC pattern for a particular product has to take into account the market the product is in. For example, if a product is showing no growth or decline, it may still be very successful if the market as a whole is in decline. Another complication of the PLC is that a product that is in overall decline may be losing its customers from one market segment but increasing appeal or holding steady with another. Ski areas, for example, have been very successful in attracting an increasing number of snowboarders over the past decade, despite a drop in the number of downhill skiers. In addition, although the PLC concept is neat on paper, it is often difficult to determine what particular stage a product is at. Finally, even assuming that a product's life cycle position can be determined, it may not be obvious what action should be taken.

Despite these problems, the PLC is a valuable concept, since it forces the organization to analyse trends for its product in relation to the overall market and the segments within it, in order to assess future marketing requirements. Ski areas have adapted to the growth in snow-boarders (referred to above) by changing the products they offer; most successful ski areas these days have designated areas for snowboarders. A related concept for analysing destinations is that of the tourism area life cycle.

Positioning

Positioning is the bedrock of product management. The concept as the natural follow-through of market segmentation and market targeting, and highlights the three steps necessary to develop an effective position in the target market segment. The objective of positioning is to create a distinctive place in the minds of potential customers. Positioning in tourism should evoke images of a destination or product in the customer's mind – images that differentiate the product from the competition and also convey that it can satisfy their needs and wants. Effective positioning should direct all the marketing functions of a business. Advertising and promotions, as well as decisions on price, product and distribution channels must all be consistent with positioning goals. Often, these marketing functions will be driven by a positioning statement, which is a phrase that reflects the image the organization wants to create. The positioning statement for the Churchill Museum, for example, is: 'A benchmark for personality museums in the twenty-first century'. This statement encapsulates what the Museum stands for, the essence of what the museum does, and how it stands out from competitors.

There is an endless number of positioning strategies, and selection of the appropriate approach is vital to the success of a tourism organization.

Burke and Resnick (1991) have identified four key positioning strategies that are not mutually exclusive and may therefore be used individually or in combination:

1. Positioning relative to target market (*e.g.* business travellers, families with children under ten, etc.);
2. Positioning by price and quality (*e.g.* a premium product such as the Concorde);
3. Positioning relative to a product class (*e.g.* a tour operator positioning its products within a winter sports tourism category); and
4. Positioning relative to competitors (*e.g.* the Hertz Rental Car campaign 'We try harder', which drew attention to the fact that Hertz was not market leader but would work harder to catch up with its competitors).

Boutique hotels use a combination of these positioning strategies to succeed in the very competitive hotel market. Loosely defined as small, specialized accommodations, mainly in prime city locations, boutique hotels offer high standards of service, style and comfort which suit the corporate jet-setter. The main challenge for boutiques is how to keep ahead in such a fiercely competitive market. Ian Schrager, owner of the Sanderson and St Martin's Lane hotels in London, has managed to stay ahead of the game by attracting a celebrity clientele and introducing luxurious spas at his properties. In Spain, Sorat Hotels and Sol Melia have tried to differentiate themselves by emphasizing the quality of their personal service, while the UK group Hotel du Vin has made its name with the high standard of food on offer at its stylish bistros (Goff, 2003). The Global Spotlight below is an example of an unusual tourism product that has positioned itself as a unique, one-off hotel; one that has been rebuilt every year since 1990.

But at the end of the 1980s it was decided to turn things around. Instead of viewing the dark and cold winter as a disadvantage, the unique elements of the Arctic were to be exploited as an asset. In 1990 the French ice artist Jannot Derit was invited to have the opening of his exhibition in a specially built igloo on the frozen Torne River. The 60-square metre building, named Arctic Hall, attracted many curious visitors to the area. One night a group of foreign guests, equipped with reindeer hides and sleeping bags, decided it would be a good idea to use the cylindrical-shaped igloo as accommodation. The following morning the brave group raved about the unique sensation of sleeping in an igloo. Hence, the concept of Icehotel was born, and today Icehotel is world-famous for its unique concept and its fantastic works of art.

The Icehotel has been rebuilt every year since 1990, and what started off as a 60-square metre igloo has grown to an almost 5,000-square metre hotel, using more than 30,000 tons of snow and 4,000 tons of ice. Snow cannons help to form the snow over arched steel sections. The ice pillars are then put in place to give extra strength to the self-supporting snow arches. In March, ice is harvested from the River Torne with the help of tractors and special ice saws. The blocks are then stored and used to build the hotel in the winter.

The hotel is never more than six months old, because in summer it melts. As a result, the exact number of rooms varies, but during the winter of 2004/2005 it had 85. The hotel also has a reception, hall of pillars, ice art exhibition, cinema, and a church. About 14,000 guests a year spend the night in the hotel, with over 40,000 day visitors walking through the reindeer-skin covered doors. In April, the entire hotel literally trickles into the Torne River, to be resurrected during November and December the following winter, with a new architecture and new works of art. So visitors can experience a new Icehotel every year.

The temperature in the Icehotel varies between -4 and -9 degrees centigrade, depending on the temperature outside, which can dip to -40. At night, guests are supplied with a specially made sleeping bag, and are given a talk on 'how to survive in the Icehotel'. For some, this may mean sampling the wonderfully coloured cocktails served in ice glasses at the Absolut Ice Bar. Others may want to try the food at the Icehotel Restaurant which serves Laplandic gourmet food on plates of ice from the Torne River. During the daytime there are plenty of activities for visitors such as snowmobiling, dog-sledding, moose safaris and ice sculpting. Visitors can also attend concerts in an open-air venue inspired by Shakespeare's Globe Theatre in London. The 520-person theatre is a marvel of ice engineering, carefully crafted by technicians in just three weeks. However, staying at the Icehotel doesn't come cheap. A deluxe suite costs about 6,000SKr a night (£440).

BRANDING

The practice of branding was developed in the field of packaged goods, as a method of establishing a distinctive identity for a product based on competitive differentiation from other products. Branding was commonly achieved through naming, trademarking, packaging, product design and promotion. Successful branding gave a unique identity to what might otherwise have been a generic product. This identity produced a consistent image in the consumer's mind, which facilitated recognition and quality assurance. In the 19th century, products such as Beecham's Pills, Cadbury's Chocolate and Eno's Salts were early users of branding. These days, the market in packaged goods is dominated by brands, and in the last few decades branding has also been widely recognized in services marketing. A 'brand', in the modern marketing sense, offers the consumer relevant added value – a superior proposition that is distinctive from competitors' and that imparts meaning above and beyond the product's functional aspects. There is even a Museum of Brands in London, where visitors can view 10,000 consumer products covering 200 years of packaging, branding and advertising.

Branding offers a solution to some of the problems in services marketing – in particular those of consistency and product standardization. Branding can be a way of unifying services, which is why it has been particularly developed in hotel marketing. Research shows that nearly 90 per cent of bookings are made with branded hotel chains, and nine out of ten consumers can distinguish between chains, franchise operators and independents.

For large hotel companies that have a wide variety of properties, grouping them into brands can:

1. Unify them into more easily recognizable smaller groups;
2. Enable each branded group to be targeted at defined market segments; and
3. Enable product delivery, including human resource management, to be focused on creating a specific set of benefits for a specific market.

North America has over 200 hotel brands competing for business, and many hotel chains offer a family of sub-brands or endorsed brands. For example, Hilton Hotels Corporation, Intercontinental and Starwood each has seven sub-brands, while Marriott International has 12 (as well as the Ritz-Carlton chain which, to protect its exclusive image, is not normally identified for marketing purposes as part of the Marriott Group) (Lovelock and Wortz, 2007). For a multi-brand strategy to succeed, each brand must promise a distinctive value proposition, targeted at a different customer segment. There are even branded hotel floors in some hotels. American Express and the Sheraton Vancouver Wall Centre Hotel have partnered to open a floor dedicated to business accommodations for American Express credit card holders. Located on the 27th floor, the 'American Express Club Floor' features a private lounge with business service centre, direct access to boardrooms and fitness facilities, dedicated front-desk check-in and a late 4.00 p.m. check-out. According to officials, guests using the club floor pay the same price for their room as Amex's negotiated standard room rate and benefit from a host of value-added services and amenities. These include complimentary continental breakfast, all-day coffee and tea, evening hors d'oeuvres, international and local newspapers, and 24-hour room service.

In the past, branding was often seen mainly as a matter of promotion and of creating the right image through advertising and publicity. But marketing managers now recognize that successful branding involves the integrated deployment of product design, pricing policies, distribution selection and promotion. The case for branding is stronger for tourism products that offer the possibility for differentiation in several areas of the marketing mix. This is why branding has been particularly successful in hotel and restaurant marketing. Branding of restaurants, hotels and airlines developed extensively in the United States during the 1980s and 1990s, and com -panies in the rest of the world are following suit. The momentum is driven mainly by large organizations that recognize that, to remain competitive, they need to offer several products to different markets instead of relying upon a monolithic presence in one main one.

Apart from the advantages already mentioned, Middleton and Clarke (2001) suggest that branding in tourism offers other specific advantages:

1. It helps reduce medium- and long-term vulnerability to the unforeseen external events that so beset the tourism industry. Recovery time after an event such as a terrorist attack or a natural disaster is likely to be shorter for a well-established brand;
2. It reduces risk for the consumer at the point of purchase by signalling the expected quality and performance of an intangible product. It offers either an implicit or explicit guarantee to the consumer;
3. It facilitates accurate marketing segmentation by attracting some consumer segments and repelling others. For an inseparable product, onsite segment compatibility is an important marketing issue;

4. It provides the focus for the integration of stakeholder effort, especially for the employees of an organization or the individual tourism providers of a destination brand; and
5. It is a strategic weapon for long-range planning in tourism.

It should be recognized that a competitive brand is a live asset and not a fixture, and therefore its value may depreciate over time if starved of investment and marketing and management skill. Brand decay may begin if a brand is over-stretched into new products that damage its essence, or following a merger or takeover. Marketers sometimes use the term brandicide to describe the process of taking a well-known brand and extending it into a new area that will 'kill' the brand. Companies are increasingly attempting to stretch their proven expertise into new areas. Walt Disney Inc., for example, has recently entered the produce business. Disney's cartoon characters are popping up on fruit and vegetable packaging across the US, as growers clinch licensing deals with entertainment companies hungry to cultivate positive images among health-conscious parents and children. The Snapshot below describes how chefs – some of the most successful and fastest-growing consumer brands today – are stretching their brand names into a number of different areas.

A combination of factors has made companies more eager than ever to stretch their brands further and more boldly. Advances in technology have reduced barriers to entry in new sectors. Companies have developed stronger and more knowledgeable relationships with customers, and the cost and difficulty of developing new brands is encouraging companies to exploit the brands they already have. But there can be a cost to leveraging brand equity. If a brand loses credibility in one sector, this tainted sector can contaminate everything else that bears the brand's name. So brandicide should be avoided.

The Case Study on Richard Branson how over the past 25 years, Branson has diversified his Virgin brand into a far-reaching empire, encompassing mobile phone services, a rail service and even wedding dresses, as well as his original record label and discount airline. The Snapshot below takes a look at the Jamie Oliver brand, and how, albeit on a smaller scale than Branson the celebrity chef has used his name to promote cookbooks, cookware, healthy school lunches, supermarkets, restaurants, and, of course, television shows.

PACKAGING

In the tourism and hospitality industry, packaging is the process of combining two or more related and complementary offerings into a single-price offering. A package may include a wide variety of services, such as lodging, meals, entrance fees for attractions, entertainment, transportation costs, guide services, or other similar activities. Travel packages have become increasingly popular over the years. They are attractive because they benefit both the consumer and participating businesses by providing convenience and value to the consumer and added revenue for businesses. An example of a package holiday is one on offer from Arctic Experience, a UK tour operator. In 2007, the operator was selling a three-night trip to the Icehotel in Sweden on a bed and breakfast basis for just over £1000 for a single person. This price included return flights from London.

Packaging provides several customer benefits, including:

1. Easier budgeting for trips: the customer pays at one time and has a good idea of the trip's total cost;
2. Increased convenience, which saves time and prevents aggravation;
3. Greater economy, as the cost to the customer is usually more economical than purchasing the package components individually;
4. The opportunity to experience previously unfamiliar activities and attractions; and
5. The opportunity to design components of a package for specialized interests.

For tourism operations, packages are attractive for the following reasons:

1. They can improve profitability by allowing businesses to price at a premium by adding special good and services;
2. They can streamline business patterns. Packaging during low demand periods may add attractive features to the service or product, thus generating additional business;
3. They allow joint marketing opportunities, which can in turn reduce promotional costs;
4. They can be an effective tool for tailoring tourism products for specific target markets.

The tourism industry is becoming increasingly sophisticated and innovative with its packaging. The Snapshot on weekendtrips.com is an example of the growing number of companies catering to the demand for short-break tourism experiences sold via the internet. Others are catering for the more sophisticated backpacker market. For example, Ho Chi Minh City-based Linh Nam Travel Co. has a 79-day tour of Vietnam with an itinerary of 8,000 kilometres through 59 cities and provinces nationwide.

The programme runs twice a year and tourists can choose to stay at hotels of one to three stars or take a home-stay. Others are packaging holidays for the growing interest in wildlife tourism amongst older, more affluent tourists. Churchill, Manitoba in Canada, for example, attracts 2,500 tourists a year who take trips in tundra buggies to see wildlife, primarily polar bears, but also ptarmigan, Arctic fox, Arctic hare, snowy owls and lemmings. Tour packages range from CDN$2,200 to $7,000 for two nights including accommodation and transportation to and from Winnipeg. A 2004 study found that 75 per cent of Churchill's visitors were American, and about 15 per cent were from abroad, primarily Japan, Germany and France. About 10 per cent of visitors were Canadian.

NEW PRODUCT DEVELOPMENT

According to the *Los Angeles Times*, 700 new products are introduced every day. Many of them fail, and many new ideas take years before becoming a reality. The BridgeClimb in Sydney is a prime example of the latter, and the Snapshot below explains how it took nine years for the idea to become reality. Safety concerns and other issues kept the unique tourism product on hold for nearly a decade. Developing new products is different from maintaining existing ones, and planning for both kinds of product will differ according to whether the products are targeted at existing markets or new ones. According to Holloway and Plant, a company has four alternatives when developing new products.

Market Penetration

Firstly, the company can follow a market penetration strategy by modifying an existing product for the current market. Improvements to an existing product can transform it, so that prospective purchasers view it as a genuinely new product. The case study at the end of the chapter highlights a number of ways in which ski resorts are modifying their service offerings to provide new experiences for their customers.

Market Development

The second strategy, market development, calls for identifying and developing new markets for current products. If an existing product is launched to a new market that is unfamiliar with it, that product is also, for all intents and purposes, a new product. When Banff Mount Norquay in Canada introduced hourly tickets, they attracted a new market of skiers - locals who would not normally ski due to lack of time.

PRODUCT DEVELOPMENT

The third strategy, product development, involves developing a genuinely new product to be sold to existing customers. Over the last few years, fast-food companies have developed new healthier products for existing customers. Subway, for example, has positioned itself as a healthy fast-food alternative, turning its low-fat, low-calorie food into a marketing coup. When the company learned that Jared Fogel, a once 425-pound (193 kg) college student, lost 245 pounds (111 kg) on a diet consisting of Subway turkey and veggie subs, Fogel was recruited to endorse Subway products in numerous (successful) promotions. The Snapshot below on Sydney BridgeClimb is an example of a genuinely new product sold to tourists visiting the Australian city.

Diversification

Diversification growth makes sense when good opportunities can be found outside the present business. Three types of diversification can be considered.

Firstly, the company can seek new products that have technological or marketing synergies with existing product lines, even though the product may appeal to a new class of customers (concentric diversification). Secondly, the company may search for new products that could appeal to its current target market (horizontal diversification). Finally, the company can seek new businesses that have no relationship with the company's current technology, products or markets (conglomerate diversification). An example of diversification comes from Four Seasons, the hotel company that moved into new territory in 2003 with the launch of a luxury catamaran cruise in the Maldives.

SYMBIOTIC OF TOURISM PRODUCTS MANAGEMENT

Wildlife sanctuary, Marine parks, Aero products and Water sports, Flower festivals are the example of tourism products which are a blending of nature and man. Nature has provided the resource and man has converted them into a tourism product by managing them. National parks for example, are left in their natural state of beauty as far as possible, but still need to be managed, through provision of access, parking facilities, limited accommodation, litter bins etc.

Yet the core attraction is still nature in this category of product. These products are symbiosis of nature and man. In case of adventure sports tourists can be participants. The basic element of adventure is the satisfaction of having complete command over one's body, a sense of risk in the process, an awareness of beauty and the exploration of the unknown. Adventure tourism can be classified into aerial, water based and land based.

Aerial adventure sports include the following activities:

- Parachuting, which involves jumping off from an aircraft or balloon and descending by means of a parachute. The infrastructure required, includes an aircraft, parachutes and large landing zones
- Sky Diving, which involves a sky diver jumping off an aircraft or balloon at a much greater height without deploying his parachute initially and opening it after some interval at a pre determined height.
- Hang Gliding, which involves running off a mountain or being towed by a winch and essentially flying like a glider where the directional control is achieved by a shift in his own weight by the pilot.
- Para Gliding, is the latest aero-sport which has taken the world by storm. A Para Glider is a specially designed square parachute, along with a harness attached by lines.
- Para Sailing is a simple sport that involves towing a parachutist to a height of a few hundred feet in the air and then descending by means of a parachute. As a year round activity, Para sailing can be done on land and water.
- Bungee Jumping, which requires no equipment except a 'bungee cord' made of nylon fibre of enough elasticity to be able to absorb the shock at the end of the jump. The jumper makes a headlong jump into empty

space and the resultant rush of adrenalin makes the experience very exhilarating.

- Ballooning, where a balloon is attached to a basket by steel wire ropes. By regulating hot and cold air, the pilot can steer the balloon along any charted course.

Water based adventure sports include the following:

- White water rafting which is one of the most important and exciting water sports, which involves riding down water rapids in an inflatable raft which is used to negotiate fast flowing rivers.
- Canoeing and Kayaking are adventure sports which begin upstream where the water is wild and white. The gradient best suited for canoeing is the stage near the river's entry into the plains where the trip can be combined with a natural holiday in a forest. Kayaking is appealing as it enables innovation on the river by one or two oarsman seated in tandem.
- Adventure sports in the waters of the sea like wind surfing, scuba diving, snorkeling, yachting, water skiing, etc. also offer thrilling activities to the tourists.

Land based adventure tourist products include the following:

- Rock climbing which originated as a means of practicing techniques for ascending high mountains. It was earlier provided as training to mountaineers but has now evolved into a highly developed sport. The climber moves up, using knowledge of rope handling, climbing, securing one to another, etc. Very sophisticated techniques and equipments are used nowadays to ascend or descend on very steep terrain.
- Mountaineering requires trained physical ability and suitable equipment. The higher peaks need better equipment which is also costly. The challenges which mountains like the Indian Himalayas pose attract mountaineers from various countries.
- Trekking the mighty Himalayas which spread across five Indian states form a sweeping arc and compress in its expanse a wide geographical variety and contrasting cultures.
- Skiing is the practice of sliding over snow on runners, called skis, attached to each foot. There are three types of ski resorts, the first are large towns, second type are alpine villages and the third resorts built for skiing.
- Heli skiing is a type of alpine skiing where the skier is dropped to the top of a mountain by a helicopter and then he slides down on his own.
- Motor Rally is a sport that tests the navigational skills of man and his endurance with the machine. Motor rallies, grand prix racing, hill

climbing rallies, vintage car rallies, sports car racing, etc. are some forms of this tourism product.

- Safaris were earlier taken on camel, horse and elephants as an excursion for hunting or a journey. As a modern tourist product now safaris are taken on jeeps and in the form of caravans. Viewing and enjoying nature, meeting the local villagers, seeing their traditions, customs and lifestyle, entertainment and camp fires are some of the characteristics of modern safaris. Eg, Egypt desert safaris. Horse and elephant safaris are arranged in most of the national parks and wildlife sanctuaries.

EVENT BASED TOURISM PRODUCTS

Where an event is an attraction, it as an event based tourist product. Events attract tourists as spectators and also as participants in the events, sometimes for both. The Ocktoberfest organised in Germany, Dubai and Singapore shopping festivals, the camel polo at Jaisalmer, Kite flying in Ahmedabad attracts tourists, both as spectators and participants. Whereas in case of the Snake Boat race of Kerala can be enjoyed witnessing it. Event attractions are temporary, and are often mounted in order to increase the number of tourists to a particular destination. Some events have a short time scale, such as the Republic Day Parade, others may last for many days, for example Khajuraho Dance Festival or even months like the Kumbh Mela. A destination which may have little to commend it to the tourist can nevertheless succeed in drawing tourists by mounting an event such as an unusual exhibition.

SITE BASED TOURISM PRODUCTS

When an attraction is a place or site then it is called a site based tourist product. Site attractions are permanent by nature, for example Taj Mahal, The Great Wall of China, The Grand Canyon in Arizona, Eiffel Tower, Statue of Liberty, Temples of Khajuraho, etc. A site destination can extend its season by mounting an off season event or festival. A large number of tourists are attracted every year by the great drawing power of Stratford on Avon in England because of its association with Shakespeare, the city of Agra in India with its famous Taj Mahal, Pisa in Italy for its famous Leaning Tower. Some new features have been added to the same product to keep the tourist interest alive in the products. For example now visitors can see Taj by night, music shows have been organised with Taj as the backdrop so that there are repeat tourists.

MAN- MADE TOURISM PRODUCTS

Man- made tourism products are created by man for pleasure, leisure or business.

Man- made tourism products include:

CULTURE

- Sites and areas of archaeological interest
- Historical buildings and monuments
- Places of historical significance
- Museums and art galleries
- Political and educational institutions
- Religious institutions

Cultural tourism is based on the mosaic of places, traditions, art forms, celebrations and experiences that portray the nation and its people, reflecting the diversity and character of a country. Garrison Keillor, in an address to the 1995 White House Conference on Travel and Tourism, best described cultural tourism by saying, "We need to think about cultural tourism because really there is no other kind of tourism. It's what tourism is...People don't come to America for our airports, people don't come to America for our hotels, or the recreation facilities....They come for our culture: high culture, low culture, middle culture, right, left, real or imagined—they come here to see America." Two significant travel trends will dominate the tourism market in the next decade.

- Mass marketing is giving way to one-to-one marketing with travel being tailored to the interests of the individual consumer.
- A growing number of visitors are becoming special interest travellers who rank the arts, heritage and/or other cultural activities as one of the top five reasons for travelling.

The combination of these two trends is being fuelled by technology, through the proliferation of online services and tools, making it easier for the traveller to choose destinations and customise their itineraries based on their interests. Today we can witness large masses of people travelling to foreign countries to become acquainted with the usages and customs, to visit the museums and to admire works of art. One way of hastening the beneficial effects resulting from tourism is to bring the cultural heritage into the economic circuit, thus justifying the investments made at the cost of the national community, for its preservation.

Taking an economic view of the cultural heritage of a nation may not altogether be justified, considering that the preservation of its culture is one of the basic responsibilities of any community.

But considering the financial obstacles especially for the developing countries, this may appear to be a rational approach. Hence mass tourism can contribute unique benefits to the exploiting of the cultural heritage of a nation and can serve indirectly to improve the individual cultural levels of both citizens and travellers. Cultural resources have another specific characteristic, which many tourists want to experience the exotic.

There will be a great urge on the part of the tourist to visit and become acquainted with the ancient civilization in their quest for novel human knowledge. Culture means the prospect of contact with other civilizations, their original and varied customs and tradition with their distinct characteristics. This entire process creates a powerful motivator towards travel. Various Museums also attract tourists like Madame Tussauds Museum in London, the Louvre Museum in Paris, Smithsonian Washington Museum, Museums of famous painters like Salvador Dali, Pablo Picasso, Natural History Museum, British Museum, Museum of Modern Art are also popular tourist products. Sites of archeological interest like remains of Mohenjodaro and Harrapan civilizations, museums for fossils and dinosaurs.

Sites for historical interest like city of Hiroshima and Nagasaki, sites of holocaust in Germany, tombs of various leaders and emperors. Historical buildings like Warwick Castle, Tower of London, Stratford-on-Avon which is Shakespeare's birthplace, the Roman Baths are all popular with tourists. Even historical cities like Varanasi in India get a lot of tourists due to its status as one of the oldest cities of the world. Stonehenge in United Kingdom, The White House, Buckingham Palace and other places of political significance, are also great tourist draws.

TRADITIONS

- Pilgrimages
- Fairs and festivals
- Arts and handicrafts
- Dance
- Music
- Folklore
- Native life and customs

A pilgrimage is a term primarily used for a journey or a search of great moral significance. Sometimes, it is a journey to a sacred place or shrine of importance to a person's beliefs and faith. Members of every religion participate in pilgrimages. A person who makes such a journey is called a pilgrim. Secular and civic pilgrimages are also practiced, without regard for religion but rather of importance to a particular society. For example, many people throughout the world travel to the City of Washington in the United States for a pilgrimage to see the Declaration of Independence and the Constitution of the United States. British people often make pilgrimages to London to witness the public appearances of the monarch of the United Kingdom.

A large number of people have been making pilgrimages to sacred religious places or holy places. This practice is widespread in many parts of the world. In the Christian world, for instance, a visit to Jerusalem or the Vatican is considered auspicious. Among Muslims, a pilgrimage to Mecca is considered a great act of faith. In India there are many pilgrimage centres and holy places belonging to all major religions of the world. India is among the richest countries in the world as far as the field of art and craft is concerned. Tourists like to visit and see the creative and artistic treasures of various countries.

Every country has certain traditional arts like soap sculptures and batik of Thailand; gems and jewellery, tie and dye works, wood and marble carving in Indonesia; ivory, glasswork, hand block printing, sandalwood, inlay work; are some of the examples of traditional art that attract tourists. There are many forms of dance in the world like Salsa, Hip- Hop, Jazz, Flamingo, Ballet and Traditional Dances. People who travel like to watch these dance performances and sometimes even take some introductory classes.

Music can be either traditional or modern. Traditional music like folk music and classical and country music is specific to every region and country. Modern forms include Blues, Rock, Pop, Jazz, Rap, Techno and Hip- Hop. Music also adds to the attraction of a destination. Fairs and Festivals capture the fun loving side and bring out the joyous celebrations of the community. Festivals like Christmas, Easter, Thanksgiving, Eid, Ramadan, Diwali, and Holi and so on, also bring people to destinations where the celebration can be enjoyed. Some popular Fairs which cater to fun and work are Pushkar Mela in Rajasthan, Prêt fair in Paris, Magic Fair in Vegas for garments, Hong Kong Fashion Week and various job fairs where people are recruited.

ENTERTAINMENT

- Amusement and recreation parks
- Sporting events
- Zoos and oceanariums
- Cinemas and theatre
- Night life
- Cuisine

Tourist products that have entertainment as their main characteristic are many. Just to name a few there are amusement and recreational parks like Disneyworld in United States, Hong Kong, Paris, Singapore and theme parks in various countries and cities like Appu Ghar and Fun and Food Village in Delhi, Essel World in Mumbai and so on. Tourists may come to attend sports events and it is also an opportunity to explore the country. The fundamental concept is that all tourist activities have an influence on providing economic benefits and have a powerful influence in some definite locality, like the Olympics in Athens has given immense benefit to all in tourism business in Athens in particular and Greece in general.

Many countries organise year round sports events like swimming meets, athletic meets, weight lifting events, cricket matches, baseball and football events and many more such events which encourage tourism. India will be hosting the Common-Wealth Games on 2010 and it is anticipated to give the tourism industry a big boost. Night Life is one of the prime attractions in a holiday. Tourists like to especially visit areas in cities where the night life activity is promoted. These areas are usually lit up with street stalls like flea markets and food areas. Bars, night clubs, casinos and very often open air bands attract and add to the psychological satisfaction and experience of tourists.

Cuisine is very often an understated but highly important part of any holiday. Now-a-days there is cuisine from all areas of the world which is found at most tourist destinations. Specialty restaurants serve Indian, Continental, Chinese, Italian, Japanese, Thai, Indonesian, Fast food, Mexican, Mediterranean, and Arabic and so on. However, tourists usually like to eat the local food of the areas they visit.

BUSINESS

- Conventions
- Conferences

People who travel in relation to their work come under the category of business tourism. However such travel for business purposes is also linked with tourist activity like visiting places of tourist attraction at the destination, sight seeing and excursion trips. Business travel is also related to what is termed today as convention business, which is a rapidly growing industry in hospitality and tourism. A business traveller is important to the tourism industry as it involves the usage of all the components of tourism. He travels because of different business reasons- attending conventions and conferences, meetings, workshops etc. Participants have a lot of leisure time at their disposal.

The conference organisers make this leisure time very rewarding for participants by organising many activities for their pleasure and relaxation. The spouses and families accompanying the participants are also well looked after by the organisers. The organisers plan sight seeing tours and shopping tours for the participants and their families. In India, cooking classes for learning Indian food cooking from the various states, visits to the craft bazaars where tourists see how artisans make clay pots and other handicrafts, they visit tie and dye units to see Indian printing eg. Batik printing etc. Women tourists enjoy henna demonstrations. Conferences are events which require meticulous planning and efficient implementation, co-coordinating various activities so that the right things happen at the right time.

There are a number of players in the convention business. On one hand are the customers or the consumers and on the other hand are the principle suppliers like hotels, transporters, convention centres, tour operators and travel agencies, tourism departments, exhibition organisers, sponsors etc.

FORMS OF TOURISM PRODUCT MANAGEMENT

By now you must be aware of what a tourism product is and what its peculiar features are. It is necessary to understand the components of the tourist product from the point of view of the consumer. The product for the tourist covers the complete experience from the time he leaves home to the time he returns. The tourist product today is developed to meet the needs of the consumer and techniques like direct sales, publicity and advertising are employed to bring this product to the consumer.

The tourist product is the basic raw material, be it the country's natural beauty, climate, history, culture and the people, or other facilities necessary for comfortable living such as water supply, electricity, roads, transport, communication and other essentials. The tourist product can be entirely a man-made one or nature's creation improved upon by man. A consumer can combine individual products in a large number of ways.

There would be many possible destinations, each with a number of hotels, each to be reached by more than one airline. Thus, the potential choice facing the consumer is very large. The large number of tourist destinations have placed at the disposal of a tourist a very large variety of tourist products in abundant quantity from a large number of competing destinations. This eventually, has led to the adoption of the new concept *i.e.*, the marketing concept in tourism by various countries promoting tourism. Tourism, basically, is an infrastructure based service product. The nature of the service here is highly intangible and perishable offering a limited scope for creating and maintaining the distinctive competitive edge.

The effective marketing of tourism needs constant gearing up of infrastructure to international standards and presupposes in its coordination with the tourism suppliers. In strategic terms, it calls for the action of an integrated approach to management and marketing. In operational terms, it means the implementation of a better defined, better targeted market-driven strategy for realizing the defined objectives.

The important point to note here is that marketing is applied to situations where the choice can be limited to a relatively small number of brands giving the consumer a reasonable choice. The process of selection thus becomes easier. In the field of tourism this process is taking place by the increased use of 'package tours'.

A package tour is a travel plan which includes most elements of vacation, such as transportation, accommodation, sight- seeing and entertainment. The tourist product is a composite product, whether it is sold as a package or assembled by the individual himself or his travel agent. There are many tourism products that are available to the consumer today.

In modern times these products, whether traditional in nature like culture and pilgrimage, or modern like adventure, conventions and conferences, health, medical, etc. are being packaged, promoted and priced appropriately to woo as many tourists as possible. Tourism products can be classified as under for a better understanding of each of their peculiar characteristics.

TRANSLATING CUSTOMER NEEDS TO PRODUCT CONCEPT

We have already said that a firm must be able to assess what its customer value is—what its customers perceive as benefits received from the firm, versus what it cost the customers to access and receive those benefits. This assessment must be done both at the aggregate, segment level and at the individual, customer level, where appropriate. The aggregate, segment-level assessment orients the firm's thinking about overall product strategy. When a firm directly interacts with its customer, the individual, customer-level assessment helps the firm configure the product within that strategy to the individual customer.

In keeping with the view that a product is really a bundle of benefits, the core value in any product for any firm is the primary benefit that the firm provides. The supplementary product includes as parts of the solution additional benefits that augment the core product. Typically, a large part of the supplementary product is comprised of services. The example presents in a graphic this view of any product offering. For the most part, the core product is a commodity, as in the example of Commerce Bancorp. All banks offer deposits, withdrawals, and investments and banking products such as checking and savings accounts, and fixed and variable income securities, and today most banks offer mutual funds.

These products comprise the core product for banks. How these products are different from bank to bank is represented in the supplementary components of the total product. Commerce Bancorp offers free checking and money orders and does not compete on its lower interest on its savings accounts and CDs. Thus, Commerce Bancorp differentiates itself on a number of different supplementary benefits to the customer, ranging from the quality of its customer interactions to a number of facilitating services such as bathrooms in its branches. Similarly, most if not all banks have an online presence, but customers at banks like Allfirst Financial can talk with bank personnel via their home personal computer.

The hotel industry is one that grew out of its room-and-board days to a total product offering that today includes a multitude of facilitating services. "Room and board" was the commodity. As all hotels in a certain level, competitors in the same segment, began offering the same set of supplementary services, such as room service, meeting and conference rooms, a swimming pool, a gift shop, personal grooming salon service, business services, cable, or Internet service in each room, these became commodity and part of the core product.

By March 2001, 78 precent of all Ritz-Carlton hotels offered highspeed Internet. While only two hotel chains—Omni and Westin hotels—have laptops available for guests, most hotels in that class offer two phone lines. Thus, over time, as competing firms add supplementary services, these previously differentiating value components become a commodity and lose their differentiating ability.

Consider the recent "advances" in the form of supplem-entary services in the hotel industry. Electronic kiosks can not only check you in with your room key and print your bill at checkout, but can also be an electronic concierge providing a guest with directions or maps to locations of interest. Human butlers are back in the hotel industry. A growing number of hotels at the top end will provide a bath butler to prepare your luxury bath, a technology butler to solve your gadget problems, a private butler to pack your clothes or make your plans.

If you are traveling with a baby or young child, you can find a hotel that offers a room for a nanny and kiddie perks such as baby-sitting, some one to read a bedtime story with live actors, or toys and activities for the child. If you are bringing a pet along, some hotels will even offer you special pet services for a fee! Over time, hotels in the premium category will all be offering some or all of these supplementary features.

These features become part of the standard offering and reduce themselves into a commodity for that category of hotels. You can expect that the "technology butler" service will be adopted by hotels for the business traveller segment, briefly providing a differentiating feature only very quickly to become standard fare. In designing superior customer value, a firm must translate customer needs to the specifications of a solution in terms of core and supplementary benefits.

All hotels need not have the same core product. That statement might seem confusing. Consider the Station Inn, in Pennsylvania, between Pittsburgh, and Harrisburg. It sits 125 feet from the railroad tracks. Railroading buffs sleep at the hotel just to see the freight trains, about 60 of them in a space of 24 hours. Same industry as hotels—but a somewhat different core product. Precise definition of a product can only emerge from deep inspection of the "What business are we in?" analysis.

If product differentiation is derived from the enhancement that the supplementary product provides the core benefit, what constitutes supplementary product? Starting with the familiar: customer service is a common supplementary product (sometimes mistaken as the only element in the supplementary product). There are elements of the supplementary product, such as billing and payment that are also common to all firms. They are required to facilitate the core product. These must also be viewed as part of the supplementary product to the extent that they affect customer value.

A firm can add to the customer value when its billing and payment process is customer focused or can detract from customer value if it is unpleasant in the customer's experience. Thus, there are some supplementary features that are found in all products that may not necessarily be recognized as such. Services marketing scholar Christopher Lovelock visualized this concept as a flower with petals. Think of the supplementary product as composed of elements of the total value bundle that facilitate and enhance (or detract from) the primary benefit sought in a product. Visualize these elements in three broad categories: facilitating services, quality of customer experience, and brand image.

FACILITATING SERVICES

Facilitating services are all those features of the product and activities of the firm that serve to facilitate the consumption of the core product. All firms have to provide some of these services at some level. Large retailers such as Sears, Walmart, and Lowe's will provide assembly and installation services for a fee and sometimes for no charge. Table outlines the four broad categories of facilitating services—complementary services, customer education, customer access, and customer service. Customer-focused firms differentiate themselves by excelling in these facilitating services.

Complementary services are those related to the consumption of the core product. Some are almost necessary, like the waiting area in a physician's clinic or parking facilities at a hotel. Passengers on long international flights enjoy a wide range of inflight entertainment activities such as films, TV channels, and even casino-style gambling or electronic shopping and services such as being able to rent a car or book hotel rooms from the technology at their seats. Some complementary services are product differentiators. For example, recognizing that some of its customers were coming in to the bank to conduct their business bringing little children with them, some Wells Fargo branches have a play area with television cartoons, Nintendo, and the like—and even sells toys to children. Washington Mutual offers calculators, pens, and piggy banks for a small fee. To compete for advertising within its *Mutual Funds* magazine for instance, the publisher, Time, Inc. offers its advertising customers anything from primary research and use of its subscriber list to assistance in customizing gifts and promotions to readers or sponsorship featured on special cover-wraps.

Only with an intimate understanding of the customer's value chain consumption (and creation) activities can firms begin to see what opportunities there might be to facilitate the consumption of the core product. Sometimes complementary products are outsourced and provided directly to the customer by the supplier, as Wells Fargo did when it invited Starbuck's to open locations at some of its branches. Ultimately, these complementary products ought to be consistent with the positioning strategy for the product. When a complementary feature is offered by all competitors in a particular product category, it becomes a commodity and part of the core product for that category and ceases to be a product differentiator.

Customer education is a form of facilitating service in that it provides information to the customer about the firm or the product in such a way that it facilitates the acquisition and consumption of the product. Instruction manuals and product support via telephone, fax, or the Internet are examples of customer education. Consider what some banks are doing to be more accessible for customers looking for assistance. Tellers and managers are dressed in khakis and casual shirts to appear approachable and friendly. Bank of America has tested concierges in their lobby to help direct customer questions. Home Depot provides free classes on home improvement projects. Once again, the service feature might be a necessary component of the total product, but how it is designed and delivered may be a source of product differentiation.

Customer access has to do with everything that the firm does to make its products available to the customer and to facilitate the acquisition and consumption of the product. The hours of operation and location are a simple example of customer access for a service. The various touch points that are available to the customer to access the services of the firm or to reach someone within the firm would be a measure of the customer access. The methods of billing and payment for the product would relate to access to the product and can be a product differentiator.

For example, the convenience of payment by credit card was once a source of competitive advantage. Convenience and ease of use is a critical component of customer value for any product. Services such as financing options are also related to this idea of customer access. If these are not customer-focused, they will fail the customer and the firm. Customer service is a key facilitating service and includes the commonly understood activity of businesses related to product complaints or failures, product returns, refunds, and such. The accommodation of special requests or adapting to unusual or irregular customer situations would be an example of customer service as well. Poor customer service reduces customer value and risks losing the customer.

Quality of Customer Experience

When the total product provided by all firms contains the same set of facilitating services, the product is not necessarily a commodity. The quality of the service offered remains a source of differentiation and therefore a supplementary feature of the product. Perceived quality enhances, and lack thereof reduces, the value of the core product. For example, even when Internet service is offered by all hotels, the quality of the customer experience with the Internet service is still a differentiator.

One hotel may require you to get into a closet, fish out the cables and force you to shape yourself into a yoga pose to hook up those cables to your laptop, while another hotel may offer wireless Internet access from anywhere on the property. All airlines provide seating and, depending on distance and class, also provide meals and entertainment while transporting you from point A to point B. Differentiation in seating can come in legroom and comfort. First-class services can offer six and a half feet of seat length, single seats, pajamas, and privacy partitions between seats. The quality of the entire customer experience is most definitely a source of differentiation. Brand image is a supplementary feature of the product in that it adds to customer value. Brand image is the sum total of all the perceptions and attitudes about a brand. The image of the firm in the general media as well as for each individual customer provides a measure of the perceived quality of the product.

The reputation of a firm is usually a result of the firm's product and actions. Where there is very little tangible evidence of the product, as in the case of Web-based services, an entire industry of so-called "reputation managers" has emerged. These reputation managers are Web sites that rate the reputation of others! A firm's image is an implicit source of differentiation in the market. Brand image is the ultimate differentiator. When all else can be seen as equal, the brand image captures the essence of the difference in customer value among the alternatives available to the customer.

Firms have to determine what their total product offering is and what it should be. The value bundle of core and supplementary product needs to be designed based on what the customers expect as standard from all providers of a solution in a product category.

The supplementary product might also contain features that are sources of differentiation among solution providers reflecting the positioning strategy of the firm. Firms must constantly watch the various solutions that are being offered. Sometimes the threat of competition comes from newer business models. For example, online broker ETrade surprised the banking business when it began to open ATMs with new services. A deep and broad analysis of customer needs could reveal value-creating opportunities.

To determine how best to match the total product as the superior solution to fit customer need, the firm must understand the customer's value chain. This is an integral part of the product concept development of the customer-focused firm. A thorough understanding of the customer needs and the customer value chain will help the firm conceive its product from the customer's point of view. Firms that best relate their own value chain to the buyer's value chain, said Michael Porter, will enjoy a sustainable differentiation strategy.

The value chain is essentially a chain of value-creating and value-consuming activities, where the value created as output from one activity becomes the input to another value-creating activity that in turn creates value as input for another activity, and so on. Thus, any activity can be assessed by the value it creates versus the value it consumes. This is why activity-based costing practices make a lot of sense.

As already said the value creating activities *within a firm* are those that contribute to the creation of either the core product or the supplementary product. The value created by these activities is derived by the processing of the productive factors of the firm—its people, facilities, and equipment. There may be assets or value components sourced from external suppliers or intermediaries that contribute towards producing either the core or the supplementary product. Some outsourced services may even be delivered directly to the customer. When any value component of the total product is outsourced, as in the case of a retailer offering customers outsourced financing options for purchases, or airlines outsourcing catering services, there is the obvious issue of quality assurance in the value creation that is outside the control of the firm.

Externally (to the firm) when you relate other firms' value-creation activities into a value chain, you see that the value created by one entity contributes to the value created by the next entity in the value chain. The same idea is referred to by economists, in the context of forecasting, as "derived demand." The demand for a product is dependent on the market for another product, such as aluminum and aircraft sales for example. We know a homeowner who gets a home improvement job done receives (customer) value from the home contractor who in turn is receiving value from the retailer who in turn receives value in the form of products and services from the supplier or manufacturer.

Looking for Customer Value Opportunities

An understanding of the role that the firm's product plays in the customer's value chain could open up value-creating opportunities. A customer-focused firm has a detailed picture of the customer's consumption domain. When a firm views value consumption activities, it can see if there are other value creating opportunities that it can leverage from its assets. The watchmaker Swatch, for example, offers wrist watches with the technology that allows them to function as electronic passes at ski resorts in Switzerland or for public transportation in Finland. Wrist gadgets can now serve not only the function of telling time, but also making phone calls, playing music and videos, browsing the Internet, or sending e-mail.

This example defies categorization of product. What is the product? It is a wallet or a pocketbook, as well as a telephone, a personal stereo, a personal VCR, and an Internet communications device! The exercise of determining what revenue opportunities Swatch's value-creating assets would offer forces a complete redefinition of the product. As we saw the (product) solution is conceived to take advantage of opportunities to meet the needs in the customer's life with the assets that the firm has. Swatch has found a way to provide value to a recreational activity—skiing—and a functional activity—public transportation. It is contributing to the "customer access" components of the ski resort's and public transportation's product. By enabling customer access, information technology provides a whole range of supplementary benefits to a variety of products. Contrast this with the example of a firm that does not understand the value of complementary product components and the customer's value chain. A customer came out of a movie theater in Kendall Square, Cambridge, and experienced a 40-minute ordeal trying to leave the theater's parking lot. She spent 30 minutes standing in line in frigid weather to pay the $2.50 parking fee and a further 15 minutes to exit the parking lot. When complaining to the management of the movie theater, she asked if she could pay the parking fee as she bought the movie ticket. She was told that the parking lot was owned by a different company and the theater would not take responsibility for the customer's bad experience at the parking lot. In contrast, the airline SAS has been known to provide an annual dinner to taxicab drivers in Stockholm because the SAS management wants the drivers to treat passengers on the way to and from the airport with professional courtesy and respect. Clearly, firms that are customer-focused conceive their product differently from other firms, because of their intimate knowledge of the customer's consumption activities.

Information about the customer's consumption cycle, therefore, is a key prerequisite to exploring the opportunities that might be tapped. An understa-nding of how the customer actually benefits from the solution and the information of how, when, where, and with whom the customer consumes the product should provide some interesting revelations of what the firm is doing and can be doing in the composition of the total product solution for customers. Thus, Procter and Gamble sends its researchers to homes to observe how people actually use laundry detergent. When Samsung was trying to break into the microwave business in the late 1970s and early 1980s, their design engineers observed homemakers shopping for microwaves at the retail store. You can stay ahead of the curve by offering value through supplementary product that your customer information tells you customers will be willing to pay for. Even if the value-producing feature or activity cannot be priced separately, you may be able to command a premium for your superior customer value. Being customer-focused is critical in identifying opportunities for establishing superiority in customer value.

All decisions about the product and, therefore, the value-creating activities of the firm are based on an understanding of the value-consumption activities of its customers. What are the decisions and what are the issues to be considered in determining the total product by a firm? The three major decisions constituting the product strategy are: the product concept, the operations design, and the value creation and delivery process alredy—displayed.

The product concept defines the customer to be served and what value is to be provided. The operations design defines the productive assets of the firm required to create and deliver that value for that customer. Together, the product concept and the operations design define the scope and configuration of the productive assets that can be leveraged to produce the specific customer value that maximizes profits to the firm.

The *value creation and delivery process* executes the product concept with the operations design. In developing the product strategy, the firm makes a fundamental decision in answering the question of how the product will be positioned among all potential solutions to the customer's need. This positioning question poses an asset- and market-based decision that comprises two perspectives.

- The *market-based perspective* looks outward at the market and asks what customer needs can be most profitably served by the firm.
- The *asset-based perspective* looks inward, at the firm's assets, and asks what assets of the firm can be most profitably leveraged by the firm.

The market-based perspective drives the product concept and the asset-based perspective drives the operations design. Thus, the initial step in developing product strategy involves two critical analyses. The product concept requires analyses of the various segments in the marketspace, while the operations design requires analyses of the firm's productive factors. These two sets of analyses are essential to determining what value-creating activities the firm should engage in to generate the maximum revenue from its assets.

A market analysis to determine what would be the most profitable segment mix for a configuration of the productive assets of the firm is the foundation for product strategy. First you need to identify the segments and the solutions that are currently available to the segments. The target market selection or the selected market segments to be served can be based on the profitability and size of each segment that the firm's assets are best positioned to serve. Here, a formal comparison of all the current solutions from the customer's perspective is necessary. Based on this analysis, the firm is able to determine what it can provide better than the alternative available to the appropriate target market, thus framing the firm's competitive advantage. Only after such customer needs analysis is it possible to specify what would be the desired customer value in the product offering.

The intended customer value in the product offering can now be translated into a detailed picture of the product concept—what the core and supplementary product ought to be. Remember that the customer value also reflects the customer's implicit assessment of the firm's solution compared to competitive offerings and, indeed, all solutions that are available to customers in the segment.

To ensure that the product concept can effectively be superior customer value, the core product should combine the imperatives that have become commodities in the product category with the appropriate features in the supplementary product to reflect superiority in customer value. Thus, the product concept embodies the product differentiation and the superiority in customer value. The operations design decision rests on how best the assets of the firm can be most profitably leveraged and follows a sequence of questions that pertain to the productive assets and capabilities of the firm and how they should be deployed: What people, facilities, equipment assets are needed to create and deliver the product?

Which employees' skills and knowledge would be needed? When and where would specific human capital be needed and for how much time? Similar questions are asked about the facilities and equipment of the firm. Of course, when the asset or resource is not available within the firm, it seeks suppliers or outsources that part of the value creation. Ultimately, the question is what competitive advantage the firm is capable of and how the assets needed should be configured.

The process decisions are about determining the specific activities of the value creation and delivery. The process of making the product and delivering it to the customer must be detailed. The value creation and delivery activities required are set in a specific sequence. The firm must deliberate on the structure, content, and process of creating and delivering the product to the customer.

No product differentiation from supplementary product can be seen in isolation. If the total benefits from the product are not worth the costs that the customer incurs in acquiring and using the product, the product is likely to fail. The more carefully the firm designs the process with the customer in mind, the more likely the process ensures ease, convenience and quality for the customer. Thus, the customer-focused firm designs the creation and delivery process with the customer's percep tion of benefits and costs in the value consumption process.

Firms must also recognize that since customer value is dynamic, they need to continually monitor and improve this customer value. Ignorance of the need to innovate to sustain competitive advantage is a common mistake committed by the complacent firm. The argument is sometimes made that the firm's priority of customer focus minimizes the attention to innovation. Customer focus and innovation are not contradictory, an either/or strategic decision.

Indeed, to be customer-focused would mean that the firm is continually looking for new ways and solutions to meet customer needs—and to be aware that customer needs evolve as well. Now we can know what the firm needs to do to ensure that it is creating and delivering customer-focused value that can be sustained. To sustain superiority in customer value the firm must ensure that management continually assess its market and its assets to ensure that the choice of customer and the value being created and delivered by the firm maximizes the profit goals of the firm. How well is the customer value in the product concept translated to the operations design and the value creation and delivery process? Is the superiority in customer value being executed. The answer lies in the customer's judgment. Customer-focused firms will let the customer decide whether the firm's value creation and delivery is customer-focused. Continual customer satisfaction assessment information needs to be available for the customer-focused firm to improve by changing the product concept, the operations design, and the value creation and delivery process, or to continually reassess whether its assets and capabilities are being leveraged to realise the maximum profit potential. To ensure customer-focused value creation and delivery, firms must assess customers' perceptions of the benefits they receive as well as the costs incurred by them.

As an ongoing assessment of customer value, firms must continually assess customer needs and customer satisfaction. As customer needs change, the value bundle needs to be reviewed in terms of its product concept, operations design and delivery.

An assessment of customer satisfaction presents an opportunity to improve customer value. The smart firm will continually monitor customer satisfaction to understand what customers perceive as the benefits they are getting from product compared to the costs that they incur. Based on customer satisfaction, does the value bundle need to be modified and redesigned?

Are the assets and capabilities of the firm being leveraged for maximum sustainable profits? If the expected customer value cannot be delivered with the existing value-creating assets, then the firm has two choices. Either it acquires or outsources the required value-creating assets and capabilities, or it determines that the target market decision needs revisiting.

Managing Customer Interactions

The process of delivering value is a tricky and detail-rich exercise; it requires careful planning, using techniques such as blueprinting to visualize the entire customer experience. From the customer perspective, some service encounters are critical incidents requiring more attention than others. All service encounters must be staged for a customer-focused experience just as in the production of theater.

Why does Kimberly-Clark manage the discount retailer Costco's inventory of its diapers? The firm has a salesperson live near the Costco headquarters, and a data analyst responsible for overseeing stock at 155 Costco stores in the western United States. Similarly, Procter and Gamble stations 250 people near Wal-mart's headquarters in Bentonville, Arkansas. Large retailers are asking suppliers to more actively manage the movement of products from factory to retail store shelves.

PandG estimates that stock-outs amount to 11 per cent of an average retailer's annual sales. When firms like Kimberly-Clark pay more attention to how its immediate customers—the retailers—create value to their customers, they demonstrate that they are being customer focused. In fact, the Kimberly-Clark salesperson passed on information on how customers place packages in their shopping cart that played into package design for diapers. Wayne Sanders, chairman and CEO of Kimberly-Clark, attributes this change to the information age.

Prior to the industrial revolution, a service orientation and the individual-to-individual interaction was the predominant mode of competitiveness. Assembly-line production distanced the firm from the customer due to the sheer number of customers and the physical distance between the customers and the firm brought about by the wonders of modern transportation. Manufacturing goods became the engine of individual and collective (national) economic growth.

Mechanization far outpaced services and replaced producer-customer interaction, relying instead on intermediary institutions to provide a specialized set of competencies that the producing firm lacked. Businesses lost sight of the customer. Now, information technology has brought this full circle, back to the customer.

We call it the information age because what has changed in our time is that new technology has revolutionized the way information is handled. Another equally significant revolution is the change in the customer's domain. Customers not only have access to more information on products and service offerings, they also have the ability to interact with the providers of products and services in ways not previously possible. Providers can also present enhancements to customer experiences from the functionalities presented by technology. Service providers must, however, also manage customer participation when they utilize technology.

When firms take advantage of online marketplaces, it might be necessary to make changes in organizational structure so that value creation and delivery processes are adjusted to the addition of the online delivery. Two key technologies underlie this information age technology phenomenon: the Internet and wireless communications. What customer access to these technologies has done is to bring customer interactions to a new level and to the front and centre in how a firm deals with the customer. These interactions are essentially service encounters with the customer.

Much has been said about the service encounter—customer interactions with the firm. In a way, all customer relationship management (CRM) solutions are basically technology support to ensure that the firm maximizes returns from customers by enabling customer-focused interactions. The service encounter is truly "where the rubber hits the road"—where the prospects of customer loyalty are materialized or lost. It is where promises made in advertising are honoured or reneged on, and where expectations of customers are disappointed or met. It is where all the assets of the firm need to be brought to bear. Service encounters with the customers are also laden with the challenges of a product that is produced and consumed in real time, where failures are bound to happen. When the firm designs the value creation process with the customer in mind, it will be prepared for all predictable eventualities. When the service fails, smart firms have smart processes, that recover and learn from the failure. They have service recovery and knowledge management processes in place.

As firms compete more and more on services, the management of the customer interaction becomes critical to ensure superiority in customer value. As the core product is a commodity, and most facilitating services approach the commodity state, the competitiveness comes from how the customer is treated by the firm at each and every encounter. This chapter discusses a method for designing the value delivery process with special attention paid to the service encounter and the critical incidents in the value creation and delivery process. A framework for designing the service encounter based on the theatrical metaphor is offered as a way to examine the customer focus of value creation and delivery.

Analyzing customer interactions can be very rewarding. Amazon constantly tracks the reasons for every customer contact. It has made numerous changes to its value creation and delivery process based on customer input. The customer service function at Amazon is considered a research lab for ways to improve the Amazon customer experience.

We can turn to the unique characteristics of services to obtain a clear understanding of what is involved in a customer interaction. Something intangible is always exchanged in the interaction (intangibility). Without a customer, there is no interaction and the separation of production and consumption is irrelevant (inseparability).

To conduct the interaction, the firm has the resources and infrastructure in place that "perish" when not utilized (perishability). Each interaction is unique (variability). From these characteristics, emerge situations that are challenges and opportunities typical to the service firm.

We need to keep these in mind as we design the process of creating and delivering customer value. At the most general level, all customer interactions occur in a certain place (or space), at a certain time, for a certain duration, between certain entities, in a certain manner for a certain purpose. Consider these as ingredients in a customer interaction and categorize them into elements of structure, content, and process.

When the customer interaction is mapped onto the consumption activity cycle, the objective of the interaction becomes the driving force behind the design of the interaction in terms of its structure, content, and process.

- Structure relates to who or what entities are involved in the interaction.
- Content relates to the subject, the task, and its significance in the interaction.
- Process relates to the sequence of steps in the interaction.

The primary decisions that would configure the structure of the interaction involve the nature of the interaction—what entity should represent the firm, should the interaction be face-to-face or not, what technology can be utilized, where should it occur, and so forth. As a complementary question about the customer: What entities from the customer's domain are involved in the interaction? Similarly, decisions determining the content of the interaction should centre around the task and include what information should be required in the interaction, what should transpire between the parties, and what value should be created and consumed in the interaction. Decisions about process would include a script of the interaction and the roles of both parties in the interaction. Any of these decisions must be based on the information that the firm has about the customer's consumption cycle and on preferences regarding these dimensions of the interaction. For example, technology may provide the firm with scale economies, but the customer may want to disengage from the script and interact with a person instead. Ultimately, the important question is what value is being created in the interaction.

As we saw earlier the execution of the product concept as the delivery of the product involves a process, a sequence of activities. Therefore, designing the product must necessarily include a design of the delivery process. Lynn Shostack proposed a technique called "blueprinting" to detail the process design in the delivery of services.

The service blueprint is a map or flowchart as a visual representation of the process of service delivery. Essentially, the blueprint design is diagramed in three steps. In the first step, all types of customer interactions with the firm are listed. Next, these interactions are arranged in sequence of occurrence. In the final step, processes within the firm that are required to create and provide each customer interaction are mapped. How and what information, materials, facilities and equipment, and people are processed must be included in the service blueprint.

The customer-focused blueprint is one that is designed with the customer in mind. With the activities in the customer's consumption cycle in mind, processes within the firm need to be designed in such a way that the desired value added in the solution is reflected at each and every encounter with the customer. Commerce Bancorp, for example, encourages its employees to make suggestions in streamlining the service delivery process. Commerce Bancorp employees receive a fifty-dollar reward for finding something about a process that does not contribute to customer value and instead is an impediment to serving the customer; the bank immediately adjusts its operations.

Even as a simple representation of the value creation and delivery process, the service blueprint has a variety of important strategic, analytical, and diagnostic uses. In designing the delivery of the product, it can be used to determine the uniqueness of the service process. When compared with competitive blueprints, where and at which points in the process the firm derives its competitive advantage and superiority in customer value become evident.

Thus, the service blueprint can be used in a strategic analysis of the differentiating features and benefits of the service delivered by the firm. Only with such comparative analysis of the service blueprint is it possible to ensure that the value creation and delivery processes are commensurate with the superior customer value planned in the product concept and operations design.

The service blueprint has two major dimensions that characterize the nature and scope of the service delivery process: complexity and divergence. The complexity dimension reflects the number of steps or activities in the process. A highly complex service process has a great variety of activities during the series of customer interactions. Some of these activities occur in the front stage and some in the back stage, away from the customer's view.

A so-called line of visibility determines what the customer sees or does not see. The customer-focused firm will need to examine everything that the customer sees and experiences to determine whether the service delivery at the service encounter is contributing to or detracting from customer value. The divergence dimension reflects the degree of flexibility at each customer interaction.

The greater the divergence, the greater the customization built into the service—the greater the number of options the customer is given to choose from at each interaction. Therefore, supplementary product benefits such as customization must be mapped into the service delivery process. Complexity and divergence decisions will determine the position of the firm's offering compared to competitive offerings. Competitive blueprints can be compared to determine how competitive value bundles differ from each other. It becomes clear that the positioning of each competitive offering is reflected in the service blueprints.

The patient experience is very carefully orchestrated to support the entire concept of the "Shouldice Method." The surgical procedure itself is probably the least sophisticated element of the whole process. The recovery process is more important than the surgery. Every step in the blueprint is designed for a speedy recovery and an overall "enjoyable" experience—despite the anxiety and pain of the surgery.

The method is known for a very low recurrence rate and high customer satisfaction. The hospital even has patient reunion parties each year that are sometimes attended by as many as a thousand former patients. For this service, its critical steps are not in the surgical procedure but in in the recovery process and the total customer experience. All customer interactions depicted in the blueprint are not of equal importance in terms of criticality towards customer value—some are more important to the customer than others. It is imperative that the firm employ its knowledge of customer expectations so that the critical interactions are highlighted for priority when allocating resources of the firm. This is the primary application of the blueprint technique.

Jan Carlson, CEO of the SAS airline, popularized the notion of the "moment of truth" in services. While each customer interaction is a moment of truth, those product features and customer encounters with the firm that are considered critical to the satisfaction of the customer are considered *critical incidents.* The critical incident technique has been applied in the managing of services to understand what can make or break the customer's experience. The method was initially developed for the U.S. Air Force in simulations to help in cockpit design and pilot training.

A simple question to the customer soliciting a verbal description of a typically satisfying and a typically dissatisfying experience with the product and firm would yield valuable information on what might constitute a critical incident.

The incidents to which the customer attributes a satisfying or dissatisfying experience are those that are critical to customer satisfaction. When a particular point in the service delivery process keeps recurring in customer descriptions of satisfying and dissatisfying experiences, it becomes clear that it is a critical incident. These incidents can also uncover "failpoints"—points in the process that are especially likely to fail to perform as desired.

Some are internal to the firm and cannot be obvious to the customer, while others occur during direct interactions with the customer. For each of these, the design of the process should ensure "fail-safe" methods and have a system recovery process in place. Fail-safe processes require a metric that triggers the recovery processes.

Thus, benchmarking the performance at the failpoints is critical to the successful implementation of the product concept and operations design to deliver the desired customer value. For firms that rely on intermediaries to bring the product to the customer, critical incidents may lie outside the firm's control. Consider, for example, what Handspring, Inc. does to make sure the customers of its products are served well at the retailer. The firm sends its employees from channel marketing posing as customers to retailers such as CompUSA and ensures that its product is stocked and well displayed and that the floor salespeople are presenting the product to the customer in the way Handspring had instructed them to do. Microsoft hands out a free Casio pocketPC to every sales rep who completes its training. These examples show an awareness that customer interactions at these intermediaries are failpoints and need to be monitored.

Critical incidents help in assigning the appropriate level of resources within the firm. Thus, the service blueprint is useful from a quality control perspective. Customer evaluations of a firm's service can be linked to specific customer encounters in the blueprints and all processes directly affecting or affected by the critical incidents must be monitored for quality. Customer-focused quality control efforts can be focused on critical variables that can be controlled. Service recovery procedures must be designed into the process at these points. Interactive technologies provided by the information age revolution are now an integral part of the design of the value creation and delivery process. These technologies work through the three primary productive components of customer value—the people, the infrastructure in facilities and equipment, and processes and systems of value creation and delivery. Consider all the ways in which the customer can interact with a firm. Each touch-point can be made by the converging technologies of today.

For example, in some interactions the location of either buyer or seller becomes irrelevant. Customers can interact by wireless or wired means, which can be by voice, video, or text, initiated by either party; they are constantly getting cheaper and better in features and functionality. The basic difficulty with any of this newer interactive technology is that the objective and role of the technology can be lost sight of and the technology itself become the focus. The final measure is whether the technology is contributing towards sustainable profits for the firm by improving customer value.

The benefits of interactive technology come in the form of efficiency and efficacy. Efficiency is reflected in increasing productivity and efficacy is reflected in improved customer value. Both of these outcomes contribute to the bottom line of the firm.

For a firm competing on service, interactive technology is critical to sustain profits because of what it can do to customer value. Maximize the return from interactive technologies by deploying it at the critical points; prioritized by its customer value-creating power. For example, a common source of dissatisfaction and irritation to the customer is the length of waiting time before being served.

Any point in the process where there is likely to be a wait is a potential critical incident requiring the firm's express attention. If there are interactive technologies that can be used to effectively manage the customer in these situations, customer value is not threatened.

All the service components in the total product, being susceptible to the inherent characteristic of being produced and consumed in real time, force customers to the experience of "wait." Demand and supply need to be matched as closely as possible.

To avoid idle capacity, services adopt the queuing (and scheduling) approach to processing customers, resulting in a certain amount of wait before the process begins. In multi-stage processes, which many services are, in-process waits are common as well. The problem of course is that no one wants to wait. Customers will wait for a certain amount of time that is reasonable to them as per their expectations. What is reasonable is a very subjective judgment, of course—one that requires analysis of the factors that determine the perception of waits.

Maister's work on the psychological cause and effects of wait suggests a way to reduce the negative consequences where wait is a given.

- Preprocess waits feel longer than in-process waits. Allow the customer to begin the process by completing the first step in the value delivery process.
- Unoccupied waits feel longer. Keep the customer in wait occupied with activities, preferably related to the product or service.
- Uncertain waits feel longer. Keep the customer informed about how long the expected wait is to likely to be.
- Unexplained waits feel longer. Keep the customer informed about why they are having to wait.
- Inequitable waits feel longer. Serve customer based on priority, determined by what is considered just in the ambient society.
- Value of the service. Ensure that the customer value you are providing is clearly superior to any alternative.

The most important common thread through all of these suggestions is that they all have to do with managing the customer perceptions. The firm is better placed if the customer perceptions can be influenced favourably by managing customer role and expectations in the value creation and delivery.To varying degrees, customers play a role in the production of products and not just in the consumption. Firms that realise this have paid serious attention to how the customer fits in the organization. In services, the role of the customer is abundantly evident. Customers engage in a coproduction role. In services or in the service component of the product, customers are coproducers in self-service configurations.

All services as we saw earlier involve some kind of customer participation, as in the case of providing required information to the tax preparer, for example. Even when placing the order with the provider, the customer is essentially contributing to the production of the product by providing input into product specifications.

When the customer is interacting with the firm and this interaction has some relevance to the production of the product, by definition we have the customer engaging in coproducing the product. Service firms instinctively manage the role of the customers in their participation in the service. Restaurants have menus, professors have syllabi, airlines have their method of emplaning passengers according to a certain priority, etc. Sometimes managing customer roles may be in the form of a complementary service.

For example, Universal is experimenting with a calming zone adjunct to its roller-coaster rides, for people who need help with coaster-phobia before they get on the ride. UPS and other package delivery firms instinctively accommodate special customer requests as to where their packages should be deposited if the customer is not at the location of delivery.

It is a matter of perspective. If we take the notion of value creation a step further, we could argue that even in the case of packaged goods, the value hasn't really been created to the customer until the customer actually begins to use the product.

Value creation and value consumption are both inextricably interwoven into a continuous and overlapping set of activities. This is an important issue in a service orientation.

In the case of services, customer interaction is a given. And the firm must include the customer in the design of its operations. The customer-focused firm by always keeping the customer in central view manages the role of the customer in the value creation and the value consumption activities. For example, providing excellent product assembly instructions improves the value created for the customer in an "easy to assemble yourself" product.

Conversely, even with a well-engineered product, poor instructions reduce customer value. Recent product innovation studies have shown that some firms are equipping customers with the tools to design and develop their own products, ranging from minor modifications to major new innovations. PTC (formerly Parametric Technology) is a world leader in computer-assisted-design (CAD) technology, whose software solutions bring suppliers and customers together so that a client can use the software during product development to virtually interface with upstream and downstream players.

Ultimately, anything that the firm can do to manage the customer's role in the value creation as well as value consumption process is an imperative for the customer-focused firm. As mentioned earlier, Procter and Gamble is recruiting families to allow a team of their ethnographer-filmmakers to observe their daily routines to get a better sense for how their customers use household products.

The actual use situation says a lot about how a product should be designed. It would also be a way to learn how the customers should be instructed in the appropriate use of the product.

How does a firm take a systematic approach to managing the customer? First, the firm identifies all the activities that the customer enacts in the value creation as well as value consumption blueprint. Next, the firm scripts the role for the customer at each activity.

Firms then have to determine how best to communicate and educate the customer in playing the appropriate role.

Customers' performance of their roles will depend on their ability and inclination to perform those roles. The consumer's ability will depend on consumption skills that the customer's past experience may have provided. The customer's inclination will depend on the personal characteristics of the customer. Familiarity with the service and service provider could affect the ability and the inclination of the customer in the role performance.

In the case of services and the service components of a product, customer role is managed by the service provider. The service provider's production skills and motivation could affect the way in which the service provider manages the customer's role. The service provider's familiarity with the segment and the specific customer will influence the service provider's skills and motivation in managing the customer's role performance. The service provider's production skills are reflected in its operations and customer interaction skills. The personal characteristics of the service provider can affect the service provider's motivation. When designing the service delivery process, it is important that the firm incorporate these factors on the customer's role performance.

Bibliography

Anil Passi: *Oracle E-Business Suite Development & Extensibility Handbook*, Tata McGraw-Hill, Delhi, 2009.

Arun Dutta: *A Modern Approach to Management and Business Studies*, Pearl Books, Delhi, 2008.

BAJAJ: *E-Commerce: The Cutting Edge of Business, 2/e*, Tata McGraw-Hill, Delhi, 2005.

Bastin Gerald: *Oracle: E-Business Suite Manufacturing & Supply Chain Management*, Tata McGraw-Hill, Delhi, 2003.

Bholanath Dutta: *International Business Management*, Excel Books, New Delhi, 2000.

Cristian Darie, Karli Watson: *Beginning Asp.Net E-Commerce In C#: From Novice To Professional*, Dreamtech Press, Delhi, 2005.

Darie: *Beginning ASP.NET 1.1 E-Commerce: From Novice to Professional*, Springer Publication, London, 2000.

Darie: *Beginning ASP.NET 3.5 E-Commerce in C#: From Novice to Professional*, Springer Publication, London, 2000.

F.L. Bascunan: *International Business Management*, Global Vision Publication, Delhi, 2011.

Foster: *Basic Business Statistics: A Casebook*, Springer Publication, London, 2006.

G.S. Prakasa Rao: *An Introductory Mathematics to Business and Economics*, Akansha Publication, Delhi, 2011.

Gail L. Cramer, Clarence W. Jensen and Douglas D. Southgate: *Agricultural Economics and Agribusiness*, Wiley Publication, London, 2011.

Gomez-Perez: *Ontological Engineering : With Examples from the Areas of Knowledge Management, E-Commerce and Semantic Web*, Springer Publication, London, 2011.

Hellsten: *Beginning Ruby on Rails E-Commerce: From Novice to Professional*, Springer Publication, London, 2003.

Himanshu: *Agri Business Management*, Ritu Publications, Delhi, 2006.

Large and Small, That have Shaped the Course of Modern Business, Jaico Publication, Jaipur, 2003.

J S Amarnath and A P V Samvel: *Agri-Business Management*, Satish Serial Publication, Delhi, 2008.

Kamal Sharma: *Encyclopaedia of E-Commerce*, Anmol Publication, Delhi, 2006.

Ken Black: *Applied Business Statistics: Making Better Business Decisions*, Wiley Publication, London, 2012.

Laxaman Tandon: *E-Commerce*, Mohit Publication, Delhi, 2006.

Michael Papazoglou & Pieter Ribbers: *E-Business Organisational & Technical Foundations*, Wiley Publication, London, 2003.

Michael Wash: *54 Tools and Techniques for Business Excellence*, Westland Publication, Delhi, 2001.

Mitlesh Dhunna: *Fundamentals of International Business Management*, Cyber Tech Publication, New Delhi, 2011.

Nandan Kamath: *Law Relating to Computers Internet and E-Commerce*, Universal Law Publishers, Delhi, 2012.

Nina Verma: *E-Commerce Taxation : Prospects and Challenges*, Global Vision Publication, Delhi, 2012.

P Srinivas Subba Rao: *Entrepreneurship and Small Business Management*, Discovery Publishing House, Delhi, 2001.

Padmalochan Hazarika: *A Textbook Of Business Statistics*, S. Chand Publisher, Delhi, 2010.

Prasant Salwan: *Best Business Practices for Global Competitiveness*, Sterling Publication, Delhi, 2003.

R V Murthy: *International Business Management*, GNOSIS Publication, Delhi, 2008.

Rajagopal: *Agri-Business and Entrepreneurship*, Anmol Publication, Delhi, 2001.

Rajesh Talwar: *Indian Laws of e-Business*, Vision Books, Delhi, 2001.

S.N. Choudhary: *Agri-Business : Marketing and Management*, Oxford Book Company, Delhi, 2012.

Shipra Chawla: *A Textbook of Business Communication*, Dominant Publication, Delhi, 2012.

Thomas R. Trautmann By Gurcharan Das: *Arthashastra : The Science of Wealth : The Story of Indian Business*, Penguin Books, London, 2012.

V S Mahajan: *Art of Successful Business, Family and Social Life*, Deep and Deep Publication, Delhi, 2008.

Index